The Social Psychology of Aging

UNDERSTANDING AGING
The Psychology of Adult Development

General Editor
James E. Birren

Editorial Advisory Board
Stig Berg, Dennis Bromley, Denise Park, Timothy A. Salthouse,
K. Warner Schaie, and Diana Woodruff-Pak

During this century life expectancy at birth has increased more for the average person that it did from Roman times to 1900: there are a greater number of old people today and they live longer than ever before. Within universities there is pressure to educate younger students about the scientific facts of adult development and aging as well as to train professionals to serve an aging society. The past twenty years have seen an exponential growth in material published.

This new series of modular texts has been designed to meet the need to integrate, interpret and make this new knowledge available in an efficient and flexible format for instructors, students and professionals worldwide. Each book will present a concise, authoritative, integrated and readable summary of research and theory in a clearly defined area. Bridging the gap between introductory texts and research literature, these books will provide balanced coverage and convey the excitement and challenge of new research and developments. The modular format allows the series to be used as a complete sequence in primary courses on aging, and also book by book in more specialized courses and in primary courses in other fields.

Published

The Social Psychology of Aging
Michael W. Pratt and Joan E. Norris

In preparation

The Psychology of Aging: An Overview
James E. Birren and Timothy A. Salthouse

The Cognitive Psychology of Aging
Denise C. Park

Personality and Aging
Jan-Erik Ruth and Peter Coleman

The Psychology of Aging and Mental Health
Michael A. Smyer and Sara H. Qualls

The Neuropsychology of Aging
Diana Woodruff-Pak

The Social Psychology of Aging

A Cognitive Perspective

Michael W. Pratt

and

Joan E. Norris

BLACKWELL
Oxford UK & Cambridge USA

First published 1994

Blackwell Publishers
238 Main Street
Cambridge, Massachusetts 02142
USA

108 Cowley Road
Oxford   OX4 1JF
UK

Library of Congress Cataloging-in-Publication Data
Pratt, Michael W.
    The social psychology of aging: a cognitive perspective / Michael
W. Pratt and Joan E. Norris.
        p.   cm. — (Understanding aging)
    Includes bibliographical references and index.
    ISBN 1–55786–491–8 (alk. paper). — ISBN 1–55786–492–6 (pbk.:
alk. paper)
        1. Aging—Social aspects. 2. Aged—Psychology. 3. Social
perception. 4. Cognition in old age. I. Norris, Joan E.
II. Title. III. Series.
HQ1061.P687   1994
305.26—dc20   94–4312
                                                                     CIP

British Library Cataloguing in Publication Data

A CIP catalogue record for this book is available from the British Library.

Typeset in 10½ on 12½ pt Bembo by Graphicraft Typesetters Ltd, Hong Kong
Printed in Great Britain by T.J. Press Ltd, Padstow Cornwall

This book is printed on acid-free paper

For our Parents

Contents

3 Thinking about the Self   39

4 Thinking about Other Persons   64

5 Thinking about Relationships   94

6 Thinking about Society 115

7 Decision-making, Wisdom, and Moral Judgment 142

8 Communication: Social Cognition in Action 176

List of Figures

List of Tables

Preface

Last Christmas, Mike Pratt's parents, Ted and Louise, now in their 80s, set out to stuff their turkey for the family dinner. They have always sewed the bird up after it is stuffed, part of doing things "with care," in contrast to their lazy child, who is just happy to get it into the oven any way he can. Unfortunately, Louise can no longer see well enough to thread the needle or to stitch. Ted, on the other hand, can see quite well, but doesn't have the dexterity in his fingers any more to sew. A truly complicated collaboration ensued, which drew on everyone's resources. The final product may not have been beautiful, but it tasted fine, and did make for a good family story.

Over the past ten years, a series of family incidents, many much more momentous than this one of course, have piqued our interest in how older individuals adapt to their changing and often challenging life circumstances. Many of these developmental adaptations have involved trying to compensate for problems or limitations by using social relationships and resources in some way or another. This book is the product of trying to discover what we know about how these and other sorts of social processes operate in the lives of older adults, and how they may facilitate, or perhaps at times hinder, older individuals' coping.

The book is a review of psychological research and theory on social aspects of the experience of aging. Because this is an area in psychology in which actual evidence is only beginning to be collected, the primary effort has been to raise issues and questions for future consideration, rather than to provide definitive answers. Kurt Lewin, an early social psychologist, argued that there is nothing so practical as a good theory. What that has meant for us as authors is that we required an appropriate framework for considering what the important questions about aging and social psychology ought to be.

Our focus in this book is on the adult's experience of his or her social world. Understanding how people organize and construct the meaning of their social lives is central, we believe, to the project of social psychology (and of psychology in general). Thus, social cognition in adulthood is the central core of our presentation in the chapters which follow. We consider the ways in which meaning-making about the world may change in later life and the central role of such meaning-making in organizing the experience of social interactions and social systems for older adults' daily lives.

Our bases in cognitive social psychology and in cognitive developmental psychology have led us to our own, certainly personal, views of how best to provide coverage of this field. The focus on how adults in maturity experience and construct their social worlds has selective implications for coverage of the social psychology of aging, of course. It means that we have placed relatively less emphasis on some other strands of research. For example, we have been little concerned in the book with evidence tracking overt *behavioral* change across the lifespan (e.g., changes in institutional participation rates of different types with age). Similarly, the effects of broader social–cultural forces, such as economic or historical events, are discussed only as they are mediated through processes of social and individual understanding. Thus, the book focuses squarely on research on the processes and development of social understanding and their implications across middle to later adulthood.

Like some mysterious island, this question of how we perceive and reason about the social world of ourselves and others has been explored by adventurers from two different coastlines on the world map of psychology. Social psychologists, moving towards a more cognitive compass point in recent years, have become increasingly interested in the complex thoughts, explanations, and rationales that intertwine with and support everyday social life and action. A number of fine books on this approach have been written. Moving from the opposite coastline, theorists of cognitive development, particularly those in the Piagetian tradition, have become increasingly interested in how development occurs in the ways that children view their social worlds. Again, a number of valuable discussions of this topic have become available in recent years.

Despite these pioneering cartographic efforts, however, there so far has been limited consideration of social cognition within a lifespan context. Development in later-life social thinking has been occasionally studied, and widely speculated upon, in discussions of conceptions like "wisdom" and "social competence". But there has been no attempt so far to draw together the broad strands of this research and to summarize what is known about social thinking and its role in everyday social experience as people grow older. This book is designed to begin such an exploration. Like the maps of old, there are many uncharted territories, marked only in the crudest fashion in the present summary. But just as the ancient maps were preludes and indeed dynamic contributors to the process of more exacting exploration, so we hope that this book can serve in some modest way to encourage questions and research on lifespan social thinking and social psychology.

The chapters attempt to give up-to-date summaries of the general research literature on various territories in this domain. However, the book has been prepared for students and readers with only a general knowledge of basic psychology. We have attempted to keep our terminology readily accessible, and, throughout the book, have sought to provide many case examples and real-life illustrations of the points we are making, some drawn from our own research and some constructed to be prototypic regarding important issues. We have also tried to highlight the implications of the research for practitioners in the field of gerontology. Thus, the book should be appropriate as a supplementary text for advanced undergraduate and graduate courses in lifespan development and aging, in gerontology, and in social psychology.

Like the explorers described above, the authors approach this topic from somewhat divergent directions. Michael Pratt is a developmental psychologist by training, interested in the social context of thinking across the lifespan. Joan Norris is trained as a social psychologist, with a continuing research interest in social interaction and relationships in later life. These particular backgrounds have undoubtedly led us to emphasize the continuities between these disciplines and lifespan research and theory more than would many other writers. In particular, a focus on continuity with work on earlier parts of the lifespan is evident throughout, partly due to interest and expertise, and partly in the belief that integration of the study of development *across* the lifespan is a worthwhile and ultimately necessary endeavor. As well, a continuing interest in the cultural–historical school of development proposed by Vygotsky (1978) and others, which emphasizes the social context of cognitive development in earlier life, is here extended and expanded to adult social cognition. It has seemed to us that this focus is particularly apt with respect to the domain of social cognition, since thinking about the social world is surely grounded in social experiences throughout life. Of course, alternative frameworks for social cognitive development are plausible as well. By drawing out such parallels and interpretations across the lifespan, however, we hope to foster both theoretical and practical work on development in social thinking and the factors which influence it.

Much of the research reported by both Pratt and Norris in this book was supported by the Social Sciences and Humanities Research Council of Canada. We thank the Council for its generous support of our interests in this area over the years [We also thank the many respondents who have been an indispensable part of our research. We have quoted from some of them throughout the book, but in all such instances names and other identifying information have been changed to protect their confidentiality.] Wilfrid Laurier University also provided financial support for the preparation of the manuscript, for which we are grateful.

As authors concerned with the role of social support to sociocognitive development, we would be incredibly remiss if we did not thank the many who have served in this capacity for us. First, we thank Jim Birren for his interest and (we hope) good judgment in allowing this manuscript to find a home in this series, and for his thoughtful commentary during the editing process. Our first executive editor at Blackwell, Susan Milmoe, worked to improve the clarity and style of this manuscript, we hope to some effect. A number of colleagues and students read and commented on many of the book's chapters, including Philip Cowan, Brian deVries, Bruce Hunsberger, Barry McPherson, Gary Reker, Ellen Ryan, Joseph Tindale, and Rhett Diessner. To all of them, we are very grateful. The book has surely benefitted from their comments; the errors and infelicities that remain we must claim as our own. We also thank Susan Curror, Margo Gallant, Silvana Santolupo and Nancy LaPointe for their help in manuscript and bibliographic preparation. Thanks also to Alison Truefitt and Donald Stephenson for their careful editorial assistance. Last, but by no means least, we thank our families for their patience and understanding, as this book struggled through many peaks and valleys on our own personal life maps over the past several years.

Acknowledgements

The authors and publishers gratefully acknowledge the following for permission to reproduce copyright material: the Far Side cartoon by Gary Larson on p. 68 is reprinted by permission of Chronicle Features, San Francisco, CA. All rights reserved. The Gary Larson cartoon on p. 194 is reprinted with permission of the Farside © 1987, Farworks Inc., distributed by Universal Press Syndicate. All rights reserved. The publishers apologize for any errors or omissions in the above list and would be grateful to be notified of any corrections that should be incorporated in the next edition or reprint of this book.

1

An Introduction and Orientation

Could you tell me about a situation where you had to decide what was the right thing to do?

Well, this was 20 years ago, and I'm not even sure I've decided this yet. My daughter was 21 then and she still doesn't know about this. She was going with a chap. They were sort of engaged and he was totally unsuited to her and I wrote my sister and said that what my daughter needed was to be away for a while, would she invite her to visit for her 21st birthday? And my sister did, and she went away and came back and her whole outlook was changed. And interfering in her life was a moral decision for me.

What was the conflict?

She was 21 and I had tried very hard not to interfere in their lives. When the children were 21 we gave them matched sets of luggage which was symbolic that when they came back they were visitors in our home. And it also meant to us that we had no more right to interfere in their lives . . . That if we hadn't brought them up adequately by then, we'd lost our chance. So doing it without telling her was the conflict for me.

What happened?

She went, she had a great time, and she came back with a little bit more cosmopolitan outlook and realized herself that the relationship was wrong. She was only gone for three weeks, so if the relationship had been strong at all, it would have been able to survive that three weeks.

Do you think it was the right thing to do?

Absolutely . . . If it had just gone on from habit it would have been disastrous. And three weeks' holiday for her wouldn't have been enough to break a relationship. I think she just needed to be a little distanced from the situation.

Do you consider the situation to be a moral problem?

It was for me. Because it was blatant interference. I think the problem was that I didn't tell her. If I had just said, "How would you like to go away," or "I think it would be wise to give your relationship a holiday or take a break from it," I think it would have been a little more open, a little more honest with her. Doing it without telling her was the moral problem.

What does morality mean to you?

It means actively not hurting anybody else. Going out of your way to avoid hurting and to alleviate hurt if you come across it (Pratt, unpublished data).

Could you describe to me a situation where you weren't sure what was the right thing to do?

This decision came about two years ago. We had planned for three years to bring my husband's mother here to live with us . . . When she came it went wrong from the day she arrived. And because you plan a thing you think you should carry it through. I always believed in the extended family; we should care for her, you know . . . We changed the house around, we did everything to make it nice for her and it went wrong from the beginning. Finally I had to decide who was going to go into the [hospital], me or her. You know, and it was a religious decision too, because I prayed about it. She felt I didn't give her enough attention, I didn't hold her hand, I went out and left her alone sometimes . . . She was here so I could look after her totally. I finally said one day, "OK, then we'll find you somewhere you'll be happy". And we found a place right away and it was within our means . . . So that decision took a lot of agony because we were limited with money. It couldn't be too far away because we knew we'd be running back and forth still caring for her, but she'd be with people her own age. She'd have the company she wished or whatever. And I think that was one of the very most difficult decisions that I ever made.

What was the conflict for you?

I couldn't give her the attention she wanted. It was guilt . . . It was a guilt trip from the word go for me. This wasn't our only problem of course. But she walked around the house and she wanted to be mistress of her house again. I realize that was a conflict. She had given up her home. We wanted her to have somewhere that could be like her home, that we could furnish with her things . . . I felt that I was going back on the job because we'd promised, we'd planned, and I couldn't fulfil the plan . . . I was at the point that I couldn't do anything more. So what I considered was her comfort and that I had other things that I had to do. I wanted to be sure that I was doing the right thing, that I wasn't being harsh . . .

Do you think it was the right thing to do?

Yes, she's been much happier. She's happier there but she still pulls the strings and she calls daily for things.

Do you consider this situation a moral problem?

Yes, because I gave my word and I had to break it. I can't exactly grasp why we didn't get along. I feel I kind of failed. I should have been able to and I couldn't (Pratt, unpublished data).

Two women in their late 60s, describing issues in their lives that have raised important moral questions for them. These are generational matters that turn on social relationships and the duties and obligations that are associated with family life. They are difficult problems, but part of the natural rhythms of the life cycle and they come to most of us, in some form, in time. What does it or should it mean to be the parent of a child becoming an adult, or to be the daughter of a failing adult, becoming in some way child-like again?

These are complex questions, ones that might be analyzed at many different levels. At a societal level, family life involves a number of roles and expectations, standardized but also variable across cultures. At a biological level, these behaviors may be strongly shaped by physiological and neurological mechanisms based on genetic inheritance that guide the special generosity of our actions towards our kin. But at the psychological level of the individual and her experience of her family life, these patterns of action and decision-making are largely shaped by how the individual understands and interprets the situation, the choices, and the principles involved. In a word, the way in which people think about their social world and its qualities is front and center to any account of its psychology, and social psychology as a discipline has increasingly come to emphasize this point (e.g., Fiske & Taylor, 1991).

How people do this sort of social thinking, how they understand and cope with a social and biological world that inexorably forces on us life choices like those faced by the women above, is the focus of this book. In particular, it is concerned with similarities and differences in such social thinking across the adult lifespan, how any differences should be understood, what impact they may have on the aging individual's social experiences and behavior, and what their practical implications are. By focusing on the cognitive aspects of social psychology, we attempt to provide a lens for understanding the individual's social life. However, we do not wish to ignore or deny the broad range of non-cognitive aspects of social experience. Rather, we have sought to link these aspects to the cognitive, interpretive processes we believe are central. To continue the metaphor introduced in the preface, let us begin by surveying what we consider the current, albeit primitive, map of the territory of social thinking in adulthood.

Defining social cognition

What is social cognition? A definition by John Flavell (1985), one of the most active developmental researchers of this topic, provides a starting point. "Social cognition takes humans and human affairs as its subjects; it means cognition about people and their doings" (p. 119). Flavell provides a figural representation of his notion of social cognition (see figure 1.1). This deceptively simple figure actually captures a range of distinctive phenomena which fit under the broad umbrella of social cognition for Flavell, and for us. It serves as a useful survey map of the territory we wish to consider in this book.

Two important distinctions are explicit in figure 1.1. Social cognitions can refer both to thoughts about others and to thoughts about the self (O versus S in Flavell's picture). And social cognitions may refer both to thoughts about the person's inner states (top) or to thoughts about the relationships and interactions *between* persons or groups (bottom). As described in the plan of the book below, these distinctions are represented

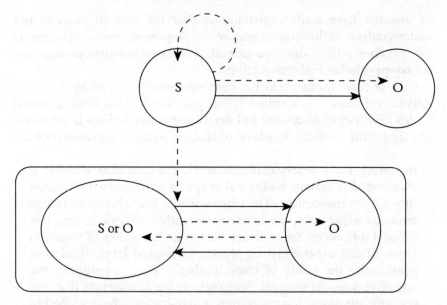

Figure 1.1   A representation of social cognition; from Flavell, 1985 (figure 5.1)

explicitly in the way in which the chapters are organized. As Flavell (1985) notes, one can also think about what individuals or groups *ought* to do, as well as what they actually do, and this aspect of social cognition is represented in research on the topic of social judgment. Finally, social cognition plays a central role in what people actually do in social situations, and so the dashed and solid arrows of figure 1.1 should interconnect in some complex way. In the present book, the implications of social cognition for communication processes between individuals are discussed as one example of this complex relation of social thinking and doing.

Today, the topic of cognition is so central and pervasive in psychological research and theorizing that it is difficult to imagine it was ever absent. Yet 30 to 40 years ago, psychology was defined and prescribed as the study of *behavior*, and all theorizing on the topic of thinking (let alone "social thinking") was literally taboo. This revolution has had a dramatic impact on many fields and disciplines associated with psychology (e.g., Gardner, 1985), including the fields of social psychology and of lifespan development and aging. Ideas about how thinking and knowledge may best be understood and represented are discussed and argued at center stage in a range of theories important for understanding later life. As discussed in chapter 2, at least four different schools of theorists have made contributions over the past 30 years to our understanding of lifespan cognitive development: those representing the **psychometric**, **developmental**, **information-processing**, and **social–psychological** perspectives.

Each of these frameworks has been profoundly shaped by the "cognitive revolution." As Gardner (1985) points out, what is most central to this new way of discussing and describing in psychology is the necessity for positing a distinctive level of analysis termed "representational":

> In opting for a representational level, the cognitive scientist is claiming that certain traditional ways of accounting for human thought are inadequate. The neuroscientist may choose to talk in terms of nerve cells, the historian or anthropologist in terms of cultural influences, the ordinary person or the writer of fiction in terms of the experiential or phenomenological level. While not questioning the utility of these levels for various purposes, the cognitive scientist rests his discipline on the assumption that, for scientific purposes, human cognitive activity must be described in terms of symbols, schemas, images, ideas, and other forms of mental representation (Gardner, 1985, pp. 38–39).

Gardner's description applies equally well to the cognitive aspects of each of the various theoretical frameworks we will discuss. The patterns of such symbol use in representation across the lifespan, the ways in which these may differ or remain the same in later adulthood, are the stuff from which theories of lifespan cognitive development are made. As the quotation also notes, use of this representational level does not imply disinterest in, or a devaluing of, other "levels" of description, such as the social or the neurological. As the social psychology of later life is discussed in this book, it is this level of mental representation within the individual (and between individuals in joint activity and communication, we would add) that is central in our analysis. And the complex and reciprocal ways in which social representation and thinking in later adulthood are linked both to the social experiences and interactions of the individual, and the larger social and cultural systems through which people's lives are constituted, provide the focus of our story.

Why is it important to focus specifically on the issues of *social* understanding and representation in later adulthood? First, of course, these problems are inherently interesting, and ones with which humans have had to be concerned, since the beginning of the species, in managing their practical, everyday affairs. Every time you consider why someone did what he or she did, how another feels, or what he or she might do next, you are drawing on sociocognitive knowledge and skills. Obviously, all sorts of everyday social actions and interactions, both nice and not so nice (trying to assist someone to feel better, trying to trick someone into doing something for your own ends) are grounded in these skills.

Second, adults are particularly likely to conceptualize their own intelligence and cognitive skills within a social context as they grow older (Willis & Schaie, 1986). "Getting older, getting wiser," at least in a social sense, seems to characterize many people's views of personal aging. What can the study of lifespan social thinking in psychology contribute to an understanding of whether, and how, this might be so? This book considers these issues in terms of the research findings in this area to date. In considering these questions, several specific themes regarding lifespan cognition will be highlighted.

Themes of the book

Three central themes dominate this book. They are relevant to research, as well as to issues of policy and practice, related to older adults. An intergenerational work situation can serve to illustrate them.

A large corporation employs 20-year-olds and 60-year-olds in the information systems department. An analysis of the daily productivity of these workers finds that the young, relative to the old, carry out more computer analyses, write more new programs, and need to consult manuals to existing programs less frequently. Based on such observations, management might be likely to conclude that memory, creativity, and problem-solving skills deteriorate as workers age, and perhaps to base their hiring and managerial decisions accordingly. Nevertheless, there are three features of this scenario involving age differences in adult "skills" that we hope to convince the reader need closer examination. First, it is assumed implicitly that the work and its context are viewed and understood in the same way by both the older and younger adults, so that the "performance" of the two age groups can be readily and directly compared. Second, the question of average age differences often takes precedence over the study of individual performance variations within groups in such situations. Third, it is assumed in this situation that cognitive competence is located *within* the person; the role of the social context in performance is ignored.

The main points that we wish to make in this book concern these three themes, and thus we will elaborate on each one. First, performance and performance differences in cognition must be understood and interpreted within a lifespan developmental and adaptational context. The goals, purposes, and cognitive frameworks of older adults may be distinct from those of younger individuals in important ways. For example, the logic of abstract problem-solving tasks presented in a work setting or in an experiment may operate quite differently for a young adult in the beginnings of formal operative competence compared to an older adult with a wealth of qualifying evidence and "wisdom" with respect to real-life implications. The abstract logical games of adolescence may make little sense in the context of mature adulthood (e.g., Labouvie-Vief, 1985). One reason that social cognition is an interesting context for study is the obvious link between thinking about the social domain and the everyday tasks of getting on with one's life. We hold that knowing about the way individuals understand the world is central to meaningful psychology, and has important implications for intergenerational relations. We also argue that such understandings are embedded in each person's place in the life course, and that we need to appreciate that place as part of our theorizing. In terms of our work-related example, it could be that older employees' potential losses in speed and efficiency on the logic tasks of computer analysis may be offset by expertise regarding what is practical in real-life situations (e.g., Rybash, Hoyer, Roodin, 1986).

In this book, we will stress the importance of a lifespan developmental framework for understanding social experience in later adulthood and aging. That should not imply, however, simply a comparison or description of how the young differ from the middle aged and from the old on specific variables. Our second theme is an obvious one, but one easy to overlook in a literature geared to description. Age, in and of itself, is not an explanation of anything. Instead, we must observe individual variability exhibited by persons at all ages, and the explanatory factors (be they skills, processes, interests, purposes or whatever) which may be linked to these. The natural emphasis on age/stage-related descriptions of adulthood has tended to obscure this fundamental point. Variability *within* age groups is of great theoretical and practical interest for any serious lifespan account of sociocognitive development. By considering individual performance differences in our employment example, management may discover that some older workers do much *better* than the typical younger employee. Clearly, it will be worth examining the strategies of very successful adults as models for workers in all age categories.

Thirdly, the current generation of cognitive psychologists, from Piaget to information-processing theorists, has tended to de-emphasize the social, interpersonal nature of much of everyday thought. Cognitive competence is seen and studied as inherent within the person. Lev Vygotsky, the Russian developmentalist, long ago stressed the important role that adults play in children's acquisition of sophisticated cognitive skills. Vygotsky (e.g., 1978) stressed the *joint* problem-solving activities of adult and child as the root of these acquisitions. It is unlikely, however, that this interpersonal, collaborative cognitive activity disappears as children become adults (e.g., Dixon, 1992; Meacham & Emont, 1989).

Informal observations of older adults' daily activities suggest the role of interpersonal processes and projects in various aspects of everyday problem-solving (from reminders like "Did you put out the garbage yet?" to strategic group processes such as "How can we facilitate better relationships among our co-workers?"). This is not to deny that much of this problem-solving is "internalized" and carried on by individuals. But in terms of the present example, attention to the social context and processes of work may be critical to understanding how tasks get done, and to facilitating such performance for all age groups.

Plan of the book

The book is organized around the issues identified in figure 1. Chapter 2 is a review in relation to aging of the four centrally relevant frameworks of psychometric theory, information-processing theory, developmental theory, and social–psychological theory. It also discusses some of the critical issues that must be addressed by any theory in describing lifespan development, such as the sources and nature of growth and change, and their patterning across the lifespan.

Chapter 3 reviews the evidence regarding the self in later life. Thinking about the self as "agent" (self-efficacy, coping), as "object" (self-concept and personality), as "process" (life narratives and the life-story), and as "knower" (metacognition) are described. The evidence regarding these views of the self in later adulthood is reviewed and summarized, and the ways in which these perspectives impact on the aging social self are discussed.

Chapter 4 reviews evidence on aging and the processes of thinking about other persons. Studies of attention, memory, and representation of other individuals and their behaviors are reviewed in terms of both developmental patterns in later life and their practical implications for everyday social thinking and interaction. We also consider how the wider society views the older adult in terms of issues of ageism.

Chapter 5 moves to a consideration of the "relationship" section of figure 1.1, reviewing evidence and theory regarding how people feel about and experience attachments and close relationships between individuals in both family and friendship contexts. It covers how these relationships are formed, maintained and lost as people grow older, and addresses how development in these interactions and relationships affects participants.

Chapter 6 next describes research on older adults' thinking about and involvement in the major social institutions and roles outside of the intimate domain of family and friends, including work and retirement, and neighborhood and community. We also discuss religious participation and thinking in later life, and the older adult's experience of and perspective on the political system.

Chapter 7 then reviews and summarizes evidence on adult age differences in evaluations and practical judgments about what *ought to be* in social life and relationships, including research on social problem-solving, wisdom, and moral judgment in later life. The links between such judgment processes and what people actually do in their social lives and interactions are discussed as well.

Chapter 8 considers the evidence about how social cognition is manifested in later life in one particularly critical social-interactional system, verbal communication. Age differences and similarities across adulthood are summarized at a range of levels, from basic sounds to complex dialogues, and issues raised for intergenerational communication are particularly highlighted.

Finally, chapter 9 summarizes the themes from these reviews and discusses their implications both for further research in this field, and for practitioners working with older adults.

Each of the chapters is organized in relatively parallel fashion, beginning with an introduction to the problem, and a brief discussion of how the various theoretical frameworks are relevant. The important research and evidence is then reviewed and summarized in the body of the chapter. Each chapter ends with a summary and conclusion, in which the evidence is related to the central themes and applied to specific examples or cases introduced earlier in the chapter.

In reviewing the evidence across these diverse areas, we have focused on description of the major findings regarding age differences and similarities across adulthood (the "what" of aging and social development). Investigations into explanatory factors which might account for patterns of differences are still limited, so there is less consideration of the "hows and whys." However, wherever appropriate, some discussion of these questions is included. In particular, we have sought to discuss the central social categories of gender and ethnicity, and their moderating influence on the social experiences of later life, throughout the various chapters where relevant evidence is available.

Finally, a word needs to be said regarding the emphasis on theory in the following chapters. Why should one bother with theories at all? Can't the *facts* of later-life development simply be stated where they are known, and the gaps noted where they are not? The history of science makes it clear that the answer to these questions must be no. The only way to understand, interpret, and collect facts in a coherent fashion is to utilize a guiding framework for investigating the events of the world. And these guiding frameworks must constantly be kept explicit, so that their role in the process of science is clear, and open to debate.

It is only because of this process of rigorous theorizing and theory-testing that science can help us move beyond "common sense" descriptions of the world, which may be right sometimes, but also may be quite wrong. It was always common sense, for example, that the sun circled the earth. Just watching the sky for a day, the facts were clear! But this obvious "fact" had to be understood in a very different way, by Copernicus, Galileo and others, if a more powerful and appropriate description of astronomical observations was to develop (e.g., T. S. Kuhn, 1962). This need for theory may be little comfort to the reader, assaulted by a cacophony of multiple views in the pages to follow. But only through hearing its diverse theoretical "voices" can the reader get an honest picture of where adult developmental theory currently stands, and, most importantly, how it moves forward and grows.

As well, the authors feel compelled to warn readers about the complexity of research evidence in such a developing area. Because the number of studies on any particular problem is typically small, it is often difficult to separate the wheat from the chaff. The reader will undoubtedly feel some sense of frustration, given the conflicting findings and the uncertainty with which conclusions can be drawn. In reviewing this research, we have tried to attempt an honest, but critical, summary of where the field is at present, as well as sketching where we would like to see it go in terms of questions raised and answers sought. In the final chapter, we will try to draw this commentary together, and to relate it to practical concerns. Again, however, there is a certain richness and excitement in this diversity and disagreement, as well as confusion and complexity. We hope we have been able to convey some of this sense of the normal challenges and workings of our science, as we seek to understand the social lives of older people.

2

Theoretical Perspectives on Lifespan Social Cognition

How can two children from the same family be so different? Why do people tend to age at about the same rate? Such fundamental questions regarding development have long challenged human curiosity. Modern lifespan developmental theories in psychology operate in the context of long philosophical traditions concerned with responding to such issues regarding human development. In the first section of this chapter, two of these focal issues are considered. First, the contributing role of biology and heredity versus experience and the environment as *sources* of development is considered. A second issue concerns that of *patterns* of development. Is change across the lifespan smooth and continuous, or more abrupt and stage-like?

The second section of the chapter focuses on several issues more specific to lifespan developmental theory. The first of these draws on the concepts of Baltes (1987) and others regarding the relative gains and losses in development across the life course, from infancy through old age. A second issue, also stressed by Baltes (1987), concerns the importance of seeing the patterns of individual human development within the historical and cultural contexts in which such growth and change is embedded. Finally, a third topical issue is briefly discussed – the potential for change or alteration in characteristics within new or different environmental contexts, i.e., the plasticity of development (Baltes, 1987). As Baltes points out, each of these three lifespan issues provides a starting point for integrating findings on later patterns of development with those observed in childhood.

The third section of this chapter covers four major theoretical perspectives of importance to the study of lifespan social cognition: **psychometric**, **information–processing**, **developmental**, and **social–psychological** frameworks. For each of these frameworks, in turn, a brief historical discussion of their application to issues of later adult cognition is provided. This approach aims to put the recent development of these theories in an historical context, and to illustrate the major shifts within these perspectives in contemporary psychological views of aging. Some theoretical and methodological contributions arising from the use of these perspectives in studying older adults are also included.

General developmental issues

Heredity–environment interactions

Mike's uncle, Charles Pratt, was always a strong, solidly-built man who liked to eat, but with retirement and less exercise in his late 60s, his weight increased. One cold January day, as he was driving his truck on the highway, he suffered a massive heart attack. He somehow managed to drive home, walked up his long driveway, and then collapsed and died at his kitchen table.

Physicians and researchers continue to debate the role of both environmental factors (such as diet) and genetic influences on heart disease. Did a too rich diet and too little exercise conspire to shorten Charles's life, or was it mainly a genetic predisposition lurking in his body's cells? Of course, the issue is not merely academic to the rest of his family.

Just as in the case of medical disorders, the debate between those favoring a predominant role for genetic and/or biological factors in psychological development, and those arguing for the primacy of experience and the environment, has had a long history (e.g., Konner, 1982). Developmental psychologists of today at least give lip service to the idea that each of these sources plays a crucial role, in *interaction with* the other, in specifying the course of growth and change (e.g., Scarr & McCartney, 1983). Experiences must occur to some biologically-specified organism, and each organism must grow within some environmental context.

For some specialized developmental patterns, this interaction is beginning to be understood. For example, the recessive hereditary disorder of phenylketonuria (PKU) afflicts only infants who receive a specific defective gene (the unit of heredity carried on chromosomes in the nucleus of each cell of the body) from both their mothers and fathers. This defective gene is associated with a particular biochemical disorder of functioning, an inability to break down the amino acid phenylalanine, which then builds up in the brain and blood-stream, and causes an atypical growth pattern characterized by severe, lifelong mental retardation. Understanding this genetic–biochemical pathway has led to an environmental treatment for PKU, however. By altering the diet of infants carrying these genes, to avoid the intake of phenylalanine, a relatively "normal" cognitive outcome can be achieved. Thus, a genetically-based disorder can have quite different outcomes, depending on its interaction with different (dietary) environments.

Most genetic–environmental interactions are not yet so well understood. However, there is some hope that similar environmental treatments may be able to control the negative effects of gene defects in such later-life-onset disorders as Huntington's disease or some specific subtypes of Alzheimer's disease (Finch, 1989). At the least, the rapid advances being made in mapping the genes we carry on our cells' chromosomes suggest that, in another one or two decades, the genetic influences on many lifespan developmental behavior patterns will begin to be understood (e.g., Konner, 1990). As the examples of Huntington's disease and Alzheimer's disease indicate, these genetic influences extend across the lifespan, and may not be expressed until later adulthood.

Interest in how genes and environment interact in development has led to the growth in recent years of the field known as developmental behavior genetics (e.g., Plomin & McClearn, 1990). Plomin and his colleagues have begun to study possible genetic influences on later-life social processes using the methods of this behavioral genetic approach (e.g., Bergeman, Plomin, Pedersen, McClearn, & Nesselroade, 1990; Plomin & McClearn, 1990). In this research on a Swedish sample, identical twins (those from a single egg), who share 100 percent of their genetic makeup, were compared with fraternal twins (from two different eggs), who share only 50 percent of their genes. For each of these twin groups, some had been raised together, and some apart, making possible a number of comparisons of the role of genetic and environmental influences (Plomin & McClearn, 1990). So far, these studies have suggested that genetic influences on personality differences, at least, may decline somewhat in later life. Examples here included anger levels, activity levels, and sociability. Environmental influences, especially from environments that differ between persons (called *non-shared environmental influences*), tend to increase, presumably as people's experiences become increasingly different from one another over the lifespan (Plomin & McClearn, 1990).

The study by Bergeman et al. (1990), focusing more directly on issues relevant to social cognition and experience, assessed both the quantity of social support networks reported by these older (aged 50 to 80) twins, and their perceptions of the networks' adequacy. The findings suggested that size of the person's social network was little influenced by genetic factors. However, perceptions of the adequacy of social support were substantially more similar for identical than for fraternal twins, indicating genetic influence on this "sociocognitive" measure.

This result illustrates the complex nature of genetic–environmental interaction in later-life development. Social support is an environmental factor, and one which has an important role to play in later-life psychological functioning (e.g., Antonucci & Akiyama, 1987). It seems that the individual's sense of satisfaction with such support is critical in feelings of well-being (e.g., Krause & Markides, 1990). However, Bergeman et al.'s results suggest that such *perceptions* of environmental support may be partly mediated by genetic mechanisms. Of course, the details of how these genetic–environmental interactions operate in social perception remain to be worked out (Bergeman et al., 1990).

These findings on possible genetic influences do not indicate that environmental experiences are unimportant to development. It is precisely through the ways in which our human capacities and dispositions, from whatever source, *interact* with particular environmental opportunities that the course of development across the lifespan is shaped (Konner, 1990; Scarr & McCartney, 1983). Clearly, then, the dynamic interplay of both genetic and experiential sources will be crucial to an adequate account of development. For human social behavior and cognition, this story is likely to be exceedingly complex. As noted, there has been limited study of how genetic–experiential interactions influence later-life development to date. Given the focus on applications in this discussion, this book will emphasize the role of environmental factors in shaping the course of later life, since this class of factors is currently more amenable to intervention. However, as individual variability in social development is described and reviewed below, the potential complexity of the forces shaping these adult pathways, both environmental and genetic, should be kept in mind.

Continuity/discontinuity in development

Nature provides many examples of life courses characterized by sharp transition points. As a child, Mike remembers bringing home many a drab cocoon, to wait in eager anticipation for the dramatic emergence of an adult butterfly from this seemingly unpromising source. The development of human cognition over the life cycle has been similarly described in such "discontinuous" terms by contemporary "stage" theories, such as those of Piaget (e.g., 1970) and Kohlberg (1984). In contrast to positions emphasizing qualitative shifts in development, however, other theories of human cognitive growth have argued for much more continuous, quantitative changes over time. A good example here are many versions of information-processing theory (e.g., Kail & Bisanz, 1982). These theories, to varying degrees, model development as the accumulation of gradual changes in skill in various basic processes or activities through practice and experience.

Why should it matter whether development is viewed as involving broad structural changes in patterns of factors (the "stage" position) or comparatively specific changes in particular individual variables (the "continuity" position)? As just noted, beliefs about these patterns in development are often at the heart of differences in theoretical frameworks meant to describe development, as well as in the type of research which flows from these frameworks (e.g., Salthouse, 1991). Furthermore, implications for stimulation and/or remediation may be quite different, depending on which pattern is presumed to hold. Specific skill practice, for example in speed of arithmetical calculation, is a good teaching strategy for improving problem-solving according to the continuity position, but may not make much sense if one believes that the child must grasp the meaning of number in a new way to make real gains in mathematics understanding (e.g., Piaget & Inhelder, 1969).

The cognitive–developmental stages of Piaget entail the clearest claims for the discontinuity position. Piaget (1970) argued that the same stages are *universally* present in the same sequence (in all humans everywhere), that these stages form a *hierarchy* of cognitive adequacy (such that each stage is logically more advanced than its predecessor), and that these stages are *general* (across all sorts of problems and topics in the individual's current reasoning). Thus, all children can be expected to achieve Piaget's concrete–operational stage, for example, entailing an organized understanding of logical and quantitative operations in the world. This stage is logically more adequate than the pre-operational stage which must precede it, and concrete operations are applied by children to reasoning about all sorts of physical and social problems which they encounter (e.g., Cowan, 1978).

Piaget's stages characterize developmental changes in cognition up to young adulthood, but they do not depict further qualitative changes in thinking in later life. Theorists of lifespan development have sometimes argued for patterns of discontinuity in adulthood as well, but they have generally been inclined to weaken or discard one or more of the strong Piagetian assumptions just noted in making their case.

Probably the most widely questioned of these is the argument for broad generality in application of the stages (e.g., Flavell, 1985). A great deal of research evidence indicates that children may be at quite different levels of thinking on different topics simultaneously, and many current "neo-Piagetian" theories tend to incorporate this idea (e.g., Fischer & Pipp, 1984; Case, 1985). With respect to adult development, even Piaget (1972) himself suggested that his final stage of formal operations may only be attained by adults in their areas of vocational and/or educational expertise, and not in other areas of their thinking. Similarly, recent theorists of adult cognitive development have argued for "specialized skills" that may be retained and even enhanced as people grow older, but that are "encapsulated" and not reflected in thinking in other domains or topic areas (e.g., Rybash, Hoyer, & Roodin, 1986). Such positions are generally easier to reconcile with the less stage-like development posited by information-processing frameworks, as might be expected (e.g., Case, 1985).

The requirement of a hierarchical ordering of the stages has been relaxed by many lifespan theorists as well. Many of the stages discussed by theorists of adult development are held to follow a standard sequence in their unfolding, but are not strictly hierarchical, in the sense that later ways of viewing the world are logically more comprehensive than earlier ones. This would apply to such stage models as Erikson's (1950) or Levinson's (1978), for example. Grappling with Erikson's issue of "intimacy" as a young adult is not *logically* inferior in any way to coping with the "generativity" concerns of middle age. Similarly, Kohlberg's stage theory of moral development has been criticized as a description of later-life development because its most advanced stages may represent alternate endpoints in development, rather than a strict, hierarchical sequence (e.g., Gibbs, 1979). Kohlberg's (1984) own discussions of "soft" stages of adult moral and religious development point in a similar direction. Such relaxations of the strict hierarchy notion of stage sequence seem to accommodate the greater diversity in developmental pathways that is held to characterize adulthood compared with childhood (e.g., Schaie, 1990).

Finally, the notion of universality in stage sequence is weakened in most adult developmental frameworks. Seeing alternative pathways and possible endpoints to development argues that not everyone travels the same road in the same way. A recent issue in later-life sociocognitive development has been the question of whether age is the best criterion measure for investigating the development of adult reasoning patterns (e.g., Labouvie-Vief, DeVoe, & Bulka, 1989). These investigators, studying people's conceptions of their own emotional processes, showed that measures of developmental complexity of reasoning were better predictors of level of performance on this emotions task than was chronological age in adulthood. Such findings (cf. Labouvie-Vief, Hakim-Larson, & Hobart, 1987) also undermine a notion of universality of stage sequence attainment, by decoupling development from the universal factor of age, and linking it to the contingent factor of complexity of individual reasoning patterns instead.

Overall, then, discontinuities in cognitive development, of the strong type posited by Piagetian theory during the early part of the lifespan, are believed by most to be less in evidence in later adulthood. Though stage-like models of adult development have been suggested by many, theorists have generally accommodated the properties of these models to the apparent diversity of cognitive pathways in adulthood. And many recent models of cognitive development acknowledge that underlying quantitative changes in the efficiency of processes of thinking may account for seemingly qualitative shifts in performance, thus bringing together the stage and information-processing positions on cognitive growth (e.g., Case, 1985, 1992; Siegler, 1991).

Lifespan issues

Gain/loss balance over the lifespan

As a child, Mike attended rather fundamentalist Christian religious services. He spent lots of time coloring attractive biblical scenes and learning stories about interesting people. However, these usually pleasant Sunday school experiences were sometimes marred by what he recalls now as frightening exhortations to pray to the Almighty to spare our sin-sick souls for another night. Views of the child's early nature as innately "sinful" have been shared by many, including proponents of a variety of religions, as well as of Freudian psychoanalytic theory (Kessen, 1965). Such frameworks naturally tend to view the story of development as one of mastering a dangerous human nature through hard-won gains in the human rational faculties (e.g., Shaffer, 1989). Conversely, others have seen development as the story of a long fall from the blissful innocence and grace of childhood into the corruption of the world (Kessen, 1965).

Despite these divergent psychological views on the child and the processes of some aspects of early development, when the focus is specifically on cognition, the overwhelming view has been one of growth and positive change during the early part of the life cycle (Baltes, 1987). In contrast, the primary view of cognitive change in later life, certainly the perspective emphasized by much traditional clinical and neurological research, has been one of loss (Baltes, 1987; Labouvie-Vief, 1985; Salthouse, 1991). Later adulthood is seen as host to a range of more or less serious cognition-impairing disorders, such as Alzheimer's disease, and even those older adults free from such specific conditions have generally been believed to suffer from increasing handicaps in basic cognitive processes such as memory and attention.

These patterns of differences in developmental change over the lifespan have been observed as well in the area of social cognition. For example, Walker (1989) has shown that rates of gain in the acquisition of Kohlberg's stages in moral thinking are much faster in children over a standard two-year period than they are in a comparison group of adults at midlife. And these gains in moral judgment reasoning may well become actual losses in very late adulthood (e.g., Pratt, Golding, Hunter, & Norris, 1988).

Of course, this is not just an arcane view shared by researchers. In many cultures, cognitive losses in later life are part of the standard "folk psychology" about development as well. For example, Heckhausen, Dixon, and Baltes (1989) examined lay people's views in Germany about the patterns of personal development across adulthood. Various adjectives were rated for the extent to which they showed a developmental change, either positive or negative, in adulthood, and views on when these changes began and ended were solicited. Results showed that raters from 20 to 80 years of age exhibited considerable consensus on a pattern of greater expected "losses" than gains in many characteristics in later life (especially after 80), as well as predominantly many more gains in earlier adulthood. Nevertheless, even in late life, a number of gains were also attributed, in adjectives with positive connotations such as "wise" and "dignified." Thus, despite a strong consensus on a shift toward losses in later adulthood, a cultural belief in some countervailing gains was also evident in these findings.

As Baltes (1987) notes, it is for precisely these reasons that lifespan developmental theorists in the social sciences have stressed the notion of a relative gain/loss *balance* in development as a way of integrating contemporary theorizing about both ends of the life course. Despite the differences in cognitive change from early childhood to late life, some gains in later adulthood in certain areas may be possible and should at least be considered (Baltes, 1987). Baltes cites the emerging area of "wisdom," discussed later in chapter 7, as a possible case in point. And, conversely, the possibility of cognitive losses in earlier life should be explored as well. An example here might well be a decline in the freshness and spontaneity of children's drawing occurring with the onset of schooling and the later technical focus in youngsters' art (e.g., Gardner, 1973). At any rate, the notion of relativity conveyed by this idea of evaluative balance raises important implications for perspectives on change across the lifespan.

An even stronger proposal is that *every* change over the lifespan inherently implies both gains and losses (Baltes, 1987). The notion here is that acquisition of a new skill or specialization entails certain new risks as well as new potentials. For example, Elkind (1967) has suggested that the acquisition of Piaget's highest stage of formal operational reasoning by the teenager means greater skills in solving logical problems, but also new risks in terms of the possibilities of "egocentric" confusions between the adolescent's views of herself and her understanding of how others view her. Memories of awkward social situations in adolescence, when the whole world seemed to turn on one's every *faux pas*, make these developmental risks vivid for many of us.

Contextualization of adult development

Mike's father, Ted Pratt, was born in 1911. In addition to the fact that this now makes him a man of a certain age, it also means that he has experienced a particular historical and social context. He was born at the end of a year when people worried about the "dangerous" tail of Halley's comet (as the Earth passed through it on the comet's 75-year-long journey about the sun). Ted came of age in the greatest worldwide economic depression of modern times. And, as he reached retirement age, the long Cold War showed its first tentative signs of thaw. Lifespan developmentalists have particularly stressed that patterns of growth and change across the life course must be understood and given meaning within specific historical and sociocultural contexts such as these (Baltes, 1987). Thus, in thinking about development, one is not just an older man in his 80s, but an 80ish North American male in a late twentieth-century historical context.

Neugarten and Datan (1973) have emphasized the need to distinguish at least three types of time dimension in considering lifespan development: life time or chronological age, social time, and historical time. Chronological age is of course the prototypic index of life time for describing human development, and the one most salient for students of the systematic laws of growth and change over the life course. But social time, including the extent to which the individual is either synchronized or not with cultural expectations about the life course for his or her cohort or age group, is also of great importance. For example, Caspi, Elder, and Bem (1988) showed that males who were shy in childhood were more likely to be delayed in their entry into stable occupational roles as adults. In turn, such "off-time" delays with respect to normative social expectations were linked to continuing lower levels of occupational achievement and less occupational stability across the lifespan. However, the consequences of childhood shyness for women were quite different, presumably because their personal trait of "shyness" did not interfere with normative roles of these women (homemaker, mother) at this historical time (the 1940s, Caspi et al., 1988). Thus, a complex interaction of life, social, and historical time here appears to produce distinctive developmental trajectories in adulthood.

As another illustration, the role of particular historical "moments" in influencing child-rearing and development has been extensively studied by Elder and his colleagues (e.g., Caspi & Elder, 1986). This research has focused on how the experience of financial hardships in the family engendered by the Great Depression of the 1930s led to different life courses for individual adults. Caspi and Elder suggested that the experience of coping with financial adversity in the 1930s may have actually benefitted middle-class women in their later life. These women expressed more life satisfaction in their 70s than those who had not experienced Depression-linked hardships, presumably because such hardships allowed them to develop better social and cognitive coping resources for dealing with the (sadly) somewhat similar life situation of being old in the 1970s (Caspi & Elder, 1986). However, such an enhancement effect of hardship was not present for working-class women, whose satisfaction at 70 was actually diminished if they had experienced greater Depression hardship. These complex findings suggest that the impact of particular historical events depends strongly on what resources individuals bring to these experiences (Caspi & Elder, 1986). But they also highlight the critical "filtering" role that such unique historical events can play in shaping the developmental trajectories of individual lives.

Of course, the historical context of aging in European and North American society has shown extensive changes as a result of wider societal forces over the past several centuries (e.g., Hareven, 1982). Sociological and historical studies of the status and role of the older person in past times abound. One well-known approach has been modernization theory, which argues that the status of the elderly has declined with the advent of industrialization and modernization in society, and the attendant disruptions to an older, agricultural order in which the elderly were traditionally venerated (e.g., Cowgill & Holmes, 1972).

This linear, idealized story of sociohistorical changes in views of the aged is much too simple, however. Considerable detailed research indicates that the status of the elderly was not necessarily higher in earlier, pre-industrialized society (e.g., Quadagno, 1982). Furthermore, the "isolation" of the elderly from kin relations in modernized societies is complex and certainly not uniformly greater than in earlier centuries (e.g., Hareven, 1982). While the debate on modernization theory has been an interesting and important one in social and historical research, it is beyond the scope of the present book on the social psychology of aging. We should, however, keep in mind the central impact which larger social and economic forces may have on the experiences of individuals at any particular moment in history.

Just as development takes place within particular historical times, it also occurs within particular, culturally defined "settings" or contexts (e.g., Laboratory of Comparative Human Cognition (LCHC), 1983). But these contexts are not simply the person's physical surroundings – the playground or the supermarket. Contexts are obviously social, and involve the activities of people who "serve as environments for each other" (LCHC, 1983, p. 333). To the extent that activities involve specified normative expectations, they can be seen to represent "cultural practices." A culture, then, is represented at the psychological level by participation in a network of such specified contexts for individual experience (e.g., grocery shopping).

What, then, are the implications of a lifespan focus on developmental context? Clearly, it should remind us that different developmental cohorts are unique due to their particular social and historical settings. This does not mean that no commonalities linked to age and developmental status can be established, but that other aspects of experiences which are correlated with or linked to age must be considered in interpreting lifespan trajectories (Schrootes & Birren, 1990). Two older adults, each born in 1911, share more than just their current ages. They also share a particular set of historical circumstances, located within a specific cultural framework. Research designs that follow parallel age changes in different cohort groups over time (termed longitudinal sequential designs, Schaie, 1965) are one way of attempting to distinguish among some of these timing factors. Conducting such studies across varied cultural settings is important as well.

Plasticity across the lifespan

As the saying goes, "You can't teach an old dog new tricks." When Mike's daughter, Adelle, was little, Mike and his wife decided that a puppy would be a great addition to the family, and they promptly spoiled this new acquisition terribly. In particular, they could never get the dog to come when called unless she felt like it. After many struggles with this problem, Mike became convinced that it was simply "wilfulness" genes. However, after some years, when the dog, now grown older and even more "wilful," went to stay with Mike's parents, Mike was amazed to find that his parents succeeded in training her very well. Evidently, there was more potential for change than he had imagined, based on his less-than-effective training regime. Good thing! In fact, despite the adage above, most of us North Americans share a powerful belief in the general possibilities for human, as well as canine, change (e.g., "Today is the first day of the rest of your life"). Naturally, the potential for different developmental paths than those exhibited presently is of great interest to the lifespan theorist of development.

Such within-person variability is referred to as plasticity in development (Baltes, 1987). It does seem probable that some declines in plasticity in development occur in later life (e.g., R. M. Lerner, 1984). Nevertheless, many lifespan theorists argue that there is evidence that considerable plasticity is maintained across the lifespan. These questions have generally been examined through training research, of which there has been an increasing amount with older adults in recent years (e.g., Willis, 1990). Of course, this theoretical issue also has very important practical implications with respect to responsiveness to interventions to remediate difficulties or problems in cognitive functioning across the lifespan as well.

Investigations of developmental plasticity over the lifespan might usefully be viewed as falling into two broad categories, which differ in both the extensiveness of the interventions involved, and in the underlying conception of the issues being studied (Baltes, 1987). Thus, training interventions of relatively brief duration have been used to assess the role of so-called "performance" limitations in the individual's response deficits for both children and adults (e.g., Flavell & Wohlwill, 1969). Longer-term and more extensive interventions have been used to examine questions of "learning potential" among both young and old (e.g., Ferrara, Brown, & Campione, 1986).

As will be discussed below, Piagetian research with children has been extensively criticized in recent years on the basis that performance factors in standard assessment procedures may mask children's underlying competence, and lead to errors of diagnosis (e.g., Gelman & Baillargeon, 1983). For example, relatively brief training of attention allows young children to show robust conservation of number skills at a much younger age than predicted by Piagetian theory (Gelman, 1969). Similarly, when older adults are given brief training in the use of simple memory strategies, their recall of names to faces is greatly enhanced (Gratzinger, Sheikh, & Friedman, 1990). The argument in such studies is that individuals "have" an underlying competence, but are unable to demonstrate it due to some performance limitation (e.g., a tendency to be distracted by the physical arrangement of a row of objects in conservation tests). Considerable evidence of such plasticity in overcoming performance limitations in specific task situations is apparent in recent studies of older adults (e.g., Willis, 1990).

A more extensive notion of plasticity is implied by interventions which focus on assessments of the individual's "potential" (Baltes, 1987). Vygotsky's conception of the child's capacity to learn more or less effectively with supportive social environmental assistance from adults (the "zone of proximal development," Vygotsky, 1978) has been studied through extended learning interventions in recent research (e.g., Ferrara et al., 1986). Here, the notion is not one of allowing the individual to exhibit a competence already present, but rather to assess the potential to acquire a competence which is truly just beginning to emerge. A similar conception underlies recent work on "testing the limits" in older adults (e.g., Kliegl, Smith, & Baltes, 1990). In this work, the "reserve capacity" to acquire new skills across the lifespan is investigated in relatively extensive training procedures. As predicted, age has been shown to interact with such learning procedures. Thus, younger adults exceed older adults much more extensively after training than before, indicating greater "reserve capacity" in the younger group (Kliegl et al., 1987). Nevertheless, older adults show considerable potential for gains in these studies. As the evidence on social–cognitive development in later life is considered throughout this book, the limited amount of research on training, and the indications of plasticity in development that are implied, will be highlighted.

Four theoretical frameworks

The psychometric perspective

The psychometric tradition in cognitive psychology has focused on the use of standardized assessment procedures designed to measure individual differences in "intelligence." At the beginning of the twentieth century, Alfred Binet and his co-worker, Henri Simon, developed an assessment instrument for use in testing Paris school children for the practical purpose of identifying those who were intellectually "backward," and in need of special class placement. From this initial work has grown a plethora of assessment methods and tests for measuring variations in cognitive abilities across the lifespan. It is fair to note, however, that many of these tests were initially developed for use with children, and were based on the criterion (prediction measure) of scholastic performance, like the original Binet–Simon measure itself (Schaie, 1990). Several major issues have detracted from both the use and conceptualization of these tests throughout the century, including the extent to which the tests assess intelligence in "real life," the extent to which the abilities measured are genetically or environmentally determined, and the extent to which intellectual ability is a single entity or many different things (e.g., Orasanu et al., 1977).

A dominant early hypothesis within this perspective was that there was a single, unitary intelligence, which was largely genetically determined (e.g., Spearman, 1904). Early investigators of this perspective in relation to lifespan development suggested that this unitary intelligence of early life became differentiated into more distinct abilities in adulthood, and then "de-differentiated" again into a single ability structure in later life (Balinsky, 1941). However, the evidence for any "unitary" conception of intelligence as a single entity has been severely criticized (e.g., Gould, 1982), and studies of later adulthood have failed to support any notion of "de-differentiation" with aging (Schmidt & Botwinick, 1989).

In the 1960s and 70s, further analyses of psychometric test data across adulthood led to the proposition that there were distinct *types* of intelligence, which aged in different ways. Cattell (1963), Horn (e.g.,

1982), and others proposed a distinction between *fluid* and *crystallized* intelligences, which underlie performance on different types of ability tests. Fluid abilities support skills on novel tasks, involving learning of new activities (e.g., arranging sets of blocks to copy novel visual patterns on the block design test of the Wechsler Adult Intelligence Scale). Crystallized abilities support tasks that involve using cultural information already learned (e.g., general information or vocabulary tests). Both types of tests are included in most standardized measures of intelligence. When these two ability structures were separated, it was argued that fluid intelligence peaked in early adulthood and then declined, whereas crystallized intelligence remained constant or even showed increments into later adulthood (Horn, 1982). However, careful investigations of age changes, using *longitudinal* studies that follow the same individuals as they age, have shown less marked decline than expected in fluid abilities, and at a later point in the lifespan (e.g., Cunningham & Tomer, 1990).

More recently, theorizing has challenged the psychometric paradigm on the question of the extent to which standard assessment procedures actually represent examples of "everyday" intelligence (e.g., Sternberg & Wagner, 1986). The school-based criterion of standard intellectual assessment for children is essentially irrelevant in adulthood (Schaie, 1990). This raises important issues about what "intelligence" *is* in adulthood (of course, these questions are very important in childhood as well). Many have proposed that social/practical dimensions of intellectual ability must be assessed more adequately to measure intelligence in adulthood (e.g., Baltes, 1987; Sternberg, 1985). Efforts to understand what is meant by later-life intelligence, including concepts such as "social intelligence" and "wisdom," are just beginning to emerge in the lifespan psychometric perspective. They will be reviewed in the chapters which follow.

What are the important contributions of the psychometric framework to lifespan sociocognitive development? As indicated, psychometric approaches draw on evidence collected from standardized test batteries, obtained under highly controlled procedures, and designed primarily to investigate individual differences in cognitive performance across the lifespan. The data obtained from these standard assessments are particularly suited to the investigation of changes over time in cognitive functioning, and most of the longitudinal research on cognitive development in adulthood to date has used psychometric tests (e.g., Schaie, 1990). This framework has also encouraged theorists to ask important questions about the meaning of "intelligence," about the role of social knowledge and skills, and the ways that such cognitive processes are related to real life, even if the answers to these questions are still uncertain.

The information-processing perspective

Over the past 30 years, the dominant model in psychological research on adult cognition has been an "information-processing" framework (e.g., Salthouse, 1985). This theory treats human thinking as fundamentally parallel to the processing of information that takes place in a computer. As computer technology and theory have developed, the applications of this analogy to human thinking have also grown. Salthouse (1985) noted that this approach seeks to describe specific components of human thinking at a level between actual behavioral phenomena (e.g., recalling one's fifth birthday party) and neurological mechanisms (e.g., changes in brain synapses with experience).

There are several key features that distinguish this perspective from other approaches to cognition (Kausler, 1991). Information-processing theories postulate both structures (e.g., a long-term memory storage "system") and processes (e.g., retrieval activities to access specific memories from this system) as part of their models of information processing. This structure and process distinction is formally parallel to the "hardware" and "software" components of computer systems, respectively (Kausler, 1991). Second, the mental operations involved in processing information describe a sequence of short-term "stages," each of which takes a real, though brief, amount of time (Kausler, 1991), just as do computer processes. Thus, *quantitative* changes in either the capacity of a structure, or in the rate of a process, could be involved in age-related changes in cognitive performance. This "mechanistic" framework, focusing on the efficiency of specific component processes in thinking, differs fundamentally from the qualitative "organismic" perspective on development proposed by Piaget (see the next section), which focuses on transformations in the broad patterning of mental structures in describing growth and change (Kausler, 1991). A third feature of these models is the postulation of some sort of "executive" or control component, a "central processor" which oversees and regulates the role of various component systems in task performance (e.g., Kail & Bisanz, 1982).

Early lifespan research within the information-processing framework, comparing young versus older adults on identical laboratory tasks, yielded considerable evidence of possible decline in cognitive functioning (Datan et al., 1987). Older adults were found to perform at lower levels on attention, memory, perceptual-motor, and problem-solving tasks of a variety of sorts, compared with their younger counterparts. Longitudinal studies of older adults, actually tracking changes in individuals over time, have often supported these findings of decline as well, though not necessarily as clearly or dramatically (e.g., Arenberg, 1988).

These early results led to a conviction in the 1970s and 80s that some specific deficiency in processing must account for the general pattern of cognitive performance losses in the aged. As Kausler (1991) suggests, this perspective, labeled "resource theory," has been a modern-day theoretical crusade in search of the Holy Grail of a specific "lack" that might account for adult cognitive changes with age. Two very popular explanations have been based on the analogies of either shrinking space or temporal slowing. The notion of "working memory," a limited capacity system where information is assembled, transformed, and utilized in problem-solving, is the best example of the space metaphor. According to this model, older adults are seen as losing territory, just as young children may be viewed as acquiring it (e.g., Light, 1991). Many studies of apparent aging deficits have been conducted from this perspective, and it will be a common theme in the chapters to follow.

An alternative explanation of aging deficits focuses on a general slowing of cognitive processing rates with age (e.g., Cerella, 1990; Salthouse, 1985). As processing slows down, the efficiency and accuracy of performance suffers because component systems in problem-solving may not be able to maintain information long enough to pass it on effectively to others. Such a change in the latter part of the lifespan is apparently paralleled by a general speeding of processing rate in early development (e.g., Hale, 1990). Other explanations (e.g., changes in deliberate strategies for processing information) have also been proposed, though space and speed are the most common (e.g., Light, 1991).

One important criticism of the information-processing framework has been directed at its reliance on laboratory evidence to investigate and model human thinking. As Salthouse (1990) noted, there is a kind of paradox in the apparent fact that older adults function quite well in the real world, often in positions of influence and importance, despite the evidence amassed in the laboratory for cognitive decline! How can this be? Salthouse (1990) discussed a number of potential explanations of this discrepant pattern. One possibility could be that the laboratory findings describe processes that are simply irrelevant to real-life think-ing. In fact, there has been considerable controversy among information-processing theorists in general on this point (e.g., Banaji & Crowder, 1989; Cohen, 1989).

Another potentially more interesting explanation with regard to aging and everyday performance, however, turns on the ideas of *compensation*. This is the notion that individuals may maintain their level of competent performance, despite the loss of some capacities, by reorganizing the ways in which they carry out a task. The work of Salthouse (1984) on skilled typists provides a possible example. Older typists are slower in basic reaction times than younger counterparts, but they are able to maintain their overall words-per-minute rates by looking further ahead and processing larger "chunks" of text at a time. This example, and others like it (e.g., Charness, 1989), may provide a model for compensatory processes in the maintenance of skilled socio-cognitive performance.

What have been the contributions of this information-processing perspective to adult social cognition research? The strength of this ap-proach is its analytic perspective on the mental structures and processes in reasoning and problem-solving. Cognitive performance is studied by decomposing the component processes involved, in controlled con-ditions, to understand their roles in detail. Given this emphasis, it is no surprise that this approach has primarily encouraged and utilized con-trolled experimentation in laboratory settings. For example, memory performance for a social stimulus such as faces might be studied under different conditions of storage and retrieval (see chapter 4 for a descrip-tion of such work). There is, as noted, a contemporary emphasis among some researchers to use this framework to study real-life cognitive performance as well (e.g., Cohen, 1989). The emphasis on specificity in this framework should provide more precise targets for both assess-ment of cognitive skills and problems and for interventions.

The developmental perspective

This perspective on social cognition in adulthood has been dominated by the work of the Swiss philosopher/biologist-turned-psychologist, Jean Piaget. The central feature of this perspective has been Piaget's emphasis on the child's continual attempts to construct "meaning," to understand and interpret the world that experience presents to him or her. Piaget's theory of the universal construction of four stages in such human "meaning-making" began to have a substantial impact in the early 1960s on North American developmental psychology. Though Piaget's interests were primarily in cognition about the physical world, his developmental theories were readily adapted to describing thinking about the social world of other persons, relationships, and the self. Probably the most influential proponent of Piaget's views in this context was Kohlberg (e.g., 1969). He formulated a six-stage model of moral reasoning (discussed at more length in chapter 7), and applied Piaget's stage framework to thinking about gender and other aspects and categories of social development. Kohlberg's students and colleagues have continued this tradition in social cognition research (e.g., Damon, 1981; Selman, 1980; Turiel, 1983).

Piaget himself, and most of the researchers just mentioned, have had little to say about the later portion of the life cycle (Kohlberg, as discussed in chapter 7, is an exception). Nevertheless, the availability of Piagetian childhood measures (such as the famous water pouring assessment of the young child's failure to understand the conservation of amount during transformations in appearance), and the implicit prediction of the theory that there should be cognitive stability across the lifespan after adolescence, made it inevitable that researchers would apply these techniques to adult cognition as well. A series of such studies appeared in the early 1970s, generally reporting that older adults performed less adequately than young or middle-aged groups on these measures, and, in fact, scored at stages comparable to child or adolescent norms (e.g., Bielby & Papalia, 1975; Looft, 1972). These findings invited the interpretation of later adult "regression" in cognitive functioning. However, longitudinal evidence of individual change was lacking in these *cross-sectional* studies, which focused on comparisons of people of different ages at the same point in time.

Despite the pattern of evidence in these early studies, interpretive questions regarding this notion of a late-life stage regression were soon raised (Datan, Rodeheaver, & Hughes, 1987). Careful research sampling showed that more educated, cognitively intact, and socially engaged elderly persons tended to do better on these Piagetian tasks than their less fortunate peers (e.g., Dolen & Bearison, 1982). As well, brief practice and training experiences with these tasks often led to considerable improvement in the performance of older adults (e.g., Schultz & Hoyer, 1976). Researchers of cognitive stage development in the earlier portion of the lifespan were also grappling with findings that young children often performed at levels better than expected by theory when seemingly minor aspects of problems were simplified or streamlined (e.g.,

Gelman & Baillargeon, 1983). These results were interpreted within a "competence–performance" distinction in developmental theorizing (e.g., Overton & Newman, 1982). The apparent stage "regressions" of elderly adults might simply reflect performance problems in delivering the goods in unfamiliar, likely irrelevant, and perhaps confusing situations, rather than signs of actual declines in underlying stage-level competence (Datan et al., 1987).

As will become apparent throughout this book, this line of interpretation is still quite common. However, since the 1980s, many theorists of adult development, with interests in Piaget's framework, have begun to take a much more radical position. These approaches have come to be labeled the "post-formalist" perspective (e.g., Commons, Richards, & Armon, 1984). What they share is the notion that Piaget's theory is not adequate to the task of describing the development of reasoning in adulthood, and that some further stage(s) of reasoning beyond Piaget's endpoint of formal operations must be posited. A wide range of proposals have been put forward for what such a stage or stages should look like, and there is surely no consensus to date on these ideas. But, these theorists argue, how can the reasoning of an early adolescent solving geometry problems, and that of Einstein, carrying out thought experiments by mentally riding a beam of light, be described as formally the same? (e.g., Arlin, 1989). From the point of view of this framework, then, the apparently "limited" performance of many adults results from an inability to understand their novel perspectives on the tasks, which are actually quite different than those of childhood or adolescence (e.g., Labouvie-Vief, 1985). These post-formalist ideas will be discussed in more detail in chapter 4.

What are the primary contributions of this perspective to an understanding of the development of social cognition? As noted, the central tenet of the Piagetian framework is the human need for "meaning-making," and nowhere is this more apparent than in social understanding and interpretation. This emphasis on the individual's construction of meanings has led to a particular methodological focus on "clinical" interviews and observations which permit the person to present his or her ways of understanding issues and problems (Cowan, 1978). The search for stages to describe people's ways of understanding has encouraged a broad focus in these interviews, while permitting participants considerable latitude to express their interpretive frameworks (e.g., Colby & Kohlberg, 1987; Labouvie-Vief et al., 1989). The value of such evidence for understanding general *patterns* of thinking, where carefully collected and interpreted, is great.

Before leaving our discussion of the developmental framework, it is appropriate to review briefly another recently influential perspective, the sociocultural model of the Russian developmental theorist Lev Vygotsky (e.g., Vygotsky, 1978; Wertsch, 1991). Working in the 1920s and 30s, Vygotsky sought to bring Marxist principles to bear on a theory of the development of the child. However, it is only in the last 15 years or so that his work has received significant attention in the West, partly in counterpoint to the work of Piaget, with which he was quite familiar (e.g., Rogoff, 1990).

In contrast to Piaget, who emphasized the role of the child as an individual "discoverer" or meaning-maker, becoming more sophisticated in thinking by examining her private experience of both the social and physical world, Vygotsky strongly emphasized the role of social and cultural forces in supporting and guiding the child's cognitive growth (Vygotsky, 1978). Adults, particularly, in Bruner's felicitous phrase, serve as "vicars of culture" in inducting the child into more sophisticated techniques of problem-solving through collaborative activities (Bruner, 1985).

Vygotsky analyzed cognitive activity in adult–child tutoring interactions as a joint, social venture, in which the adult initially provides an overall guiding function by locating the level at which the child can participate with some degree of success in problem-solving ("the zone of proximal development," e.g., Pratt, Kerig, Cowan, & Cowan, 1988). As the child participates in the activity, she becomes able to take over more and more of the problem-solving planning and function, and the adult cedes more and more control to her. Gradually, the child "internalizes" the joint interactional activity, which initially occurred between child and adult, as a self-regulatory process for guiding her internal problem-solving and thinking (Vygotsky, 1978). Thus, cognitive functions for Vygotsky initially occur on the interpersonal "plane" of social interaction and gradually become "intrapersonal" (within the mind of the child). For example, helping a tongue-tied two-year-old learn the skill of telling about past experiences may initially involve the adult in setting the stage and prompting almost all of the material ("and then Auntie gave you your new what?"). Eventually, the adult steps back more and more, as the child becomes capable of structuring and retrieving the past from memory more on her own (e.g., Fivush, 1991). And then the stories may never stop!

There are other important differences of emphasis between Piaget and Vygotsky (e.g., Rogoff, 1990), but this distinctive difference in views of the role of the social world is central. Vygotsky's perspective, along with that of other Marxist theorists who shared it (such as the linguist Bakhtin; Wertsch, 1991), provides an alternative view of individual development as arising directly and dialectically out of the matrix of sociocultural activity in which the child is naturally engaged. Vygotsky did not neglect the role of individual, biologically-based development, but he held that this early line of growth was fully transformed and altered by the social and linguistic experiences of the child with the culture (Vygotsky, 1978).

Vygotsky had little to say about development during the later part of the life cycle. However, his emphasis on socially-shared cognitive activity during earlier development has been paralleled by some recent research on collaborative cognitive problem-solving in adults (such as remembering, e.g., Middleton & Edwards, 1990). It is this aspect of social cognition as collaborative activity between adults, or as influenced by such collaborative activity, which is of importance to the present analysis (cf. Dixon, 1992). As noted in chapter 1, this provocative idea of Vygotsky and others in the developmental literature provides an organizing theme for our review of the social–cognitive aging literature below.

The social–psychological perspective

Social cognition research in social psychology has been very extensive since the 1950s. Social psychologists have consistently emphasized the importance of how the person perceives and thinks about the social world as crucial to understanding his or her responses and behaviors, even when most other branches of psychology were rejecting this emphasis under the influence of behaviorism (Fiske & Taylor, 1991). Fiske and Taylor suggest that four broad models of the "social thinker" have been described over the past 40 years: the "consistency seeker," the "naive scientist," the "cognitive miser," and the "motivated tactician." Each of these frameworks is described briefly below. However, despite this extensive history of research in social cognition, there has been very little specific attention to adult development.

In the 1950s and 60s, several models of attitude change were formulated which relied on the notion of consistency (e.g., Festinger, 1957; Heider, 1958). These theories all suggested that people sought to maintain or establish *consistency* between their various perceptions, feelings, and behaviors. For example, if you engage in some boring activity for a very small reward, your "cognitive dissonance" over the clash between your behavior and your view of the activity as not worthwhile may lead you to re-evaluate the activity as not so bad after all (Festinger, 1957). Thus, your behavior and your cognitive evaluation of the activity become more consistent. In these theories, affect or feeling states, particularly the unpleasant tension caused by inconsistency, were viewed as central motivators which led to cognitive activity to reduce this tension (Fiske & Taylor, 1991).

These consistency models were gradually displaced in the 1960s and 70s by a focus on the human as a "logician" of the social world. Based in the work of Heider (1958) and others, the attribution theory framework emphasized a model of people as "naive scientists" striving to understand, and particularly to explain, the causes of social behaviors of both others (e.g., Jones & Davis, 1965) and themselves (Bem, 1967). A formal model of how various categories of causes (e.g., personal qualities, situational influences) are combined in everyday social reasoning was outlined by Kelley (1972). Considerable research on the development of such models among children and adolescents was conducted (e.g., Smith, 1975). However, there has been very limited research on these attributional models in elderly persons (see chapter 4). Developmental research in the early part of the lifespan showed that children often failed to use these "rational" models for making attributions in understanding others (e.g., Shultz et al., 1974). However, much evidence suggests that young adults have the very same problem (Fiske & Taylor, 1991).

The considerable limitations of adults' inference processes in explaining social phenomena led to a third model in the 1980s – the adult as "cognitive miser" (e.g., Fiske & Taylor, 1991). In this model, people were seen as coping with a limited capacity to process complex information due to a cognitive system which is easily over-loaded. This view is closely linked to the information-processing models dominant in cognitive psychology, as noted above. Social thinkers, in this model, tend to operate as simply as possible, using easy short-cuts or simplified rules that work part of the time in considering most everyday social problems or questions. For example, it may be simplest to conclude that your neighbor's singing results from his cheerful disposition, ignoring the many other possibilities that may be involved as well (maybe it's choir practice!). This model does not emphasize motivational biases as sources of cognitive errors (Fiske & Taylor, 1991). Biases simply result from the use of rules which may not be appropriate or sufficient in the situations where they are applied. Because it has been argued that older adults have more limited information-processing capacities than their younger counterparts, this "cognitive miser" model may have particular implications for later life. However, the model has received very little attention in the aging literature to date.

Most recently, there has been an effort to combine some of the early interest in cognitive motivation demonstrated through the consistency theories, with the recent, sophisticated models of cognitive processing. Fiske and Taylor (1991) describe this new framework as the "motivated tactician" model. People are seen to have "multiple cognitive strategies available and [to choose] among them based on goals, motives, and needs" (p. 13). Tetlock (in press) describes a similar "people as politicians" framework, depicting the individual as using cognitive resources to satisfy or respond to a variety of different constituencies (perhaps both outside in the world and "inside," in one's mind). What these newest views share is an emphasis both on diversity in motivations *and* complexity in the ways in which social–cognitive processes may be used in the service of these motives. Their implications for issues of aging involve both an emphasis on increasing individual diversity (in both motives and skills), and a stronger stress on the role of social context in understanding the individual's performance. Though this approach has not influenced aging research to date, it clearly has the potential to do so productively, for example, in the study of later-life individual differences in patterns of thinking about social matters.

Social psychology has been broadly eclectic in its use of a wide range of different research techniques to study social cognition. Particularly characteristic of this approach, however, has been a reliance on *field* methods, or quasi-experimental research studies. These approaches attempt to introduce some of the controls, traditionally associated with the experiment, into real-world settings involving actual phenomena in people's daily lives. For example, a study by Levin and Levin (1981) on age stereotypes asked students to read the (supposed) résumés of visiting professors, and then let the faculty know if they would be attending a talk by these people. Several aspects of the résumés were systematically varied. Under some conditions, résumés describing older persons led to less willingness to attend. This field approach thus introduces controls of a more experimental nature into a relatively "naturalistic" response situation (e.g., Parke, 1979).

Summary and conclusions

This chapter has attempted to demonstrate the ways in which the study of social cognition in later life draws upon a common set of issues and theoretical frameworks with other research on development across the lifespan. Though the amount of empirical evidence on aging and social cognition with respect to many of these lifespan issues and theories is not yet extensive, the same questions about the patterns and sources of development that have guided research in other domains and at other periods of the life cycle are relevant here as well. Throughout the remainder of this book, as this evidence is reviewed, the four theoretical frameworks discussed – the psychometric, developmental, information-processing, and social–psychological approaches – will be highlighted.

The three themes of the book that were articulated in chapter 1 are tied to these lifespan issues and frameworks in important ways. The first theme focuses on the need to consider people's broader understanding of the task or problem in interpreting their specific performance and any age differences observed in such performance. This focus on the individual's "meaning-making," and how it might change with age, is particularly compatible with the developmental and social-psychological approaches, and with some of the issues raised by the discontinuity position on how development takes place. If people's interpretation of issues changes across the adult lifespan, this is likely to have important consequences for understanding their performance on relevant tasks. An emphasis on the need to be concerned with the person's own view of his or her experience is thus, in our view, a central contribution of these approaches to lifespan research.

Our second theme of individual diversity across the lifespan in the processes of aging and development is particularly compatible with the psychometric and information-processing models. Both of these frameworks tend to concentrate on within-age-group differences in characterizing patterns of thinking. This emphasis on diversity contrasts somewhat with the discontinuity position's focus on age-linked "stages" of change, by stressing the breadth of differences in most cognitive skills that can be expected *within* any age group. Both the role of social and historical context differences in development, and the emphasis on genetic–environmental interaction in change, may be particularly important in relation to this diversity theme. The issue of gain–loss balance in change across the lifespan reminds us that there will often be diversity in the functional effects of development as well as in its patterns.

The third theme, stressing the importance of the individual's social context for the ways in which skills are manifested over the lifespan, seems especially tied to an emphasis on describing the social environment of cognitive performance. The historical–cultural context of development is central to this theme (e.g., Luria, 1976), in that cognitive skills are presumably strongly shaped by the cultural context of their use (Laboratory of Comparative Human Cognition, 1983). As well, this theme emphasizes the plasticity of development, by conceptualizing variations in cognitive performance within a broader context. For example, an older adult who can no longer manage her daily routines independently may nevertheless do quite well with minimal levels of supportive supervision from a home visitor. Whether or not she still "has" these skills depends in large part on how we interpret the context of their use. It is important to avoid a too narrow focus on this question of performance as we review the research evidence below.

3

Thinking about the Self

My theory is why not think Carnegie Hall? As long as you see it there, you can strive and get up there. Once you get to the top, you can coast and rest for a bit . . . I knew that one day [my employers] were going to say, "How would you like to run an elevator in a one storey building?" So, I decided no. So I made a phone call . . . Within four weeks of doing that, I started to work. So I was 50. Past 50. Again everybody said "You are crazy; past 40, you can't get a job." I not only got a job, I got a better job. Which again to me was a tremendous lift . . . I was fortunate that it was a completely different type of job . . . All of a sudden I had to readjust my whole thinking (Mr Hentschel, a 66-year-old business executive; Norris, 1993, pp. 189–190).

Like this thing they wanted me to do. I said, "No, let [someone else] do it." I hadn't counted up all the things I do until I had to make a rational decision and I realized that I am, or course, coming to an age when I am going to have to do more of this. I am going to have to put some limits. I am on a down escalator. It is only sensible to recognize this. It doesn't involve self-pity or anything of that sort. It is just a straight fact that I have less energy this year than I had last year and next year I will have less again. If your energy output is limited, you had better keep your demands within bounds (Mr Grosberg, a 67-year-old business executive; Norris, 1993, p. 193).

Both executives are in good physical and psychological health, yet have very different attitudes toward work in later life. Mr Hentschel wants to avoid the "one storey elevator" by continuing to develop his career. Mr Grosberg, on the other hand, is willing to accept the "down escalator" which moves him away from his job. Each has chosen a course of action for later life which he feels will preserve his well-being and sense of worth. What are the reasons for their differing strategies?

This chapter explores potential answers to this question through an examination of the self in later life. The focus is on social–psychological processes which support and maintain the self-concept in the face of aging-related events such as illness and retirement. First, we consider how several theoretical perspectives help us to understand the aging self. Following this, we investigate the empirical literature related to the "selfhood" of older people. How is the self constructed and understood in later life? Answering this question involves a look at the research on self-efficacy and coping, the social construction of the self in later life, and metacognition. It should become clear that, on the whole, most older people maintain a strong sense of self throughout despite age-related losses.

Theoretical perspectives on the self

The **psychometric** perspective in psychology evolved as a means of understanding individual differences in cognitive performance within an academic setting. In gerontology, this approach has led to debates over the nature and rate of decline in abilities such as fluid and crystallized intelligence (Horn, 1982; Schaie & Hertzog, 1983). Because of this focus on scholastic abilities, the psychometric perspective, then, has limited relevance for any discussion of an older adult's actual sense of "self." Nevertheless, the methods used by researchers in the psychometric tradition have been adopted by gerontologists to assess how older adults evaluate themselves and their circumstances. Thus, many studies contain measures of morale, life satisfaction and psychological well-being (Larson, 1978).

As Larson's (1978) review makes very clear, early researchers in gerontology were preoccupied with the question of what made older people happy. Constructs such as morale, life satisfaction, well-being, and adjustment to aging emerged to define later-life "happiness," and a multitude of measures were developed to test each one. Among the most popular were the Philadelphia Geriatric Center Morale Scale (Lawton, 1972) and the Life Satisfaction Index A (Neugarten, Havighurst & Tobin, 1961). Both rely on a self-reported evaluation of the self-concept. The respondent is required to analyze his or her personality traits ("I take things hard"), the congruency between desired and achieved goals ("I've gotten pretty much what I expected out of life"), and general satisfaction with the "self" ("As I look back on my life, I am fairly well satisfied").

Recent discussions of life satisfaction in later life show the same general approach to measurement of "self" issues. There has been more concern, however, with precise definitions of the constructs to be measured as well as the psychometric properties of the scales (Kozma, Stones, & McNeil, 1991). Kozma and colleagues (1991) note that approaches to studying well-being can be characterized in one of five ways using "bottom up," "top down," telic, personality, and judgmental conceptualizations.

Researchers using the "bottom up" method of conceptualizing well-being consider well-being as a product of at least two lower order constructs such as dissatisfaction or attitude toward aging ("I'm happy because I'm healthy, have wonderful children, enough money," etc.) Those using the "top down" method assume well-being is a disposition which colours all current experiences ("How happy are you with life in general?"). Researchers employing the personality approach conceptualize well-being as a product of personality traits (e.g., neuroticism, extraversion, openness). Those employing the telic approach suggest well-being is the endpoint achieved when goals are met ("I'm happy because I became company president before I retired"). Finally, those researchers working with the judgmental approach view happiness as the result of an evaluation of current conditions and another standard ("Are you as happy as you expected to be at this point in your life"?).

Kozma, Stones, and McNeil (1991) feel that the strongest method for studying psychological well-being in later life combines both "bottom up" and telic approaches. Thus, they recommend the use of their measure, the Memorial University of Newfoundland Scale of Happiness (MUNSH), which assesses short-term affect ("In the past month have you ever felt on top of the world?") and the evaluation of longer-term experiences viewed from the perspective of old age ("This is the dreariest time of my life"). Regardless of the approach taken, however, the goal of each method remains the same: to measure the self-appraisal of old people and infer their happiness and well-being from this appraisal.

The **information-processing** approach to understanding memory and cognition has led researchers to examine changes in the nature and rate of information processing through the adult years. As we have noted in other chapters, older adults appear to handle information at a slower rate and with less efficiency than the young. There are, however, large individual differences in cognitive abilities related to reaction time, memory and fluid intelligence (Morse, 1993).

Most of the research within this theoretical perspective has been conducted using traditional tasks of cognitive functioning. Thus, little is known about the relationship between information-processing ability and thinking about the self. Nevertheless, there is some suggestive evidence that changes in memory and cognition may have both a direct and an indirect effect on self-appraisals and the maintenance of a healthy self-concept.

The direct effect of information processing on thinking about the self involves a consideration of social activity and the processing of social information. In the aftermath of the disengagement/activity theory debate (see chapter 5), there is general agreement that some form of social involvement is important to psychological well-being in later life. For successful social encounters to occur, however, social information must be processed accurately, and often quickly as well (Hogg & Heller, 1990; Norris & Rubin, 1984). If there are deficits in this processing, an older person may be prevented from adapting his or her own social behavior. As a consequence, future social interactions may appear incompetent (Norris & Rubin, 1984).

The information-processing model also suggests an indirect effect of changes in cognitive functioning on the self through self-appraisal. If losses of speed or accuracy are experienced, or even anticipated, in social and non-social tasks, the self may be evaluated more negatively than before. There is some evidence, for example, that adults who feel "old" relative to their peers may suffer from feelings of depression and low self-efficacy (Furstenberg, 1989). As well, older people who believe that their cognitive abilities and memory functioning are deteriorating may actually perform more poorly on intellectual tasks than their peers (Willis & Schaie, 1986; Hertzog, Dixon, & Hultsch, 1991).

Researchers operating within a **developmental** framework have had somewhat more to say regarding the development of the self through-out adulthood. Stage theorists such as Erikson (1982), for example, have suggested that the ultimate goal of adult life is understanding and accepting the self. This is achieved, he believes, by mastery of tasks related to healthy social relationships. During midlife, this implies a commitment to what Erikson called generativity, a concern for younger generations. Once this developmental task is mastered, adults are able to move on to the task of old age, ego integrity. Achieving integrity involves self-reflection and appraisal. If the outcome of this process is positive, all components of the self can be perceived as integrated; ego integrity has been achieved. If negative, on the other hand, the result is despair.

Despite the widespread use of Erikson's theory in discussing adult development, there is very little empirical work to substantiate his stages and connect them to particular chronological periods. Part of the problem is there are no clear markers for the beginning of "midlife" and "old age", making it difficult for researchers to identify relevant samples. The tendency of contemporary adults to move their personal markers for these ages has not helped (Chudacoff, 1989). People now in their late 30s consider themselves young rather than middle-aged; those in their 60s feel they are middle-aged rather than old (McAdams, de St Aubin, & Logan, 1993). Erikson himself acknowledged historical effects on the application of his theory: "[T]he interrelation of all the stages depends somewhat on the emerging personality and the psychosocial identity of each individual in a given historical setting and time perspective" (Erikson, Erikson, & Kivnick, 1986, p. 337). He did not, however, provide practical suggestions for dealing with these factors in empirical research on his theory.

Despite problems of sampling and cohort effects, some recent work has provided limited support for Erikson's adult stages. Ryff and Heincke (1983), for example, found that middle-aged adults rated themselves as higher on generativity than they had been in the past or would be in the future; older adults felt that they were now more reflective than when they were younger. McAdams and his colleagues (1993), in a cross-sectional study, found an increase in generative commitments and discussion about generativity between young and mid-adulthood. Nevertheless, there was no corresponding decrease from middle to late adulthood as would be predicted from Erikson's theory.

Coppola's (1987) study of Italian–Canadian nursing home residents indicated that there are probably wide individual differences in the ability of older people to achieve ego integrity, and that these differences may have a significant impact on adaptation to aging-related changes. Coppola used a measure which identified four possible outcomes of the ego integrity crisis: integrity achievement, dissonance, foreclosure and despair. Achieved integrity is the desirable status for later life; dissonance refers to entering the crisis period leading to integrity; foreclosure is the avoidance of self-reflection necessary to achieve integrity; despair refers to the inability to achieve an integrated sense of the self. Coppola found that those who had achieved ego integrity, or were foreclosed, i.e., avoided reflection, coped best with relocation to an institution. Those in despair did not adjust well and those experiencing dissonance had a variable experience. The comments of two residents suggest the role of integrity status in coping with aging and change:

> [My experience has been] really good. I thought I would have to start from the top again, but I did not. It was not a hard adjustment (Resident classified as achieving ego integrity).

> Before I came here I suffered. I am here because my kids kicked me out. I thought I would pass my life better; instead I pray to die. You are not on your own here, you have to listen always to others, even when they agitate you (Resident classified as in despair status; Coppola, 1987, p. 70).

Other stage theorists have also postulated the development of the self in old age. As noted in chapter 6, Kohlberg (Levine, Kohlberg, & Hewer, 1985) has speculated that a kind of "universal humanistic" perspective on moral problems could evolve in some older individuals. This advanced stage of reasoning is hypothesized to occur when adults rely on broad, self-chosen principles, rather than social consensus, to resolve moral dilemmas. Education and life experiences are thought to contribute to the development of this type of reasoning. Similarly, Levinson also noted the importance of life experience to personal growth (Levinson, 1978). He proposed that, at least for men, positive self-appraisal in later life is linked to the successful resolution of age-linked transitions. These transitions, occurring in early, middle, and late adulthood, arise from a continuing struggle with opposing tendencies: attachment and separation, destruction and creation, masculinity and femininity, remaining young and growing old.

As noted in chapter 2, stage approaches carry with them assumptions of crisis, change and universality. Other developmentalists, working from the perspective of personality theory, have taken issue with these assumptions, and suggested that the self is characterized more by stability than change throughout the later years. Research by Costa and McCrae using a variety of cross-sectional and longitudinal methods has been strongly supportive of the view that basic personality traits change very little, regardless of life experiences (e.g., Costa, McCrae, & Arenberg, 1980). Other researchers, more cognitive in their orientation, agree that continuity in personality is likely, but also argue that an individual's analysis of his or her life can lead to change and growth (Thomae, 1980; Whitbourne, 1987).

Social psychologists have devoted some attention to the development of the self in later life. The cognitive movement within psychology led to the development of attribution theory; the symbolic interactionist school within sociology led to the emergence of social constructionism.

An attributional analysis of the self in old age is concerned with perceptions of aging, one's own and that of others. Some theorists (e.g., Kuypers & Bengtson, 1973) have proposed that self-esteem can be severely damaged if social attributions, i.e., negative stereotypes, about aging are incorporated into the self-concept. More recently, researchers have suggested that attributional biases which protect the self can be very important in buffering the effects of negative stereotypes. Such a bias might involve considering the self as "young" relative to one's peers, despite advanced chronological age (Furstenberg, 1989).

Symbolic interactionists within gerontology have stressed the importance of older people's construction of their own aging (e.g., Marshall, 1978–9; 1986; Ryff, 1984). The assumption underlying this approach is that an individual interacts with the social world to create and manage an age-appropriate self-concept. Marshall (1986) has described this process as "the development of a model or cognitive map of the individual in relationships with other people" (p. 19). For example, if an older widow's family views her as self-sufficient and capable of autonomous decisions, she will be likely to construct her "old" self around these concepts, and seek other information from the environment which confirms this construction.

The research evidence: the self in later life

I am essentially a loner and have no interest in mixing with others in the Senior Citizen building where I live. I like people but not in group form. I am friendly in a neighbourly way, but do not like card or table games; to me, personally, they seem to be a waste of time. One stumbling block is bad memory and lack of concentration. So I miss out on many amenities provided for all of us. I feel I would not warrant anyone being able to welcome having me as a partner even if I was tempted to exert myself to try. So on games nights I prefer to stay in my own apartment and read or watch television and listen to music.

My great love is for reading for which I claim many reasons. It is of great help in taking me out of myself. While reading, I can get away from dwelling on certain frustrations and anxieties. Also, it helps relieve the guilt of indulging in so much laying down resting periods, even though I know a lot of rest is necessary healthwise . . . The enjoyment I derive from reading is great, especially books on the geography and lifestyles of other countries, probably because I spent all my married life living in the Far East and have visited many foreign countries (Mrs DiCarlo, an 80-year-old widow; Norris, 1979).

As noted earlier in this chapter, most research which deals with the "self" in old age has focused on the affective dimension of the self-concept. Such an approach would lead many gerontologists to ask about this frail older woman's happiness rather than other aspects of her sense of self. Questions about her preference for a solitary lifestyle, her passion for reading, and her perceptions that her memory is failing might be ignored. Why is this? A probable answer is researchers' difficulty in shedding the traditional biodecremental view of aging (see Norris, 1987). If aging is equated with deterioration and decline, then negative changes in psychological functioning would be expected as well. Lower morale, life satisfaction, and contentment would be part of these changes.

This perspective on aging is not popular with lifespan developmentalists who assume that change, both progressive and regressive, is possible throughout life (Baltes, 1987). Nevertheless, most lifespan researchers have still been concerned with assaults on the self-concept that may be produced by losses related to aging.

Four major areas of research have emerged as a result of this thrust. First, there is a substantial literature on adjustment to old age and the coping strategies used by older people. Second, a number of longitudinal studies have addressed the issue of personality change throughout adulthood, particularly focusing on the maintenance of adaptive characteristics such as flexibility. Third, there is an emerging area of research that considers the construction of a self-narrative, or life story, a process used by the older person to make sense of his or her life. Finally, there is a large body of literature on metacognition: how older people think about their own cognitive processes.

Coping with old age

Lerner and Gignac (1992) state that "aging in our society often implies a tragic scenario in which the elderly are increasingly victimized by social and biological processes until their progressive deterioration is interrupted by death" (pp. 321–322). They also note that despite the fact that this scenario makes old people "society's quintessential victims" (p. 321), they are surprisingly free from demoralization and unhappiness. The underlying model of aging here, of course, is one of loss; the major developmental task of old age then becomes coping with loss.

While Lerner and Gignac's (1992) view of aging may seem extreme to some, it is one which pervades the literature. Gerontologists have been intrigued by the ability of old people who have endured multiple losses, not only to carry on with the tasks of daily living, but also to derive enjoyment from life. How, for example, can Mrs DiCarlo avoid despair from the crippling arthritis that prevents her from travelling, and even makes it difficult to leave her apartment? Why, one wonders, are her books and an occasional visit from her daughter or the meals-on-wheels driver sufficient to nourish her mind and provide contentment in her life?

Disengagement theorists of 30 years ago would have answered these questions by pointing to Mrs DiCarlo's age, and hypothesizing that she had passed through inevitable, developmental changes which began in midlife. These changes would have made her more self-focused and withdrawn from the world, but still happy (Cumming & Henry, 1961; Havighurst, Neugarten, & Tobin, 1968; see also chapter 5). Happiness and a positive self-concept are preserved, according to a disengagement perspective, because growing psychological interiority and passivity make it impossible to deal with as many psychosocial demands as earlier in the lifespan. Thus, the best way to grow old is to withdraw.

There is limited support for disengagement theory. Most of the existing studies point to declines in health and the availability of social partners, rather than intrinsic developmental factors, as predictive of disengagement (Johnson & Barer, 1992). Nevertheless, the idea that developmental change produces a new approach to life in old age is not uncommon in the recent literature. For example, various authors have suggested that a kind of post-formal operational thinking emerges with age (Arlin, 1975; Sinnott, 1984). There are differing views on the nature of this thinking, but most researchers have argued that post-formal reasoning involves the ability to handle dialectical conflict and contradiction (Labouvie-Vief, 1982; Riegel, 1975).

Such dialectical processes could alter the self-concept by suggesting avenues for personal change and growth. Mrs DiCarlo's illness, for example, has challenged her ability to cope with the environment. Thus the dialectic she experiences is one of diminished person–environment fit (Lawton, 1972). She may avoid feelings of unhappiness and low self-esteem, however, if more than one avenue of adjustment to her new circumstances is available. For example, she could accept her house-bound status and build on her love of literature by taking a correspond-ence course. Alternatively, she could alleviate her isolation and loneliness by moving to an institution. Either alternative would require her to adapt her sense of self to incorporate the role of "student" or "resident."

There is limited research evidence for the relationship between dial-ectical thinking and personal growth (see chapter 4). Chandler (1975), for example, noted that older adults may engage in more relativistic thinking in later life. Differing perspectives are recognized, weighed, and personalized, enabling an older adult "to more explicitly articulate who he or she is in terms of an enhanced sense of choice and self-affirmation" (Gignac, 1991, pp. 16–17). This phenomenon is very similar to one encountered in adolescence when individuals recognize the pres-ence of multiple perspectives on any issue (Chandler, 1987).

Although it was not designed as a study of post-formal thinking, some support for this approach can be found in Norris and Tari's (1985) qualitative study of grandparents. Findings from this work suggest that life events such as retirement can cause older people to enter a kind of psychosocial moratorium. The concept of moratorium is borrowed from Marcia's (1966) description of well-functioning adolescents who, as part of their search for identity, examine their options and sample widely from a variety of activities. According to Marcia (1966), adolescents who do not engage in such experimentation "foreclose" on their sense of self, and do not achieve a mature identity. In an apparently similar fashion, the older people in the Norris and Tari (1985) study made active choices about the kind of self-development they wanted for them-selves in later life, rather than relying on the roles scripted for them by society. In this sense, they were involved in a later-life psychosocial moratorium. The busy and open lifestyle which characterized most of the people in this sample can be seen in the words of a 68-year-old retired engineer:

> I have so many hobbies that that's what keeps me going. I have a model railroad and I learn something about just about everyday in experimenting with transistorized and SCR throttles at the moment . . . and then I do latch hooking. That big tiger's face over there that's one I designed. I do that sort of thing and I do a lot of drafting, just designing things on my own. I am into the

genealogy of the family, developing family trees and corresponding
with my relatives and those of the same name who are not relatives. I am getting somewhat involved in that and then of course
I have my shopping with my wife; got the gardening to look
after, etc. Most of [these activities] I find relaxing and interesting
and I like doing them. Not because I am expected to do them but
because I enjoy it and they are things that I can drop at a moment's
notice if something new comes along (Norris & Tari, 1985).

Gignac's (1991) research also suggests that older people may engage in
post-formal reasoning when dealing with aging-related problems. In
this study, 20 people over the age of 70 were asked to discuss some of
the best and worst events in their lives and how they dealt with them.
They were also asked about their perception of change in their coping
style with age. Gignac found that some individuals used traditional
coping strategies such as avoidance when adjusting to negative events,
e.g., "I can't think of anything [that was not a good experience in my
life]. My life has been very stable – no problems, just perfectly normal,
that's all" (p. 189). Others, however, were much more relativistic in
their thinking, understanding that each situation had a number of possible interpretations which, if adopted, might have differing emotional
impact on the individual, e.g., "[Abortion] is such a difficult decision
to make. I'm not sure I could ever have an abortion myself, but I
couldn't possibly judge someone else who decided to go that route"
(p. 188).

Neither Gignac's "copers" nor her "developmentalists" appeared to
be any happier or better adjusted when compared to each other. The
developmentalists, however, reported that their approach to problems
had developed over time. This supports the notion that relativistic
reasoning reflects cognitive development not enduring personality
characteristics.

Other researchers have also become interested in coping strategies in
later life. Most often, these researchers have investigated the feelings of
personal control and self-efficacy which older adults experience despite
social and personal losses. The early literature on perceived control
suggested that old people feel relatively less able to control the course
of their lives than do younger adults (Kuypers, 1971). As Langer and
Rodin (1976; Rodin & Langer, 1977) have pointed out, this is particularly unfortunate because the old appear to benefit most from a sense
of control. Furthermore opportunities for such a sense of control are

at times diminished by their life situations. Rodin and Langer's (1977) research on institutionalized elderly patients found that a small control-enhancing intervention such as caring for a plant not only improved morale and feelings of personal control, but also lowered morbidity and mortality.

Recent research has not confirmed a universal decline in perceptions of control with age. Instead, a variable pattern emerges, with stability in most general perceptions of control and a decline only in some specific factors (Lachman, 1986). A study by Heckhausen and Baltes (1991) suggests that such specific declines may be due to attributional biases. Young, middle-aged and old adults rated a list of psychological characteristics in terms of their expected development over the lifespan, and the controllability of this change. Later-life changes were viewed as both less desirable and less controllable, and this relationship was strongest for the old group.

A study by Nurmi, Pullianen, and Salmela-Aro (1992) suggests that uncontrollable issues are more salient for the old. In this research, adults of varying ages identified their central issues and concerns and rated how much control they had over each one. The control beliefs of the old were more external than the young, but one probable reason for this was their selection of issues typically regarded as uncontrollable, e.g., adult offspring.

Age-related changes in feelings of control have implications for what older people do to exercise control, in other words, how they demonstrate self-efficacy. Early researchers proposed that older adults should show losses in the ability to actively master the environment after their middle-adult years (e.g., Gutmann, 1977; Havighurst, Neugarten & Tobin, 1968). There has been very little support, however, for the idea that there are developmental declines in self-efficacy. Instead, efficacious behavior seems very much tied to perceptions of the situation, especially fears about negative change in old age. A study by Cornelius and Caspi (1986), for example, showed that older people who believed in their own intellectual self-efficacy tended to do better on standardized tests of intelligence than those with weaker beliefs. However, simply taking such a test may have a negative impact on self-efficacy (Dittmann-Kohli, Lachman, Kliege, & Baltes, 1991) probably because the respondents' faith in their abilities had been threatened. As Berry and West (1993) have noted recently, it is important to determine in what areas people desire self-efficacy before assessing age-related effects.

Control and coping

If older adults experience some declines in perceived control and self-efficacy, then perhaps they also do not cope with life events as well as younger adults. Self-appraisal, influenced negatively by aging, might result in lower perceived control, poorer mastery and, subsequently, poorer coping. This does not appear to be the case, however. While there is some suggestive evidence that older people may engage in different types of coping than do the young, their strategies often seem more adaptive. For example, fewer defensive mechanisms such as escape–avoidance are reported by the old (Irion & Blanchard-Fields, 1987). On the other hand, "working fictions" may be employed to buffer the negative effects of old age (e.g., "I'm not really *that* old; my mother lived to be 90") (Lazarus & Golden, 1981).

This finding, then, leads to a contradiction in the literature: some losses in perceived control with age, but gains in adaptive coping. A study by Aldwin (1991) provides one explanation for this pattern. In this research, adults ranging in age from 18 to 78 were asked about the most stressful life event of the last month and how they coped with it; they also completed a measure of perceived control. Results indicated that the old perceived less personal responsibility for stressful life events than the young, and used fewer escapist strategies in coping with it. Aldwin (1991) suggested that this may because experience has taught older people that many life events, such as illness, are relatively uncontrollable, but that adaptive coping with such situations is still possible. When in his 80s, Carl Rogers (1980) noted that he believed he would "die young." This did not mean, however, that he intended to ignore an increasing lack of energy in a bid to remain productive, but that he would adjust his schedule to accommodate his aging self and maintain his feelings of youthfulness (Rogers, 1980). Mr Grosberg, whose words began this chapter, would probably agree that this is sensible approach.

Recent work by Branstadter, Wentura, and Greve (1993) also provides support for accommodation as a means of coping with advancing age. Discussing work from two larger studies, one cross-sectional and the other longitudinal, they present findings which support the view that adults invoke two strategies for managing age-related change: instrumental activities aimed at preventing or alleviating losses which might have a negative impact on self-identity; accommodative processes aimed at altering goals and frameworks for self-appraisal to make them consistent with losses in personal functioning. As people reach advanced old age, they rely more on accommodative coping methods. According to the authors, this strategy indicates flexibility and adaptiveness, not resignation or escapism.

Personality

The literature on control and coping suggests that there may be changes in the aging self brought about by the need to adjust to new circumstances. Are similar changes in later life to be expected in basic personality characteristics? The answer to this question continues to be debated within the literature, with some stage-oriented researchers (e.g., Levinson, 1978) claiming change associated with particular phases in the life cycle, and some personality theorists insisting on stability (e.g., Costa et al., 1980).

Bengtson, Reedy, and Gordon (1985) concluded that this debate has resulted in a "litter-ature" on personality, rather than in any scientific advances.

Nevertheless, more recent, highly sophisticated longitudinal studies have added weight to the argument that basic characteristics of the self do not change much throughout the adult years. An interesting cross-sectional study of monozygotic and dizygotic twins ranging in age from 27 to 86 years, for example, found that age accounted for only 2 percent of the variance on six personality dimensions (McGue, Hirsch, & Lykken, 1993). The authors concluded that genetics are very important in the development of the self-concept, and that self-concept crystallizes early in life.

There is also considerable evidence from longitudinal studies for stability in personality. As Field and Millsap (1991) have noted, findings from the Duke Longitudinal Study (Siegler, George & Okun, 1979), the Normative Aging Study (Costa & McCrae, 1977–8), and the Baltimore Study (Costa & McCrae, 1988), all of which used standardized self-reported personality inventories, indicate continuity in individual traits such as introversion–extraversion and flexibility. A recent study of adults from another longitudinal sample, the Older Generation Study, found similar results using an interview format (Field & Millsap, 1991). As well, Schaie and Willis's (1991) cohort sequential examination of over 3,000 adults in the Seattle Longitudinal Study shows continuity within age cohorts on characteristics related to flexibility and responsibility. This study, however, also revealed cohort shifts in the direction of increasing flexibility and decreasing social responsibility. Although the self-concept appears to remain stable, its core characteristics are clearly a product of both immediate and more global social influences.

Self-stories

Why did you choose architecture as your profession?

My father was an FCA and my grandfather was an FCA, so I come from a long line of chartered accountants. My brother was the first fully qualified psychoanalyst to establish himself in private practice here. In analyzing why it was that both he and I chose to differ from a well-established family business which had offices both in the UK and Canada, and enter into professions with which we had no immediate contact . . . I rather think it is perhaps more in the nature of the environment in which both he and I were raised and it had to do a good deal with the staunch pioneer stock from which we sprang five generations ago in 1829. And so, so far as I can determine, the influence was . . . from a long line of Methodists and Anglican forbearers, [who believed] that contribution to one's society was the all-important thing, that life was not taking but if you expected to enjoy the pleasant things of life, one had to make a contribution. I suspect as much as anything that both my brother and I entered our respective professions, because both had the implication of social contribution, rather than taking out (Mr Park, a 60-year-old senior partner in a large architectural firm; Norris, unpublished data).

The personality literature suggests continuity in the self-concept over the years. Does this also mean that the growth and development of the self in adulthood are unlikely? Authors of self-help books would probably take issue with this idea. An emerging area of research dealing with the social construction of the self suggests ways in which the self can grow without compromising its core stability throughout adulthood. One direction that this research has taken is the examination of "possible selves" in adulthood; another relates to the construction of a self-narrative or personal story. Neither theme has been well-researched within a gerontological framework, but both provide a useful way to understand the development of the self in later life.

Markus and Nurius (1986) have argued that an examination of possible selves – past, present, future, and ideal – can hold the key to explaining personality stability as well as personal growth throughout the adult years. They view the self-concept as dynamic, reflecting a set of self-conceptions or understandings currently active in thought and memory. Some of these self-constructions may relate to an appraisal of past events; some may be relevant for immediate functioning, and others may extend to future or to ideal selves.

Which self-conceptions are currently active will depend on the situation and whether the self-concept is challenged. If, for example, you consider yourself to be socially responsible, but others point out that your behavior is inconsistent with this trait, thoughts and feelings about all of your "selves" will be threatened. It is likely that you will either seek out confirming evidence which contradicts the new feedback, or perhaps change your behavior. The core characteristic of "social responsibility" would not be likely to change; in fact, your answers to a personality inventory dealing with this characteristic would probably remain relatively consistent. On the other hand, you, and your friends, may perceive change and growth in your attitudes and behavior.

It is interesting to consider the findings of a study by Krueger and Heckhausen (1993) in the light of these ideas. These researchers asked young, middle-aged and older respondents to judge how characteristic several personality traits were, are, or would be over their entire adult lifespan. Cross-sectional results provided support for the stability of personality; there were few differences among the current ratings of each age group. On the other hand, each cohort believed that their lives were, or would be, characterized by growth during the young and middle-adult years and decline in late old age. Proponents of the "possible self" approach to personality would probably say that these beliefs in change should have consequences for growth given the right conditions, and regardless of scores on an inventory.

Mr Park's comments, above, provide an example of how this growth might occur. He believed that he became an architect because of the values transmitted through multiple generations of his family. These values continued to guide his life, providing a way of understanding past choices, and guiding future decisions. Throughout the interview, Mr Park described his "past self" with reference to how well he had measured up to these values. He also outlined the self-corrective efforts used when he felt he was losing sight of them. For example, at the height of his firm's productivity, he sold it, noting that "the threat of becoming fully an administrative hack was the spectre that gave me the greatest dissatisfaction." On his own, he founded a new firm, one that he kept small and focused on the kind of socially sensitive projects he loved. He noted, "People on entering our buildings smile . . . That's the real satisfaction."

Throughout Mr Park's interview, and others conducted in the same study (Norris, 1993), it became apparent that each individual saw an increased merging of possible selves over the course of his or her life. Early on, there were marked discrepancies between what had been achieved so far, and what was hoped for or predicted. In middle age, future achievement was still an issue, but goals were not as lofty. In old age, the focus was more on what had been accomplished and could now be enjoyed. Ideas about future or ideal selves were virtually absent. One achieved self, rather than a variety of possible selves, seemed typical of this group of well-functioning older people.

Further empirical support for the concept of "possible selves" can be found in a recent study by Ryff (1991). Young, middle-aged and old adults were asked to judge their past, present, future, and ideal selves on dimensions related to self-acceptance, positive relations with others, autonomy, environmental mastery, purpose in life and personal growth. All age groups had different views of the change experienced or expected in their "selves." Nevertheless, these discrepancies were smaller for the old, and not always positive. For example, the young and middle-aged groups believed that their present selves were an improvement on the past version, but the old saw stability and decline as well as progress. When the present self was compared to the future, again the young and middle-aged saw improvement, but the middle-aged group also viewed stability as possible. The old, on the other hand, perceived decline.

Ryff (1991) suggests that the pattern of results may be developmental. In young and middle adulthood, it is important to aspire to a different, more positive, future or ideal self. With the foreshortening of years, however, perhaps it is more important to come to terms with what has been and what is now. There is little time remaining for great achievement, and possible declines in functioning must be anticipated. Thus, the possible selves of well-functioning older people may all be very similar, whereas the same pattern in a young person would not be adaptive.

Researchers such as Ryff (see her 1993 review) have typically considered how the development of possible selves can promote successful aging; they have rarely investigated problems with the self-concept, especially those which might come about after a critical life event. Findings from a study of middle-aged women (Helson & Wink, 1992) suggest that normative life events like menopause, launching children, and providing some care for elderly parents do not result in change to the self-concept. Other research, however, on non-normative life events such as suffering from Alzheimer's disease (Sabat & Harre, 1993) or providing round-the-clock care for a frail elder (Skaff & Pearlin, 1992) can result in a loss of self, or the deconstruction of the self. Skaff and Pearlin's (1992) study, for example, paints an alarming picture of the loss of identity felt especially by young female caregivers. These individuals reported that they did not feel any personal growth to compensate for their losses. Sabat and Harre's analysis of Alzheimer's patients is more optimistic; they suggest that social support can buffer even the almost total loss of a previous self, and facilitate growth. Clearly, more work needs to be done in this area.

Self-narratives

The concept of the working self concept implies that individuals are continually active in their efforts to construct an acceptable self (Markus & Nurius, 1986; Sansone & Berg, 1993). Some researchers have suggested that the mechanism used in this process is the creation of a self-narrative. Past, present, future and ideal possible selves become part of a continuing story (Hermans, Kempen, & van Loon, 1992; Manheimer, 1992).

The idea of possible selves suggests a highly structured view of the self-concept. While dynamic, each component of the self is readily distinguished and all are orchestrated by the centralized working self-concept. The related idea of a narrative or storytelling self is not so highly structured. Extending ideas put forward by Kelly (1955) and Bruner (1986), Hermans, Kempen, and van Loon (1992) suggested that the self has many "I's," all of whom are engaged in a dialogue which attempts to make sense of changing circumstances. This dialogical self cannot be separated into stable components, nor is there a central "I" which coordinates all the rest. Components and development of the self will depend on the psychological, temporal, physical, and social contexts. If these change, so will the dialogical self.

This view of the self has some support in the recent gerontological literature. Dittmann-Kohli's (1990) study of the construction of meaning in adulthood revealed a pattern of flexibility and adaptability among older adults. Taking what she termed a "life script" approach to her respondents' self-statements, she concluded that older persons work with the increasing limitations on their physical selves and the restrictions of their environment by reorganizing their psychological selves. As an example of this, the "stories" of the young were characterized by high expectations for self-development and achievement, those of old people featured self-acceptance and the appreciation of what had been achieved.

Research on the life review also provides support for the importance of a self-narrative to adjustment in old age (e.g., Butler, Lewis & Sunderland, 1991). This work also points to the increasing self-focus and self-acceptance acquired by well-adjusted people as they age. According to Erikson (1982), old age is a time to strive for ego integrity, a sense that the past has meaning in the present context, and that the future is not to be feared. To achieve this sense of integrity, an older person's self-narrative must be reviewed and retold, often with the assistance of supportive others (Marshall, 1974; Butler, Lewis & Sunderland, 1991). It is this sense that a personal narrative is socially constructed that has led one author to caution researchers that they might get the story they ask for, rather than the story which has developmental significance to an older person (Wallace, 1992).

Each individual's personal narrative is obviously unique. However, it seems likely that various psychosocial factors could influence the course of its construction. Cognitive flexibility could, for example, affect the way that an event such as retirement is interpreted and incorporated into the narrative. For some, it may be perceived simply as a role loss; for others, it may suggest a wealth of new possibilities for self-development. On a larger scale, historical period could affect the way an entire cohort constructs its self-narratives. For example, a recent book in the popular press (Coupland, 1991) suggests that the current "twentysomething" cohort, "Generation X," views itself as a lost generation, relative to the babyboomers who preceded it. The personal story of the "Xers" is one of cynicism, resentment, and hopelessness. Their view is that the babyboomers have it all because they took it all.

Metacognition and aging

As we have seen, construction of the self-narrative involves a great deal of self-reflection and self-appraisal. An area of research concerned with the cognitive aspects of this process is the study of metacognition. By "metacognition," psychologists have generally meant to describe a person's thinking *about* thinking, about the processes and contents of his or her own memory, attention, or judgment, as well as knowledge about how these mental processes work. The most widely studied of these "metas" has been metamemory, literally, knowing about memory.

In the 1970s, developmental researchers found that young children were generally not very knowledgeable about aspects of memory tasks or strategies (e.g., Kreutzer, Leonard, & Flavell, 1975). For example, children may fail to realize the need for immediately dialing a telephone number, because they fail to realize the limited duration of the short-term memory store. These findings suggested that children's limited use of strategies in memory tasks might be at least partly due to a deficiency in metamemory – a failure to recognize the need for special memorial activities to enhance remembering (Flavell, 1985).

In the past ten years, there has been considerable research on possible age differences among adults in the area of metacognition, and especially metamemory, as well (e.g., Lovelace, 1990). Just as in the case of children, the suggestion has been that memory difficulties in older individuals might be at least partly attributable to deficiencies in their metamemory (e.g., Light, 1991). That is, older adults might fail to *use* their intact memory skills when they should, because they do not recognize the need for them. The evidence for such deficiencies in thinking about cognition and memory among older adults, however, is decidedly weak. This section reviews three major areas of metamemory that have been studied, and summarizes what we know so far.

A central distinction that is commonly made when considering metamemory contrasts people's knowledge about the memory system, memory tasks and situations in general with their skills at monitoring the contents of their own memory system in a specific task situation (e.g., Lovelace, 1990). A number of questionnaire studies have shown little evidence for deficits in general memory knowledge among older adults. For example, the Metamemory in Adulthood (MIA) questionnaire developed by Dixon and Hultsch (1984) has a major factor that loads on strategy, task and achievement knowledge. Performance on this factor has been found not to differ by age group across adulthood (Hertzog, Dixon, Schulenberg, & Hultsch, 1987). Thus, older and young adults are equally likely to recognize that some memory problems (e.g., recognition of previously seen items) are easier than others, and require less active use of strategies. Similarly, Perlmutter (1978) found that older and younger adults were equally sensitive to the generally positive effects of interest, organization and concreteness on memory performance.

The second topic of memory monitoring refers to the person's capacities to assess the specific contents of memory in a particular task, e.g., how well one knows the material for the mathematics exam tomorrow, or the tip-of-the-tongue (TOT) feeling of knowing a word but not being able to think of it. Specific tasks or topics studied here include "feelings of knowing" like the TOT state, monitoring for response correctness once an item has been produced, and reality monitoring, which involves making judgments about the sources of information in one's memory (Johnson & Raye, 1981). As an example of the latter issue, consider that uncertain feeling of whether you have actually turned off the lights of your car, or only imagined that you did.

For the most part, older adults seem to do as well at monitoring their feelings of knowing regarding items of memory as do younger adults (e.g., Light, 1991), though TOT states may be somewhat more frequent for elders in everyday life (Cohen & Faulkner, 1986). Similarly, older people do as well as younger individuals in deciding how well they have understood material, or prepared for a subsequent knowledge test (Lovelace, 1990). For example, Zabrucky et al. (1987) showed that older and younger adults did equally well in detecting problems in texts that would lead to difficulties in understanding their meanings (termed "comprehension monitoring"), though more educated individuals in both age groups did better on this task. Older adults are also generally as good at judging the correctness of their responses after producing them (Lovelace, 1990). Pratt et al. (1989) found, for example, that older adults were equally likely to detect and correct confusing pronouns in their retellings of stories as were younger adults, suggesting that they were monitoring the quality of their productions for listener comprehension as effectively as younger adults. Older adults, however, did produce more such pronoun errors in the first place (see chapter 7).

In the specific area of "reality monitoring," older adults do appear to have more difficulties that younger persons. For example, Cohen and Faulkner (1989) asked young versus older adult participants either to perform a simple action, imagine the same action, or watch someone else perform it ("put the card next to the block"). Older participants had more trouble distinguishing whether they had performed or only imagined or watched the actions. Such findings have implications for the reliability of older adults as witnesses (Lovelace, 1990; see also chapter 4). In general, however, older persons have some difficulties in identifying the actual *sources* of their memories, which could be especially problematic when they must deal with new or unusual events, where these contexts and sources may be different than usual (Tulving, 1985).

A third topic area in metamemory concerns individuals' feelings of memory self-efficacy and confidence. The MIA questionnaire focuses on this area as well as on general knowledge (Hertzog et al., 1987; Hultsch & Dixon, 1990). Like Mrs DiCarlo, older individuals generally perceive themselves to have poorer memory capacities than younger people, a belief shared by the young. Interestingly, young and middle-aged adults also anticipate that, with age, their own memories will deteriorate (Ryan & Kwong-See, 1993).

Older people also feel that they have less personal control over their memory performance than do the young (Lovelace, 1990). These findings are parallel to the evidence discussed above that suggests lower percep-tions of control in the elderly, in some areas at least. Some researchers have shown have shown that lower memory self-efficacy is associated with poorer actual memory performance as well, in both younger and older groups (Cavanaugh & Green, 1990; Hertzog, Dixon, & Hultsch, 1991; Ryan, Kwong-See, Meneer, & Trovato, 1992). However, the direction of this correlational relationship is clearly open to various interpretations. It may be that those who remember poorly simply re-cognize this; alternatively, low feelings of efficacy may interfere with people's attempts to remember. Perhaps both processes are involved in a reciprocal fashion.

Both specific and general knowledge about memory thus seem to decline relatively little into later life (with the exception of knowledge about the sources of one's memories), but the sense of control over one's performance in this cognitive domain clearly does seem lower for most older adults. In general, metamemory scores are only modestly related to people's actual memory skills, but the links between memory performance and memory self-efficacy are interesting and deserve fur-ther study.

Tracing the book's themes

Our first theme concerns the need to focus when interpreting lifespan development on the individual's own construction of events and experi-ences. In much of the theoretical and empirical work on the self in later life, two questions have been implicit: throughout adulthood, does the self change or remain stable? Further, are there any changes in the way individuals *think* about the self?

On the one hand, personality research supports the stability of traits like neuroticism and extraversion. On the other hand, there appears to be development in the way in which people understand the self.

Influenced by a wide variety of factors – experience, life events, changes in memory, declines in health – the self in old age may become increasingly unitary and self-focused. Where once there were many equally weighted possible selves to consider, one "here-and-now" self may now predominate. This frees the older person to reflect on his or her whole life-story and construct one, logically and emotionally consistent, narrative.

Interestingly, this idea is consistent with the concepts of psychological disengagement (Cumming & Henry, 1961) and ego integrity (Erikson, 1982). Both imply that successful aging is characterized by a strong, internally directed self, less concerned with current social feedback and more with a sense of personal acceptance and peace. Contemporary theorists would disagree with the position that this process is universal and inevitable. Nevertheless, recent research findings are supportive of the tendency towards interiority in later life. In chapter 4, the positive and negative consequences of this self-focus will be explored further.

The second theme concerns individual variability in thinking about the self in later life. Despite a possible move towards greater self-reflection in later life, it is probable that individual differences in the construction and maintenance of the self will be marked. As Gignac's (1991) research suggests, for example, differences in the capacity to handle multiple perspectives on an event will affect the choice of coping strategy. The relative success of such strategies is likely to have an impact on feelings of personal control and self-esteem.

Differences due to structural variables such as gender and ethnicity also should be considered in studies of self-development. Research focusing on earlier points in the life span, for example, suggests that women's self-evaluations may be more negative than those of men (Unger, 1979). Women may be less likely than men to accept credit for their successes (Deaux & Emswiller, 1974). There has been no lifespan research in this area, so it is difficult to predict the long-term effects of such an attributional bias. One could argue that it is likely to persist given the strength of gender role socialization, and lifelong experience in gender roles. On the other hand, some research which suggests the development of androgyny in both older men and women would support the idea that such differences in self-appraisals might be reduced or even disappear (Sinnott, 1982).

Although psychologists continue to call for more comparative research (e.g., Betancourt & Lopez, 1993), little has actually been accomplished within the field of lifespan development. Research examining cultural and ethnic differences in ideas about the self in later life is practically nonexistent. This is curious considering the interests of philosophers and writers from many cultures in ideas about the self (see Manheimer's, 1992, review of European literary influences). Gerontologists have somehow remained relatively untouched (or unmoved) by these ideas (Weiland, 1992). This is unfortunate in view of the insights into understanding about the self which could be gained from more systematic study of ethnic groups within our own society. How, for example, do older immigrant women adjust their sense of self to meet the demands of new cultures? Some policy research suggests that they have difficulty (Advisory Committee for the Women and Aging Conferences for the Ethnocultural Communities in Metropolitan Toronto, 1993), but the psychological processes underlying this difficulty have not been explored.

The third theme of this book, how social encounters and cognitions are related, is readily addressed when considering the self. The "self," regardless of which theorist, researcher, or layperson, is attempting a definition, always contains social components. Even theorists who might hypothesize biological predispositions for certain personality traits would agree that such characteristics emerge within a social context.

Because of the important role played by social feedback in the maintenance of a healthy sense of self, one might predict that older people would be at a disadvantage relative to the young. There is considerable research evidence for the negative stereotypes and attitudes held by people in general about aging and the aged (e.g., Green, 1981). This social consensus could have a profound impact on the self-appraisals of elderly people. Kuypers and Bengtson (1973), for example, suggested that "Social Breakdown Syndrome" might afflict some older adults who, for one reason or another, were predisposed to accept negative stereotypes about old age. They hypothesized that a downward spiral in social and psychological functioning might come about as self- and social-appraisals matched and reinforced each other.

While there is some evidence that older people who accept the label "old" may indeed have more negative self-appraisals and demonstrate less competent behavior (Dittmann-Kohli et al., 1991), research suggests that most older people rely on their own, positive, self-definitions when coming to terms with their aging (Bengtson et al., 1985). They are able to overcome problems that one would think should lead to low life satisfaction, morale, and self-esteem. Instead, older people appear to be more adaptive copers than the young, and are at least as happy (Irion & Blanchard-Fields, 1987). Consistent with Erikson's theoretical ideas, they have achieved ego integrity.

The characters reconsidered

The comments of the four older adults discussed in this chapter provide a snapshot of their individual lives. Each picture is frozen in time, and is only one of a much larger collection, and yet each reveals something of the "self" involved.

There are clear differences among the four individuals, both in terms of their lifestyles and in terms of their philosophy of life. Mr Hentschel and Mr Park, for example, have maintained active careers into later life, and placed a high value on this activity. Mr Grosberg and Mrs DiCarlo, on the other hand, are now leading quieter lives, partly because of declining health. Regardless of their differences, however, all four are remarkably similar in their efforts to cope with age-related challenges to the self, as well as to remain satisfied with life in old age.

It is this sense of personal mastery despite perceptions of diminished control and ability which burns most strongly within the selves of these four adults. There is an acknowledgement that age brings with it some negative change, whether because of ageist stereotypes or because of personal losses. Nevertheless, there is also the conviction that a strong sense of self can buffer these effects and maintain psychological continuity. Mr Park remembers to be true to his lifelong work ethic; Mr Hentschel seeks cognitive stimulation, as he always has; Mr Grosberg remains "sensible" in his approach to achievement; Mrs DiCarlo wards off her tendency to be lonely by seeking refuge in her books. Each person is an example of the strength and resiliency of the self-concept in old age.

4

Thinking about
Other Persons

Bob Wright is a 48-year-old husband and the father of three children. His widowed father, Jim, who is 78, is coming to dinner tonight. Jim moved into a seniors-only residential community a couple of years ago. As Bob thinks about the upcoming evening, he realizes that it has been harder to discuss things with his father lately. Jim seems less tolerant of the ideas or comments of the kids and sometimes Bob has trouble getting his own point of view across to him. Bob thinks this may just reflect the fact that his dad is "getting old." Of course, the kids are teenagers now too, and can be hard for anybody to deal with. Bob's daughter has just gotten that weird new hairdo, with the orange streaks! And Bob himself has been having a lot of stress at work lately. But as Bob worries about the dinner conversation this evening, he wonders if his father's move into the residential community was such a great idea as it had seemed at the time.

In the present chapter, the current psychological evidence which could address Bob's questions will be considered. Age trends and some possible explanatory factors involved in them with respect to the topic of thinking about other persons will be discussed. An initial section reviews major theoretical perspectives on this topic. Following this, the research literatures on person memory and eyewitness testimony in older adults, on "perspective-taking" skills in later life, and then on the development of "person perception" are reviewed. Last, we consider the role of "ageist" stereotypes and biases regarding the elderly and their possible impact. In each section, some implications and applications of these concepts for adult development are discussed. Finally, the themes of the book are summarized in relation to this evidence.

Theoretical frameworks

A number of theorists in the **psychometric** tradition have been concerned with conceptions of "social intelligence," following the pioneering work of Guilford (e.g., 1965). For example, Sternberg (1986) has studied the links between conceptions of "wisdom" in everyday life (a quality believed by many to become more salient in later adulthood) and standardized measures of social intelligence. He showed that those adults who perceived themselves to be closer to the ideal prototype of "wise" in judgment and knowledge about social relations also scored higher on standard tests of "social intelligence," though not on traditional intelligence or cognitive style measures. Thus, some support for the notion of a special social expertise or intellectual ability in adulthood can be claimed.

Information-processing theories have emphasized the gradual loss of some aspects of basic cognitive capacity in later adulthood as an explanatory mechanism for observations of cognitive decline (e.g., Salthouse, 1988). Both working memory resources and/or speed of cognitive processing are hypothesized to show some decline on average in later adulthood (e.g., Cohen, 1989). Though there has been little direct research on the component cognitive processes underlying thinking about other persons, some recent work has suggested that variations in working memory span may play some role in individual differences in childhood in the ability to take the perspective of others (Lapsley & Quintana, 1989). Based on this finding, at least the outlines of a parallel account of *aging* and person understanding might be sketched, as working memory resources decline for some older adults. In addition, "simplistic" stereotyping in thinking about others has been shown to be enhanced in younger adults under conditions of stress or cognitive overload (Olson & Zanna, 1993). To the extent that this sort of overloading may be more typical among those older adults who have experienced declining cognitive capacities, we might predict greater susceptibility to such stereotyping for them as well.

Another literature on the processing of social information focuses on the series of cognitive "steps" involved in interpreting the actions of others in context (e.g., Dodge, Pettit, McClaskey, & Brown, 1986; Fiske & Taylor, 1991). This research breaks down the reception, interpretation, and response to others and their actions into an orderly sequence of information-processing procedures, and has focused on how these various steps are carried out. Differences in the utilization of such processing steps have been used to account for individual and clinical differences in children's social behaviors (e.g., in aggressiveness, Dodge et al., 1986). However, there has been little attention to these models in studying the social thought of older persons.

As noted in chapter 2, **developmental** theorists in the Piagetian tradition have been the most extensive students of the concept of perspective-taking (e.g., Kohlberg, 1969; Selman, 1980). Description of development as a stage-like pattern of increasingly sophisticated levels of considering and coordinating the perspectives of the self and the other are widespread (e.g., Miller, Kessel, & Flavell, 1970; Selman, 1980). The development of this skill or capacity of the child has been seen as essential to the growth of sophistication in many areas of social reasoning and interaction, including moral judgment (e.g., Kohlberg, 1969), communication (e.g., Roberts and Patterson, 1984), and social problem-solving (e.g., Rubin & Krasnor, 1986).

Studies of "person perception" and attributions of causality about the behavior of others have been extremely popular in the literature of **social psychology** for the last 25 years (e.g., Fiske & Taylor, 1991). These broad frameworks suggest that humans attempt to make sense of and predict the social world by inferring the causes of the actions and behaviors of others, following sets of general causal principles (e.g., Kelley, 1972; Schneider, Hastorf, & Ellsworth, 1979). Constructing underlying stabilities (e.g., traits like "aggressive") in the perception of others' qualities is a fundamental aspect of this process. Some descriptive research on the ways in which adults of different ages construe such stabilities in other persons, and explain their actions, is reviewed below.

One particular social–psychological model of importance to thinking about both others and the self is *social comparison* (e.g., Festinger, 1954). In Festinger's model, people tend to compare themselves with similar others on a variety of capabilities and qualities, in order to obtain information about the self's relative status. For example, comparing your tennis serve against potential partners can give you an idea of what level of player you are, when explicit objective information is not readily available (e.g., grins of anticipation as you step up to the service line!). Goethals and Darley (1977) suggested that social comparison draws on attributional processes in social cognition (e.g., trying to eliminate other factors that may explain your or your friend's serve besides ability, such as lack of practice).

In an interesting discussion, Suls and Mullen (1983) argued that tendencies to make social comparisons should vary over the lifespan, with older individuals being less likely or able to engage in such social comparison because of the smaller number of available peers with whom to compare, and perhaps also because of weaker levels of skills in relevant social–cognitive activities such as perspective-taking. Though there has been little relevant research, this model does stress the importance of sociocognitive factors across the lifespan in social interaction, and particularly in the construction of the self, as discussed in chapter 3. Figure 4.1 suggests that social comparison has played its role across the history of the species as well.

Social perception and aging: the evidence

In Akira Kurosawa's brilliant film, *Rashomon*, four different people involved in a rape and murder give widely varying accounts of the events that all had witnessed. Seeing this movie makes manifest the point that "knowing" the social world involves the individual in construction of a narrative story about what has happened "in reality," and that the interpretations that people give to the "same" events may diverge greatly. Testifying at a trial, as Mike did as a teenager regarding a car accident, can be an everyday life example of this "Rashomon" effect. The different accounts of the speeds, times, and sequences of events at the intersection where this accident took place were so incredibly variable that Mike was certainly glad not to have been on the jury that had to sort it all out.

All the participants in these disputed events presumably shared a set of basic cognitive processes with which they constructed these accounts. Fiske and Taylor (1991), combining the perspectives of social psychology and information-processing, discuss these processes of social cognition under three sequential categories, from the initial reception of information to the making of a response: a) attention and encoding of information, b) memory and recognition, and c) inference processes and judgment. In Fiske and Taylor's terms, witnesses might tell different versions of the "same" events because they noticed different things, because they remembered different events or qualities, or because they constructed different interpretations of these events.

These various "steps" in the processing of information are useful categories for structuring our review of thinking about persons. First, the topic of social attention and aging is briefly addressed, an area where no work has apparently been conducted to date. Then we discuss memory for faces and eyewitness memory for persons in context.

"And now there go the Wilsons! . . . Seems like everyone's evolving except us!"

Figure 4.1   The Far Side cartoon by Gary Larson is reprinted by permission of Chronicle Features, San Francisco, CA. All rights reserved

Finally, the largest section of the chapter focuses on the topics of perspective-taking and social perception, involving the patterns of inferences made by adults of different ages regarding other persons and their behaviors.

Social attention and aging

Despite the fact that there has been a great deal of interest in the general topic of attention and aging (e.g., McDowd & Birren, 1990), there does not seem to have been any work specifically aimed at age differences or similarities in how attention is distributed to *social* stimuli in particular. There is conflicting evidence that the capacity to inhibit distracting or irrelevant stimuli, either internal or external in origin, while working on a task is somewhat diminished in older persons (e.g., Hasher & Zacks, 1988; McDowd & Birren, 1990). The basic selective function of attention definitely does show some impairment in older persons on average, however, particularly under difficult task conditions (Hartley, 1992; McDowd & Birren, 1990). Given this evidence, it seems likely that the social information encoded by older persons in complex situations (e.g., encoding the name of a new neighbor while passing in the aisles at the grocery) may be somewhat less focused or efficient. Obviously, such variations in processes of selective attending could have implications for subsequent judgments or task performance by those of different ages, but to date there apparently has been no research conducted on this topic.

Person memory and eyewitness testimony

There is of course a very large research literature on the topic of memory and aging (e.g., Hultsch & Dixon, 1990). The relevant research for this chapter on social processes focuses only on memory for person-specific stimuli, i.e., memory for names and faces, and for individuals in context (Cohen, 1989).

Older adults frequently complain particularly of difficulties in the recall of names of others, though younger people have trouble with names too (e.g., Cohen & Faulkner, 1986). In some intriguing real-life memory studies, Bahrick and his colleagues have shown that people are capable of recognizing pictures of their high school classmates quite well over very long periods of time (50 years or more, Bahrick, Bahrick,

& Wittlinger, 1975). Recalling classmates names, however, posed much greater difficulties in this research. The fact that elderly persons report particular trouble recalling the names of well-known friends and acquaintances suggests that such name-blocking is often the result of some temporary fluctuation in retrieval processes, rather than a result of defective storage or encoding (Cohen & Faulkner, 1986).

The stimuli in Bahrick's study were of course yearbook photos of classmates from graduation. Anyone who returns to his or her high school reunion after 25 years knows that recognizing old friends' *current* appearance after the passage of this much time is not so easy. Good thing they make you wear those name badges.

In line with Bahrick's studies of face recognition from high school yearbooks, older adults generally have shown relatively good recognition memory compared with their performance in recall situations (Craik & McDowd, 1987). However, recent investigations indicate that older adults are more likely to make errors of "false recognition" in identifying the faces of others (Bartlett & Fulton, 1991). Specifically, older and younger individuals are about equally likely to correctly recognize familiar faces, but older adults are more likely to make the mistake of judging an unfamiliar face as familiar (e.g., Bartlett & Fulton, 1991). Why should this be so? Bruce and Young (1986) argue that there are two different retrieval processes involved in face recognition, one focusing on the physical resemblance between the representation of the face in memory and the currently observed face, and the other providing contextual information about the circumstances of previous encounters with the person's face. Based on their results, Bartlett and Fulton (1991) argued that older persons are deficient in this context recall process, and rely primarily on resemblance of facial features only in deciding whether a face is familiar to them or not. Thus, they are more likely to respond positively on the basis of physical similarities to novel faces which they have actually never seen before.

Such limitations on person memory in older adults are of special application in a very practical social context – the accuracy and reliability of persons of different ages in their eyewitness memory and testimony in the courtroom (Yarmey, 1984). Yarmey, based on a series of studies on eyewitness identification by adults of different ages, found that older adults are somewhat less accurate at recalling the details of victim and assailant characteristics in simulated slide or videotape studies of criminal assaults (e.g., Adams-Price, 1992). They also show a greater incidence of "false recognitions" of innocent bystanders to these crimes, as might be expected on the basis of the face recognition studies just noted. Interestingly, lawyers and judges assessed the elderly eyewitness as just as credible as the younger adult, though the general public and elderly persons themselves did not (Yarmey, 1984).

Despite this rather consistent evidence of some average deficit in eyewitness memory in older persons, several caveats are in order. First, there is a great deal of variability in performance among elderly adults in this situation, as for many other cognitive tasks, so that some older adults performed very well in such settings (Yarmey, 1984). Second, older adults may have particular difficulties in recalling accurate details of criminal activity carried out by those of other age groups (List, 1986). In List's study, older participants were as good at remembering the details of an elderly shoplifter's appearance and behavior as were college students, but did worse than young adults at recalling evidence about a younger thief. Presumably this was a function of greater attention or possible encoding differences when the target was more similar to the self. If only elderly persons committed more crimes, the older population might appear less disadvantaged as witnesses! Finally, there is evidence that even quite aged individuals can be trained to improve their memories for names and faces (e.g., Yesavage, Sheikh, Friedman, & Tanke, 1990).

Perspective-taking in adulthood

A crucial step in the information-gathering aspect of social inference processes, as discussed above, is believed to be the skill of construing and considering the perspectives or points of view of other persons. Research in the Piagetian tradition has focused particularly on this variable as an important factor in social thinking (e.g., Selman, 1980). By considering the point of view of others, the child is able to comprehend and behave in less "egocentric" ways in a broad range of social contexts (Piaget & Inhelder, 1969). For example, we may feel very differently about another's enthusiastic friendliness, depending on how his or her intentions are understood. Witness the current low status of politicians and used-car salespeople (those prototypic glad-handers) in our society!

Studies of children have generally shown considerable variation in the levels of perspective-taking skill displayed in trying to understand cognitive, perceptual and affective aspects of others (i.e., their thoughts, observations or feelings, Rubin, 1973). However, little systematic research has been conducted on variations in perspective-taking of different types in later adulthood. Nevertheless, the present review describes studies of adult age differences in this skill by type of perspective-taking, and then considers what is known of the various background factors which might influence these age variations.

Cognitive perspective-taking research focuses on the skill with which participants can understand or reconstruct the points of view that various others might hold in interpreting the same information or situation. As an example, Mrs Allen, a woman now in her 70s, recalled her conflict about allowing her youngest son to go far away to university:

> When my husband died, Darryl was the youngest . . . you know, I was used to him being home and enjoyed having him home, and then when he was seventeen he decided he didn't want to go to university here. He wanted to go [far away], which just about broke my heart . . . I guess the conflict was I hadn't made the decision that he had grown up. I think I was trying to hold on to Darryl for some reason – I could just see the house getting more empty every time I turned around . . . Now I think I was sort of stupid to waste all those tears I did and keep him in conflict over whether he was going to go or not when he really wanted himself to go so badly. And I think probably that I was selfish in that I was thinking more of myself probably than I was of him at the time. Because he did very, very well in university and it was what he really wanted to do and since he has got a good position and he's very happy with his work. Besides that, he keeps telling me that it was the only way to make a man out of a boy, especially when he's been spoiled by a mother . . . (Pratt, unpublished data).

Several cross-sectional studies of cognitive perspective-taking have indicated somewhat lower average performance on various developmental stage sequences by elderly persons versus younger adults (e.g., Chap, 1986; Cohen, Bearison, & Muller, 1987).

In Chap's study, older adults were judged to consider spontaneously the perspectives of the characters in a moral dilemma less fully than did younger adults when deliberating about the problem. Older adults were particularly likely to consider that there was a single "correct" point of view for reasoning about the moral issue in question (the lowest level in the scoring hierarchy). Similarly, Cohen et al. found that older adults (over 75) were less sophisticated than either a middle-aged (those in their 40s) or a young-old (aged 65 to 75) sample in their consideration

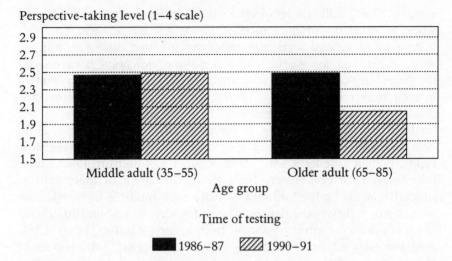

Figure 4.2 Age group by moral perspective-taking, longitudinal changes over time
Controlled for education level; significant age decline for older adults (p <.05)

of the different perspectives involved in friendship problems (e.g., two elderly friends' relationship is jeopardized by one's busy schedule).

While these studies were cross-sectional in nature, Pratt Hunsberger, Pancer, and Pratt (1994) found that there was some evidence of longitudinal decline over a four to five year period among older men and women (those in their 60s and 70s) in the extent of cognitive perspective-taking while considering moral problems taken from Kohlberg's (1969) work, such as whether a doctor should assist a terminally ill patient to commit suicide. Older adults became more likely over time to evaluate the situation as having "one right answer," using the Chap (1986) system for scoring, and less likely to see the need for reciprocal understanding among the parties (see figure 4.2).

In contrast, stability in the level of perspective-taking over the same four to five year time period was apparent in a comparable sample of middle-aged adults in their 40s and 50s (see figure 4.2). Why might this decline in perspective-taking matter? Pratt et al. (1991) found that adults' cognitive perspective-taking skill was a positive predictor of the stage level of moral reasoning exhibited by adults for both personal and hypothetical moral problems. Dolen and Bearison (1982) also found a strong positive relation between cognitive perspective-taking skills and interpersonal problem-solving scores on standard stories in an elderly sample. Thus, skills in perspective-taking in later adulthood do seem linked to other important indices of sociocognitive performance.

At a more general level, the understanding that there are multiple ways of viewing the world, and that no one viewpoint is necessarily the "true" or "correct" one, is an insight that many experience acutely in their university years (e.g., Perry, 1970). Hearing your instructor debunk your hard-won understanding of a theory propounded by the textbook can be a frustrating, if ultimately liberating, example. How does such a general understanding of "truth" develop? (e.g., Blanchard-Fields, 1989; Kitchener & King, 1981; Kramer & Woodruff, 1986; Kuhn, Pennnington, & Leadbeater, 1983; Perry, 1970) All of these authors suggest that the "relativist" idea that there are multiple interpretations or views of reality first emerges in late adolescence or young adulthood (for a somewhat contrary view on timing, see Chandler, 1987). Children and early adolescents, in this view, are "realists," who believe in a single, true reality and hold that multiple interpretations of a situation cannot simultaneously be "correct."

This topic concerns people's epistemological ideas, that is, their thinking about how we know reality and truth. Such matters have received little investigation in later life. However, Kramer and Woodruff (1986) reported on the occurrence of certain types of thinking about open-ended social dilemmas. These included issues such as whether a wife who has never worked outside the home should seek employment. Thinking which Kramer and Woodruff characterized as showing an "acceptance of contradictions" and as "dialectical" was somewhat more common in their oldest participants (ages 60 to 75), than in young or middle-aged groups.

More recently, Kramer, Kalbaugh, and Goldston (1992) have developed a questionnaire to assess these three types of thinking: absolutistic, relativistic, and dialectical. The Social Paradigm Belief Inventory consists of 27 items which are followed by three forced-choice alternatives which represent these three different views. For example, one item is:

a) Change comes neither from the inside nor the outside. It comes from an interaction of natural changes the person goes through with changes in the environment and how these changes are seen by the person [Dialectical].

b) Change comes from the inside. It comes from a change of outlook on things; no matter what happens on the outside you can always alter your view of things and you will be different [Relativistic].

c)   Change comes from the outside. It is for the most part forced on us by job changes, financial circumstances, and the like [Absolutistic] (Kramer et al., 1992, p. 183).

Kramer et al. (1992) found that preferences for dialectical thinking increased from adolescence to young adulthood on this forced-choice measure, and remained at the same level across later life. In contrast, preferences for relativistic thinking declined across adulthood, while absolutistic preferences tended to be low and showed no differences across age groups.

Pratt, Hunsberger, Pancer, Roth, and LaPointe (1990) reported on a study of religious thinking in young (18 to 26), middle-aged (30s and 40s) and older (60s and 70s) adults. Contrary to Kramer et al.'s (1992) findings, these investigators found that Kitchener and King's (1983) levels of understanding of contradictory versions of a religious issue (biblical versus evolutionary accounts of human origins) were less advanced for older adults than both young and middle-aged groups, who did not differ from one another (cf. Enright, Roberts, & Lapsley, 1983). This pattern resulted mainly from a greater tendency for older adults to take absolutistic positions. However, there was a strong negative relation between a right-wing authoritarianism measure (Altemeyer, 1988) and level of reasoning about truth conditions (more authoritarian attitudes were linked to "realist" interpretations that there is a single, "correct" truth regarding this issue).

Older adults were much more authoritarian than their younger counterparts (e.g., Pratt, Hunsberger, Pancer, & Roth, 1992), endorsing the use of power to enforce traditional and uniform social norms or standards (see figure 4.3). For example, they were much more likely to agree with statements from Altemeyer's (1988) authoritarianism inventory (the RWA), such as "The facts on crime, sexual immorality, and the recent public disorders all show we have to crack down on deviant groups and troublemakers if we are to save our moral standards and preserve law and order."

When this authoritarianism factor was controlled statistically, age differences in stages of understanding truth were eliminated (cf. Pratt, Hunsberger, Pancer, Roth, & LaPointe, 1990; Pratt, Hunsberger, Pancer, Roth, & Santolupo, 1993). Apparently, then, those older adults who are less authoritarian are more likely to view the nature of "truth" as complex and relative on this topic.

For example, one older woman, low on the authoritarianism measure, responded:

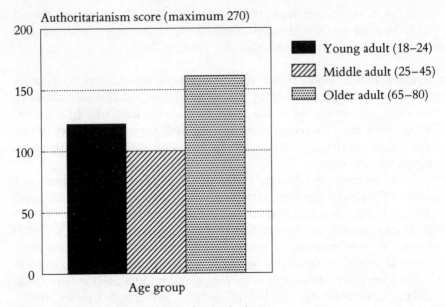

Figure 4.3 Age differences in authoritarianism
Controlled for educational background; older adults differ from both younger groups (ps < .01) by Scheffe tests

What is your view now about the origins of humanity?

I believe the scientists. I don't know, it just makes more sense. There's not enough to prove the other view. And I don't look at religion in that way, I look at religion as a way of helping people, giving them guidelines for their lives.

Is there only one right view about the origin of man?

No, there isn't. Some people are real believers in the religious aspect, they probably wouldn't believe the scientists. No, it's fine, if they're happy and they really believe in that, that's OK. I am a very flexible person . . . (Pratt, unpublished data).

These findings regarding authoritarianism and absolutistic reasoning might be particular to the religious dilemma studied in the Pratt, Hunsberger et al. (1990) investigation, of course, and research on non-religious issues would be important to test this relation between older adults' authoritarianism and their cognitive perspective-taking more fully. In view of the discrepancies between the work of Kramer et al. (1992)

and Pratt, Hunsberger et al. (1990), research on such acceptance of contradictions is needed across a range of topics and beliefs. Variations in tolerance for others' beliefs across adulthood might be especially relevant to attitude and value issues and change and their relation to aging, for example (see chapter 7).

Turning to the topic of perceptual perspective-taking, several cross-sectional studies over the adult lifespan have been conducted (e.g., Bielby & Papalia, 1975; Rubin, 1974; Rubin, Attewell, Tierney, & Tumolo, 1973). The task in these studies was generally to select or reconstruct the correct view of a display (e.g., a checkerboard) from the physical perspective of someone else. Results of these studies have generally been similar to the cognitive findings reviewed above in showing somewhat poorer perspective-taking by the oldest (over 70) adults, compared with young and middle-aged adult groups, controlling for educational differences. However, Schultz and Hoyer (1976) showed that perspective-taking by older individuals could be improved on a post-test by brief feedback experiences which reinforced the correct answers. Unfortunately, no comparison with the effects of training on younger persons was conducted, so interpretation of these training gains is somewhat uncertain. At least it would seem that such skills are somewhat modifiable in older persons, but it is unclear whether older adults particularly benefit from such feedback in comparison to other age groups.

In the affective domain, perspective-taking is concerned with the representation of the feelings and emotions of others. Several basic processes are likely involved in such understanding, including "decoding" of the facial and physical cues associated with various emotions, as well as predicting the role of situational/experiential factors in relation to feelings. Malatesta, Izard, Culver and Nicolich (1987) reported that older adults were somewhat poorer at decoding the emotional expressions of younger adults compared with the decoding performance of young and middle-aged adults. However, this relative deficiency was not true for judging emotional expressions of older adults, which were actually "read" most accurately by the older sample. The results of this research suggest that people are best at evaluating the emotions of those in their own age group, and perhaps raise some questions regarding difficulties in the non-verbal communication of emotions between generations (Ryan, 1992). It might be, for example, that intergenerational communication requires more explicit efforts to convey feelings than are needed in discussions with those of one's own age group. Interestingly, studies of facial expressions have generally indicated that older adults may be more emotionally expressive than younger groups, so there is evidently plenty to observe in these inter-generational contexts (e.g., Malatesta-Magai et al., 1992).

One other topic which is related to the area of perspective-taking skill is that of empathy (e.g., Selman, 1980). Empathy describes the tendency to share the emotional feelings of another in a situation, rather than simply to understand these feelings. Empathic tendencies are believed to develop across the early part of the lifespan, perhaps based on some very primitive elementary capacities already present in the young infant (e.g., Hoffman, 1987). Empathy for others is also believed to be intimately involved in a number of important prosocial behaviors, such as sharing and helping others in need (Hoffman, 1987).

In general, there has been very little research on empathy among older adults, though there has been some study of altruistic actions among elderly persons, discussed in chapter 7. To the extent that sophisticated forms of empathy are dependent on perspective-taking (Hoffman, 1987), it seems possible that there are tendencies for empathic responding to decrease in later adulthood. Hogg and Heller (1990) showed that older, community-dwelling women (in their 70s) tended to perform at a somewhat lower level than young-old women (in their 60s) on a measure of "relational competence." This involved providing solutions to standard vignette situations where an empathic or perspective-taking response was required. For example, participants were asked:

> Let's suppose that a friend of yours is very hurt and angry because she was insulted by another driver while at an intersection. The other driver shouted that she should not be allowed to drive a car, simply because she was being very careful about pulling into traffic. What would you say to [your friend] if this situation were actually happening? (Hogg & Miller, 1990, p. 588).

The oldest women tended to provide less sophisticated and empathic solutions, as judged by observers unaware of participant age. However, one study in a clinical tradition has shown that older adults can be quite readily trained to increase their rated levels of empathic responding in the context of being "counsellors" or sympathetic listeners to the problems of others (Isquick, 1981).

Overall, the evidence indicates that older adults, especially those in the old-old group, may be somewhat less effective at considering the perspectives of others in various ways. Longitudinal research is needed to assess the validity of these cross-sectional findings. Since perspective-taking skills in later adulthood have been linked to such diverse behaviors as moral reasoning (Pratt, Diessner et al., 1991), communication processes (e.g., Hogg & Heller, 1990), and interpersonal problem-solving (Dolen & Bearison, 1982), this might suggest some important consequences for the behaviors of elderly persons.

However, several situational and/or target variables qualify these findings of older adult "deficiency." First, adult age differences often seem to be minimized or even reversed when the perspective-taking "target" is older as well (Cohen et al., 1987; Malatesta et al., 1987). Quite reasonably, people seem to understand the point of view of peers in their own age group most readily. Second, more explicit probing, practice or training all seem to benefit older persons' utilization of these skills, at least as much as for younger persons (e.g., Malatesta et al., 1987). This seems to suggest that older adults are quite *capable* of such perspective-taking, but may need more encouragement to apply their skills to the standardized tasks most commonly studied. More exploration of non-standardized assessment procedures would be useful, as people's real-life performance in this skill area has been little studied to date.

Gender differences in perspective-taking and empathy have been studied quite extensively. It has been suggested that females are likely to be both more invested and more skilled in the interpersonal realm, and that this should translate into more sophisticated performance on indices of perspective-taking and empathy (e.g., Eisenberg & Lennon, 1983). In fact, the research evidence on this point for adults is quite mixed. As Eisenberg and Lennon noted, female superiority on indices in this domain seems to be associated primarily with self-report measures. When men and women are asked to report on their empathic experiences, women consistently report greater empathy (Eisenberg & Lennon, 1983). For example, women score higher on the Mehrabian–Epstein (1972) Empathy self-report measure, which includes items such as "Sometimes the words of a love song can move me deeply" and "It upsets me to see helpless old people."

In contrast, when physiologically-based indices of empathy are used, there is little evidence of any sex differences (Eisenberg & Lennon, 1983). These findings suggest that there may be a gender-linked cultural stereotype regarding feminine empathic processes which leads women to report themselves (and perhaps experience themselves) as more empathic than men. However, the underlying physiological differences between the sexes on which such empathic responding is presumably based seem minimal (Eisenberg & Lennon, 1983).

A number of other personal background qualities have been suggested as factors in individual differences in these skills in later life as well. Bearison and his colleagues have clearly illustrated the potential role of diversity of social experiences in maintaining or perhaps enhancing these skills in older samples (Cohen et al., 1987; Dolen & Bearison, 1982). The Cohen et al. study particularly emphasized the role of age-heterogeneous experiences in relation to consideration of the viewpoints of other age groups. As the example of Bob and his father at the beginning of this chapter was meant to illustrate, less practice in thinking about the perspectives of diverse other persons may be especially limiting for the everyday performance of elders in restrictive social contexts. However, better controls, such as actual training experiences in perspective-taking for randomly assigned participants, would be needed to establish this finding clearly.

The social lives of older groups, particularly the old-old, do tend to become somewhat more restricted in terms of all sorts of social contacts (Dolen & Bearison, 1982). Thus, this may be an especially important factor in the less adequate performance of this group reported in some studies above. Of course, the possibility of cohort differences cannot be ruled out on the basis of these exclusively cross-sectional findings, either. Younger adults today are almost certainly exposed to a greater diversity of persons from different backgrounds and cultures than their older, less urbanized counterparts in previous generations. As well, there is little systematic evidence regarding training effects on these skills, but the few results reported to date appear promising in suggesting rather large increments with fairly brief training (e.g., Isquick, 1981).

In keeping with the information-processing perspective on cognitive aging, limitations in working memory resources may be potentially implicated in any decline in perspective-taking skills that may be documented. There has apparently been no direct study of this account to date among older adults. However, Lapsley and Quintana (1989) have found that specific measures of working memory capacity in children are better predictors of actual perspective-taking performance than are age or general developmental factors. This result is consistent with the idea that conscious perspective-taking is a resource-demanding task, and that children's development in this area is facilitated by developmental gains in such available working memory capacity. Research on this question at the later end of the life cycle, where working memory capacities are declining for some (e.g., Light, 1991), might prove instructive.

What are the practical implications of age changes in perspective-taking capacities in later adulthood? Two examples of these implications concern empathy or "relational competence," as studied by Hogg and Heller (1990), and spatial capacities (Simon, Walsh, Regnier, & Krauss, 1992). Hogg and Heller found that those older adults who were higher on relational competence scores in their study were more effective in subsequent observations made of their telephone contacts with another older adult in a "dyad support" program (Hogg & Heller, 1990). The telephone contacts of higher scorers were rated more positively by observers who were not informed about relational scores. In addition, the phone partner rated these individuals more highly on such qualities as "helped me explore problems" and "liked my advice" (Hogg & Heller, 1990).

Simon et al. (1992) studied the role of measures of older adults' spatial cognition in accounting for the extensiveness of their use of their urban neighborhoods. They showed that a laboratory-based assessment of the capacity to remember and reconstruct a display from a range of perspectives of it that had been provided during a study period was the best predictor of elderly adults' use of neighborhood services and trip frequency. They suggested that such spatial skills facilitate knowledge and use of individuals' neighborhoods by making them more comfortable in negotiating travel in their environments. Though the measures used were not conventional perspective-taking assessments, these results do suggest that such cognitive skills might play an important role in the everyday social lives of urban adults. It would be interesting to conduct an investigation of the possibility of training in such skills and its direct impact on the daily lives of older adults (Simon et al., 1992).

Person perception and behavioral attribution inferences

A 7-year-old girl describes a boy she knows:

Scott, he's the gross type. He scrapes his crayon with his teeth. And he chews it, and he swallows it. I don't like gross people like that.

Gee, that could make you sick.

Yeah, [sigh] but he's never really absent (Pratt, 1975, p. 1).

In this section, studies that have investigated the complexity of conceptions of others and of the causes of specific behaviors are reviewed. The

initial impetus for this research has been studies of children and adolescents that have examined developmental trends in the types and organization of concepts employed when conceptualizing others' qualities
and explaining their behaviors (e.g., Barenboim, 1981; Livesley &
Bromley, 1974; Peevers & Secord, 1973).

For example, Peevers and Secord showed that young children produced descriptions, like the example given above, focused more on
external and non-discriminating features associated with persons ("he
has two baseball bats"), whereas adolescents and adults described more
internal and distinguishing qualities of others, such as characteristic traits,
habits, or specific inner qualities. Second, adolescents and adults were
more likely to generate descriptions with more "depth," i.e., to use
more explanatory features in their descriptions of others compared with
younger children (Peevers & Secord, 1973). Barenboim (1981) has
sketched a "stage" conception of developmental changes in person perception during this early period, from a focus on behavior in early
childhood, to more use of "internal" traits in middle childhood, and
finally to comparisons among others based on these inner psychological
features in adolescence.

What is known of the complexity of person perception in later adulthood? Only three studies using the most informative, open-ended
methodologies for investigating this question could be located. Dolen
and Bearison (1982) found no age differences (across those aged 65 to
89) in their sample of community-dwelling older people in the proportional use of the most complex levels of descriptions as assessed by
Peevers and Secord (1973). These included "differentiating" qualities
such as interests and abilities, and "dispositional" features such as traits
(e.g., kind, thoughtless). Measures of social role participation (such as
club and activity participation levels) were strongly positively related to
scores on this person perception index, however, suggesting that older
persons with more social experiences were more likely to be complex
in their views of others (Dolen & Bearison, 1982).

In a similar study, Fitzgerald and Martin-Louer (1983–84) asked
individuals from three age groups, 30s, 40s, and 60s, to respond to a
written questionnaire and describe three personal acquaintances in an
open-ended way. There were no age differences in proportional use of
the developmentally most advanced categories of dispositional information for males. However, older women used this category proportionally less than did young women (and somewhat less than older
males). Despite these *proportion* differences in the descriptions provided
by older women, analyses of total frequencies revealed that the written

descriptions of the oldest group actually contained more information overall than the two younger groups (including more total dispositional information). Thus, older adults actually provided more informative pictures of others than did the other age groups (Fitzgerald & Martin-Louer, 1983–84). An analysis of the "depth" of these descriptions, essentially a measure of the extent to which they included explanations of others' qualities, indicated no age differences, however.

Norris (1979) reported an investigation of the descriptions of others found in the journal entries of younger (20s) and older (60s and 70s) adults. These descriptions were analyzed both for their complexity of content and for depth, using the Peevers and Secord (1973) system. Results showed no age differences for proportional use of differentiating–dispositional categories in the descriptions. However, older adults provided proportionally "deeper" explanations of others' qualities than younger participants in their diary entries (Norris, 1979).

One obvious interpretive issue in these studies may be length of acquaintanceship. It is likely that older persons have known those whom they chose to describe for longer time spans, which might contribute to greater complexity in both description and explanations about the other person. Asking about persons known for equal lengths of time and/or at equal levels of intimacy, across generational groups, might help to control for this confound.

Procedures which structure the person perception task more completely have also been used to study conceptions of others. Brewer and Lui (1984) showed that elderly respondents grouped photographs of older adults into significantly more categories than did younger adults, suggesting that they have more complex representations of the set of elderly persons than do college students. In partial contrast, Linville (1982) showed that college students used more categories and more complex categories for grouping the trait qualities of younger persons than those of elderly adults. A direct comparison of the complexity of older versus younger people's perceptions of young adults has yet to be done however.

Underlying people's constructed impressions and memories of other persons are ideas and explanations for specific behaviors which lead to inferences about the qualities of persons that account for these behaviors (e.g., Schneider, Hastorf, & Ellsworth, 1979). For example, someone who is surly to new neighbors is likely to be seen by them as "unfriendly" in disposition, though alternative factors, such as stress or just a bad day, might explain such behaviors too (e.g., Kelley, 1972). Kelley's attributional models of factors involved in such inferences were

designed to specify the orderly causal "schemes" by which such everyday behaviors are routinely understood and explained by the layperson.
Again, however, there has been only a limited amount of research on
the use of such behavioral explanations later in the lifespan.

A study of the spontaneous use of explanations for behavioral information and its relation to memory for behaviors was conducted by
Hess and Tate (1991). Older adults (mean age 68) were found to be less
likely to complete sentences about a person's behaviors by providing
explanations than were younger adults (mean age 20). This was especially true when the behavior was inconsistent with the major trait
qualities of the description of the person that had been provided (for
example, explaining "gregarious" behavior in a supposedly reclusive
person). When older adults did use such explanations, however, they
were found to be just as likely to recall the inconsistent information as
were younger adults, whereas this was not the case when they did not
spontaneously use behavioral explanations (Hess & Tate, 1991). Thus,
older adults seemed just as capable of *using* such explanations in remembering inconsistent behavioral qualities, but did not do so as readily on
their own in this unfamiliar laboratory context.

In contrast, when older adults are explicitly asked to provide explanations for problem behaviors of children or other family members
with which they are familiar, they seem to produce explanations judged
to be as developmentally advanced as those provided by young adults
(Pratt, Hunsberger, Pancer, Roth, & Santolupo, 1993). However, older
adults did not use such sophisticated explanations as did younger adults
for the behaviors of others in unfamiliar, standardized story situations
(Pratt et al., 1993).

The small number of studies reviewed in this section are somewhat diverse in methodology. In contrast to the preceding section on
perspective-taking, however, these results are more consistent with a
view of stability or even increasing sophistication in person perception
and attribution in later life. This seems particularly likely when underlying competence is assessed by systematic and explicit probing. Spontaneous use of explanatory reasoning under novel conditions may not
be as high in the elderly (Hess & Tate, 1991; Pratt et al., 1993). As
usual, longitudinal research is needed to carefully assess these suggested
trends. As well, better controls over stimulus "target" persons are needed
in this work. It would seem plausible that the expertise of older adults
relative to younger groups is most likely to emerge in situations where
their life experience can provide a significant advantage (e.g., long
acquaintanceship with friends being described). However, to date, the

research in this area has not moved much beyond simply attempting to describe age differences. Studies are needed on such possible explanatory factors as social experiences and empathy differences within and across age groups. Perhaps Jim's views on his teenage granddaughter's latest hairdo are not as complex as they might be if he spent more time at the local shopping mall where the kids hang out. In fact, it might not look so bad in comparison after all!

In a study somewhat related to the topic of person perception, Heckhausen, Dixon, and Baltes (1989) examined the complexity of people's views about personal development across adulthood. Adults in their 20s, 40s, and 70s rated 358 adjectives that included a range of personality, social, and intellectual attributes. These adjectives were rated for the extent to which they show a developmental increase or decrease in adulthood, to what extent the characteristic was desirable, and when changes in the characteristic began and ended. Results showed considerable consensus between age groups on basic personal developmental patterns in adulthood, and on a pattern of greater expected "losses" in later life (especially after 80). Of most relevance to the present point, older adults showed a more complex representation of the lifespan than younger groups, in that they perceived greater change over adulthood in the entire set of characteristics, and viewed this change as beginning and ending at a wider variety of age points in the adult life cycle. Younger adults, in particular, tended to use the extreme ages of 20 and 90 as markers of the onset and closing points of changes much more frequently than did middle-aged and especially older adults. Thus, Heckhausen et al. (1989) concluded that older adults, perhaps through their own more extensive life experiences, have formulated a richer conception of aspects of the personal life cycle.

These patterns of expectations and "theories" about personality and its development across the lifespan, studied by Heckhausen et al., also appear to have interesting implications for people's own self-concepts and memories of personal experiences (McFarland, Ross, & Giltrow, 1992). In this research, Ross's (1989) model of self-perception through reconstruction of personal characteristics in the past was tested on an adult lifespan sample. Reconstruction of past personal qualities is believed to involve monitoring one's current level on a characteristic (e.g., "understandingness"), and then applying a culturally defined implicit theory about what changes generally occur across the lifespan in such a quality. For example, we generally believe that "understandingness" increases across the adult lifespan. Consistent with this, adults in their 60s and 70s remembered themselves as less understanding 30 years ago than a comparison group of 30- to 40-year-old adults currently rated themselves on understandingness. In contrast, for items that were generally believed to decrease in magnitude across the lifespan (e.g., activity level, memory ability), older adults rated themselves as higher 30 years ago than did a comparison group of young adults currently in their 30s.

There are some problems interpreting the cross-sectional nature of this comparison. The older group's qualities 30 years ago may not be well-represented by the younger comparison cohort's current scores, for example. Nevertheless, to the extent that these findings are accurate, they indicate that people's general models of the development of personal qualities over the life course may impact on the important processes of personal life review and reminiscence (McFarland et al., 1992). For example, when older adults possess a "theory of decline" regarding an important quality (e.g., memory capacity), this biased life review process may undermine positive self-evaluations. In the next section, we discuss how implicit theories about aging may also lead to the stereotyping of others.

Age stereotyping in perceiving elderly persons

A topic of much interest in the research on aging and social perception is the issue of negative stereotyping of elderly adults (e.g., Crockett & Hummert, 1987). Do people in general have "expectancy biases" regarding the performances and behaviors of adults on the basis of age? In particular, are older adults expected to perform less well than younger adults, to be less positive in their social and personal qualities, or to have more unpleasant experiences and characteristics? Such a negative view of elderly people has been labelled "ageism", referring to both the discriminatory attitudes themselves and the actions that presumably accompany this stereotyping (Butler, 1969). There seems little doubt that some discriminatory *practices* directed against older persons occur in our culture. However, much controversy has surrounded research attempts to answer the question of whether, and to what extent, ageist stereotypes or cognitive biases are actually shared among individual perceivers (e.g., Palmore, 1982; Schonfield, 1982).

Recent reviews of this research evidence show that indications of such age stereotyping vary with a number of methodological and contextual factors, so the answer to this question, like so many others in this book, is not simple. Crockett and Hummert (1987) point out that studies which have asked for people's attitudes regarding the elderly adult *in general*, as a stimulus category, tend to reveal considerable evidence of negative stereotypes. For example, Kite, Deaux, and Miele (1991) found that when both younger (20s) and older (70s) adults were simply asked to rate the qualities of a younger and older woman, and a younger and older man, common attributes based on age strongly outweighed attributes based on gender. Thus, older people, both men and women, were seen as poorer, less hopeful, grouchier, more critical, and so on, compared with young adults. However, older persons were also viewed as having positive attributes, such as being "experienced," and the older raters in this study were somewhat less likely to attribute negative qualities to the elderly adult than were those raters in their 20s (Kite, Deaux, & Miele, 1991). Nevertheless, when negative evaluations occurred at all, they were uniformly directed to older targets.

As another example, Palmore's (1977) "Facts on Aging Quiz," which measures accuracy of beliefs about elderly adults, shows that incorrect negative statements are more likely to be endorsed than are incorrect positive statements. For instance, the percentage of elderly persons in long-term care institutions was reported as much higher than is factually true. This pattern too suggests some evidence of negative bias in the population's general beliefs about older persons (Crockett & Hummert, 1987).

In contrast to these findings for general culturally based beliefs, when people are asked to respond to specific individuals of different ages, and given fuller descriptions of these peoples' qualities, they are much less likely to show age bias (Crockett & Hummert, 1987). For example, Walsh and Connor (1979) found that articles, supposedly written by either a younger or older male or female, were judged only on the basis of actual quality, and not on the basis of either author age or sex.

Obviously, context factors are critical also in how people rate others' qualities (Kite & Johnson, 1988). Rating people as counsellors versus athletes will likely lead to different patterns of age stereotyping. For example, Erber and her colleagues have recently shown that evidence of simple memory failure is viewed as more significant among older adults than among younger counterparts (Erber, Szuchman, & Rothberg, 1990). Vignettes of everyday memory problems (e.g., forgetting a phone number) were judged as more serious and as signalling greater mental difficulty and more need for memory training if they occurred in an older person than a younger person. Both older and younger raters evidenced this "double standard," though overall, older raters were less likely to see these ordinary memory failures as indicating mental difficulties. Apparently, in the context of an ability such as memory, which is strongly associated with age-linked beliefs about competence, broad "age-stereotypic" response trends can be quite readily triggered.

Similar findings for some other achievement-related areas by age group have been reported (e.g., obtaining a driver's license, Banziger & Drevenstedt, 1982). Presumably, however, in the context of other types of personal competencies (e.g., "wise counsel"), such ageist bias might be reduced or even reversed. For instance, as discussed in chapter 8, Ryan and her colleagues (1992) have shown that older adults are expected to do more poorly on many aspects of language comprehension than their younger counterparts. However, their skills at telling good stories are expected to be better.

In summary, research on this topic has revealed some evidence for a negative stereotype regarding the elderly in our culture, but one which varies considerably with topic area, and with the ways in which this bias is studied. Crockett and Hummert (1987) have argued that this research gives evidence that there are actually *multiple* stereotypes of the older individual which co-exist, and which vary considerably in evaluative tone (e.g., the perfect grandparent versus the severely impaired, Hummert, 1990). In Hummert's study, multiple stereotypes of college-age persons were observed as well (e.g., redneck, activist, perfect friend). Furthermore, these stereotypes of young adults were not at all similar to those evidenced for the elderly, suggesting that the schemata associated with various age groups are not simple extensions of one another across the lifespan. Finally, old-old individuals in the Hummert (1990) study were considerably more likely to be negatively evaluated in terms of these age-linked stereotypes than were young-old groups.

Despite the lack of gender differences reported in some of the studies of general stereotypes reviewed above, research does suggest that older women may be particularly negatively evaluated in certain contexts (Kogan & Mills, 1992). Such findings are especially prominent in studies where pictures of older men and women are used as stimuli, and appearance cues are thus especially salient. Older women are then rated more negatively compared with both middle-aged women and with older men (e.g., Deutsch, Zalenski, & Clark, 1986). Susan Sontag (1979) referred to this phenomenon as "the double-standard of aging." She suggested that the aging process leads to lowered perceptions of attractiveness for women, but to some extent, to more positive signs of maturity and desirability for men. Consider as evidence the relative level of advertising directed at the two sexes for products designed to "slow" the effects of aging in our culture.

One reflection of these patterns is that women tend to prefer sexual partners nearer their own age across the lifespan, whereas older men tend to prefer substantially younger women. This pattern was observed in singles advertisements in newspapers in our culture (Kenrick & Trost, 1989), and also cross-culturally in marital age patterns for a broad range of societies (Buss, 1989). Kogan and Mills generally interpret their findings from a sociobiological perspective, suggesting that men prefer younger women because of their capacity to reproduce, whereas such evolutionary forces are less important in women's preferences for men, who are able to reproduce across a wider age range. However, there are clearly powerful societal forces that shape these attitudes and preferences. Regardless of the explanatory mechanism, there is considerable evidence of more negativity directed toward older women in some judgment contexts (Kogan & Mills, 1992).

What about ethnic factors and variations in age discrimination? There has been a good deal of debate regarding the impact of ethnic minority status on the overall well-being of aging adults (e.g., Cool, 1987). Jackson (e.g., 1970) and others have employed the concept of "double jeopardy" to describe a conception of overall negative impact. Older African-Americans, for example, are viewed as doubly at risk in this formulation, susceptible to discrimination through processes of both ageism and racism. Indeed, demographic data do suggest that older minority status individuals are generally relatively more disadvantaged on certain measures (e.g., health, income) than are white elderly in North America (e.g., Bengonts & Morgan, 1983). And certainly both racism and ageism can be apparent, and combined, in the attitudes and reactions of members of the majority culture with power to influence the lives of older minority adults, such as service providers (Cool, 1987).

Nevertheless, on other indices of life outcomes (e.g., life satisfaction) there are no consistent differences between black and white elderly adults in the United States (Bengston & Morgan, 1983). And social contacts were actually higher for minority elderly in the Bengston and Morgan study. In fact, other researchers have proposed that minority cultural status may also serve a positive function in the social identities of older adults, by providing special roles for them in the preservation of the cultural group's heritage as well as a particular basis for close-knit social interaction (Cool, 1987). Cool provides the example of older Portuguese individuals in Santa Clara, California, an ethnic community which seeks to maintain a separate stance from majority Anglo culture. The elders' role is to act as traditional culture and language "keepers" for the younger generations, in the face of the Americanization and assimilationist pressures to which younger Portuguese are subjected. For this, they are

respected by the Portuguese community as a whole (Cool, 1987). Similarly, the old in "traditionalist" Amish cultures are valued and typically
held in high esteem (Brubaker & Michael, 1987).

Thus, elderly individuals in some community contexts may be able
to use their special minority status to establish and gain important social
resources and status. It would seem too simple to describe the impact
of minority status as either totally negative or positive in the lives and
satisfaction of older adults. Clearly, a variety of important social–
interactional processes are involved in establishing both types of effects.
More adequate longitudinal research focusing on the construction of the
meaning of ethnic minority status across the life cycle of older adults,
rather than focusing simply on ethnicity as a social category, is needed
to understand these phenomena (e.g., Cavanaugh, 1990).

One real-life arena where research on age-based stereotyping has been
conducted is the presentation of seniors on television (e.g., Rubin, 1988).
Research on the quantity of roles on television by Gerbner and associates
(e.g., 1980) has repeatedly shown that older adults are greatly under-
represented on television in relation to their proportion in the population as a whole. Despite a few recent efforts ("The Golden Girls" comes
to mind for most North American TV watchers), this underrepresentation is even more pronounced for women than it is for men. A cross-
cultural study of children's television programming suggests that this is
not only a North American phenomenon (Holtzman & Akiyama, 1985).
In this study, women over 60 made up only 2 to 3 percent of the roles
on television in both the USA and Japan, whereas they represent in
the order of 8 to 9 percent of the population in each country. The
underrepresentation of elderly men on TV was considerably less marked
in this study for both societies (shades of Sontag's double standard).

What about the *quality* of elders' roles portrayed on television? Early
studies tended to find that older adults were portrayed in quite negative
terms in the roles they did assume, as sickly, slow, and decrepit (e.g.,
Rubin, 1988). However, recent evidence on this point is more equivo-
cal. Older adults do not appear to be portrayed as in poorer health than
is true of the population of elderly adults as a whole, in either Japan or
the USA, for example (Holtzman & Akiyama, 1985). In general, the
evidence for negative stereotyping of elderly adults, on television is not
dramatic and consistent. The crotchety, but crafty, role created by Redd
Fox in the comedy *Sanford and Son* in the 1960s and 70s was a typical
mix of both positive and negative qualities. Furthermore, despite the
arguments of some (e.g., Gerbner et al., 1980), the evidence for widespread "cultivation" of negative attitudes toward the elderly through

television viewing is not very strong or consistent (Passuth & Cook, 1985).

Nevertheless, younger adults who watch a lot of television may be more subject to such a cultivation effect from stereotypic portrayals of older adults, and more investigation of this issue using careful controls for third-variable factors is certainly needed (Passuth & Cook, 1985). It certainly is difficult to think of many current network programs which portray older adults in strongly positive terms, particularly, as noted, older women. And the typical portrayal of older adults on commercials does seem associated with the sick role. Indeed, the "Help, I've fallen and can't get up" line in the commercial for a quite useful buzzer pendant worn by independently living elders has become something of a (dismayingly negative) cultural classic!

Can such "expectancies" about elderly individuals have an impact on actual social interactions with others? Almost certainly. A number of years ago, Rosenthal and Jacobsen (1968) provided a demonstration that teachers' biased expectancies about students in the classroom could affect their students' progress. Rosenthal and Jacobsen labelled this "the Pygmalion effect" (from George Bernard Shaw's play of the same name). When teachers were told that one group of students (randomly chosen) would "blossom" over the year, there was some evidence that these students did better than a comparable control group who were not so designated. Like Eliza Doolittle in *My Fair Lady* (the musical version of *Pygmalion*), high expectations by teachers translated into effective growth and learning for students.

In an interesting replication of this work with older residents of nursing homes, Rosenthal and his associates (Learman, Avorn, Everitt, & Rosenthal, 1990) examined the impact of telling nurses and aides that certain residents would show a more successful course of rehabilitation than controls. After a three-month period of such encouragement, treatment group participants were found less likely to be depressed and marginally more likely to be mentally alert on a standard test. However, they were also more likely to have become dependent on their aides in performing daily self-care activities (Learman et al., 1990).

Observations of the aides showed that they were both warmer and more infantilizing in their behaviors to the treatment group compared with their interactions with controls. This pattern may explain the somewhat mixed findings of increases in mental health but decreases in personal care skills for the target group (Learman et al., 1990). At any rate, this study suggests that such "Pygmalion effects" are likely to be present, albeit in complex ways. And it certainly suggests that positive (or, presumably, negative) stereotypes of particular groups can have an impact on the behaviors of others in the individual's social environment.

Tracing the book's themes

The first theme of the book concerns possible differences in people's orientations to the tasks of understanding other persons in later life. One important matter here is the considerable evidence that people at all ages are apparently "better" at understanding the perspectives and qualities of their same-age peers than those of other age groups. Ageist stereotyping is also less apparent among older individuals, apparently because they have more appropriate information, and a more accurate perspective with which to consider it. This finding raises important issues regarding intergenerational communication processes (Ryan, 1992), intergenerational stereotyping (Linville, 1982), and perhaps behaviors in other areas as well (e.g., intergenerational helping). It also suggests that great care needs to be taken in interpreting the performance of adults of different ages, depending on the social "target" to which they are being asked to respond.

The second theme of individual diversity in later-life performance is evident in the limited data so far obtained in this area. The research by Bearison and his colleagues (e.g., Cohen et al., 1987) suggests that variations in the types of experiences that individuals have may impact on their skills of social perception in predictable and consistent ways. The findings of Pratt et al. (1993) regarding variations in certain social–cognitive dispositions (notably authoritarianism levels) and their links to skills in perspective-taking and attribution also indicate other important factors that may play a role in later-life diversity. And the possibility of a role for differences in basic information-processing capacities in this domain of social reasoning also deserves systematic study. Interestingly, careful examination of societal stereotypes about older individuals has shown these to be complex and multiple rather than unidimensional and simple. It seems that people can't even be simple-minded in their biases! Clearly, diversity is the rule, both in people's experiences and skills and in their views of the experiences of societal roles in later life (e.g., Hummert, 1990).

The third theme emphasizes the particular role of social support in later life. Obviously, much of the preceding evidence cited on the relations of social experience variations and social–cognitive performance is relevant. As the Cohen et al. (1987) study suggested, for example, isolation from perspectives that diverge from one's own may have some serious costs in terms of these sociocognitive skills. At any rate, the social context of thinking about others' opinions and points of view in adulthood deserves much more careful study.

In an intriguing analysis of creative productivity, Storr (1988) has remarked that trends toward greater "interiority" of focus, greater synthesis and order, and a lessening of attempts to communicate with the audience can all be seen in the later works of many great artists. For example, in music, the late compositions of Beethoven, Brahms, and of Bach are all said to represent an increasing emphasis on inner development, and a lowered interest in speaking to an audience at all – creations that rather strive for a perfection of expression for the self alone (Storr, 1988). This notion of turning inward in later life has been discussed extensively under the topic of disengagement theory in the gerontological literature (e.g., Cumming & Henry, 1961; see chapter 5).

In the psychological research literature, it is generally agreed that there are both social and psychological factors which foster such disengagement processes in later life (e.g., retirement, preoccupation with approaching death), but that disengagement is not an inevitable or even a particularly satisfactory approach to aging for many adults (e.g., Norris, 1979). Indeed, maintenance of social contacts and activities is seen as a more satisfying strategy for many elderly persons as they age. Creative artists may express these later-life disengagement processes in powerful and compelling ways. However, for most individuals, extensive *social* disengagement may represent a risk factor which could impair the sociocognitive skills of person understanding as discussed in this chapter.

Reconsidering Bob and Jim

How can Bob's questions about his father, with which this chapter began, be addressed on the basis of what is currently known? The reader should be clear by now that any such answers are tentative at best. However, it does seem important to recognize that some types of "isolating" experiences may put elderly persons at greater risk of sociocognitive difficulties, perhaps particularly those which decrease contact with other age or social groups. While there are likely benefits to the current trend toward more age-homogeneous communities in modern Western culture (e.g., Lawton, 1980), there may be costs as well, for elders and, of course, for the society in which they live.

5

Thinking about Relationships

How would you describe yourself as a parent and a grandparent?

I do know that we worked hard when the kids were little and I had little spare time but I also let my housework go in order to spend time with the kids. I felt the kids were more important to me than what my house looked like. I think probably the same thing works with the grandchildren and I think the kids' happiness comes ahead of what the place looks like. I said that my parents tried to bring us up both spiritually, morally and, whether we have done a good job or not, I think both myself and my husband have tried to instill this into our children. I see them at it with their children and I try to help them too and I think if you are strong spiritually then you have the strength to withstand a lot of earth's problems. That's my little sermon. I don't know that I consciously thought about it but when you asked me that's what came to mind (Mrs McIvor, a 60-year-old farm wife; Norris & Tari, unpublished data).

Mrs McIvor's reflection on her roles as parent and grandparent shows a commitment to family relationships within the context of broader values. Her biography provided rich descriptions of long-term relationships with family members, friends, and social institutions such as her church. She described the negative side of some relationships over the years, as well as their positive features. Nevertheless, Mrs McIvor reported an overall sense of happiness with her life and characterized her relationship with her family as "delightful" and with her friends as "very satisfying."

What made Mrs McIvor evaluate her life so positively? What were her strategies for managing relationships with others? In this chapter, we will use a lifespan perspective to explore the variables producing successful relationships, like those of Mrs McIvor, in later life. Social and cognitive processes involved in forming and maintaining relationships, and in coping with their loss, will be discussed. As in previous chapters, four theoretical frameworks will be noted: **psychometric**, **information-processing**, **developmental**, and **social – psychological**. We will see that much of research on later-life relationships comes from the developmental and social-psychological literatures.

Theoretical perspectives on social relationships

Researchers in the **psychometric** tradition, with their focus on the individual, have not addressed the question of how older people think about their social relationships. Nevertheless, there are methodological similarities in the approach taken to the measurement of school-based abilities and that used in measuring social skills. Both have focused on sets of discrete abilities which can be assessed under controlled conditions using standardized tests.

As we have noted in chapter 1, the psychometric perspective has produced useful data on crystallized and fluid intelligence across the lifespan. A psychometric approach to social skill, however, has yielded less of relevance to adulthood. Researchers interested in children's social skills have had some success in measuring abilities necessary to get along with peers. Typically, observations are made of behaviors in very restricted or controlled settings; these behaviors are then coded using predetermined categories (e.g., Carr & Duran, 1985; Ross & Lollis, 1989).

As an individual ages, acquires diverse experiences, and interacts within a complicated social environment, relevant measures of social skill are difficult to construct. Some researchers have been able to measure very specific skills such as assertiveness, but typically do so with a restricted sample such as nursing home patients (Berger & Rose, 1977). When there are sample differences due to culture, socioeconomic status, or ethnicity, standardized measures of social skill lack construct validity (Franzke, 1987).

Theorists working within the **information-processing** tradition have rarely concerned themselves with older people's performance in their social environment (e.g., McDowd & Birren, 1990). Nevertheless, work on cognitive capacity does have relevance for understanding social behavior. The finding that the aged maintain fewer relationships than the young may be due in part to decreases in cognitive capacity and energy thought to occur in later life (e.g., Craik & Byrd, 1982). If, for example, memory decrements make it difficult to handle a busy social calendar, and declines in communicative ability make social interaction more difficult and tiring (see chapter 7), then it is likely that older adults will become increasingly selective in their interactions with others.

Some recent conceptualizations of social competence in adulthood fit within an information-processing perspective, as well as the psychometric framework described above. Hogg and Heller (1990), for example, have stressed that being able to evaluate the components of a social situation is important for competent functioning by older people. Norris and Rubin (1984) have made a similar point, noting that competent older adults are likely to have an extensive social–cognitive and behavioral repertoire, and the ability to select a response appropriate to the social context.

Social competence can be extremely important for people coping with the normative events of later life: for example, relocation to an institution. Adjusting to a radically new living arrangement requires that residents notice and evaluate the social features of their new home and adapt their behaviors accordingly. If successful, institutional living can be an improvement on solitary life. One new resident in a home for the aged noted:

> It has been better. I do more here. I used to just sit (Coppola, 1987, p. 74).

On the other hand, if an older person has difficulty in adapting his behavior to the new setting, the result can be misery:

> I used to be busy with my work, hobbies and my wife. Now I have nothing but time on my hands. Different people here, people have a difficult time communicating with me; maybe it is me. I have lived my life, my wife is gone, my life is over. I hope God takes me soon (Coppola, 1987, p. 73).

Among **developmentalists**, the ability and the motivation to maintain relationships into old age have been considered an important issue in the study of adult relationships. Early conceptualizations of disengagement theory, for example, had a strongly developmental focus, proposing that, due to a lack of psychological energy first seen in the middle years, older adults were likely to relinquish important adult attachments (Cumming & Henry, 1961). Researchers claimed to see evidence of declining levels of cognitive mastery. These declines led individuals to concede to social forces by withdrawing from roles such as work (Havighurst, Neugarten, & Tobin, 1968).

Disengagement theorists proposed that withdrawal from roles and relationships was evidence of successful aging. Because of this view, the theory met with controversy and was not pursued with any vigor. From time to time, however, gerontologists have explored the usefulness of a less unitary and deterministic view of the theory. Maddox (1963) and Norris (1979) have pointed to the social factors contributing to disengagement in older people. Rather than an inevitable psychological change, disengagement could be seen as a response to social losses, such as widowhood, and social forces, such as agism.

Recently, researchers have identified individual differences which might produce variable levels of disengagement in older adults. For example, some older adults may welcome the freedom of fewer social contacts and obligations as they age (Larson, Zuzanek, & Mannell, 1985). As well, they may become increasingly selective about their social relationships and invest their energies only in those which appear more rewarding (Norris & Tindale, 1994). The reaction of Joan Norris's father, Poul, to his retirement provides a good example of increasing selectiveness in social activities. Poul had always been extremely active in men's service clubs during his career as a bank manager, working without complaint at a wide variety of tasks. With a sense of good riddance, Poul dropped all of these activities and took up gardening and travelling around the world with his wife and old friends.

There is other evidence for individual differences in disengagement in work by Johnson and Barer (1992) on the very old. These researchers found that about half of their sample of adults over the age of 85 showed evidence of disengagement. This group was older and in poorer health than their peers in the study, and seemed to have taken active steps to cope with their frailty. They removed themselves from social concerns, especially those which might occur in the future, and were content with very restricted social involvement.

Johnson and Barer's (1992) disengaged old people also resisted attempts by others at more social involvement. The authors suggest that this is one aspect of the permission that the oldest old give themselves to ignore social norms and expectations. This phenomenon is particularly interesting within a cross-cultural perspective. The respondents in this study were white and middle-class, but parallel findings have been reported in other literature. Kakar (1978, as reported in Cohler, 1983), for example, described a Hindu man who shed almost all of the duties and values of his life as a businessman in preparation, not for retirement, but for withdrawal from all worldly concerns. He did so in preparation for *samyama*, a religious journey providing increased opportunity for reflection. The difference between the two situations is that North American society does not support the voluntary relinquishing of social relationships while it is still possible to maintain them. As Cohler (1983) has pointed out, some form of disengagement in the old may indeed be developmental; the response of different cultures to the process, however, varies considerably.

Some developmental researchers have noted linkages between disengagement and attachment theories (Kalish & Knudtson, 1976; Cohler, 1983). In the view of these authors, old adults may disengage because of multiple losses involving important attachment figures, friends, spouses, and sometimes children. These losses deprive the older person of a sense of security and social mastery, and lead, in Cohler's view, to a loss of "relational autonomy". Without such meaningful attachments, then, the older person may find it difficult to cope with other aspects of the social environment and withdraw from it. In extreme cases, the ensuing absence of social feedback may lead to egocentrism (Looft, 1972) or social breakdown (Kuypers & Bengtson, 1973). Within this framework, disengagement may be almost inevitable in the very old, but it is nonetheless undesirable.

This discussion connecting disengagement and attachment has appeared in the gerontological literature. As well, there has been a great deal of recent speculation from developmentalists about how to extend the concept of infant attachment to relationships in adulthood. Much of this discussion surrounds the cognitive components of attachment. Bowlby (1973) proposed that working models, or internal representations, of attachment figures are formed during early childhood. These models then influence the individual's understanding of all future relationships. Main and her colleagues (e.g., Main, Kaplan, & Cassidy, 1985) further specified that cognitive models of attachment serve, consciously or unconsciously, to screen, select, and organize information relevant to relationships in adulthood. Anxious or avoidant relationships among older adults can then be understood in terms of working models based on early insecure attachments (Sable, 1989).

Much of the theorizing about social relationships in later life has occurred within **social psychology**. The psychological perspective on this area has focused on two main themes: how relationships are constructed, and how exchanges within relationships are negotiated. The first theme concerns rules governing the formation, maintenance, and termination of relationships. The second concerns expectations of equity, deserving, and justice. Both rely on attributional analyses of relationships.

Rules and roles

Research with young adults suggests that there are implicit, but commonly understood, rules underlying friendships (e.g., Argyle & Henderson, 1984). For example, one does not violate the trust of a friend. It is not clear, however, whether there are developmental influences on the acceptance and use of such rules. Theorists who argue for increasing cognitive complexity with age (e.g., Basseches, 1986) might propose that the schema for "friend" in old age would be more differentiated than those of earlier phases. On the other hand, evidence that the old seem to be highly selective when it comes to their choice of friends (Fredrickson & Carstensen, 1990) could argue for more simplistic social perception.

Similarly, schemas for "family member" and the behavioral scripts which accompany this role appear very well defined in later life. Empirical research has demonstrated that older people have a very clear understanding about what family rules should exist and how they should operate. Commonly held rules include not moving in with your adult children ("intimacy at a distance," Rosenmayr & Kockeis, 1963; Connidis, 1989), being concerned about the continuation of the family ("generational stake," Bengtson & Kuypers, 1971), and being fully informed of family issues ("kinkeeping," Rosenthal, 1987). Whether the use of such rules has developmental implications is unclear. Some theorists have suggested that older people make more complex attributions about the behavior of others (Norris & Pratt, 1980; Blanchard-Fields, 1986). If this is true, old people may subscribe to fairly rigid rules about family roles, while still considering the many factors that affect performance within those roles.

Equity and reciprocity

Many researchers and theorists have stressed the importance of perceptions of equity and reciprocity to well-functioning relationships (e.g., Walster & Berscheid, 1978). Recently, some theorists have proposed that the old may be more concerned than the young with maintaining equity in their relationships, particularly in those which are not close (Norris & Tindale, 1994). Inequities may lead to negative, internal attributions toward the person not able to reciprocate. When the older person is overbenefitted, attributions about his or her incompetence are likely, resulting in lower self-esteem, feelings of dependency, and depression (Roberto & Scott, 1986). Such a situation could occur when an older person is receiving care from an adult child. When someone is underbenefitted, on the other hand, attributions may be made about the other person's inability to perform in a social role, with the possible result that the relationship may be terminated. This could occur when an older adult perceives that his friend has become too reliant on him for favors, but rarely returns the help.

An interesting theoretical variation on ideas about equity involves a consideration of justice and deserving (Lerner, 1981). Social behavior is governed by decisions about "who is entitled to what from whom". Under most circumstances, people rely on norms to guide their decisions. How perceived inequities in a relationship are handled is dependent on the closeness of that relationship. Those in close "identity" relationships, characterized by high similarity and identification with one another – for example, siblings – tend to forgive unreciprocated aid. Those in "unit" relationships where there is high similarity but less affection – e.g., co-workers – may be less forgiving; conflict is possible. Those in "non-unit" relationships where there is little similarity or identification – e.g., casual acquaintances – easily explain lapses as due to fundamental personal differences. Although Lerner has not applied his concepts directly to older adults, he has found some support for them in a study of sibling caregivers of older relatives (Lerner, Somers, Reid, & Tierney, 1988). Whether there are developmental changes in notions about justice remain unclear.

The research evidence

Forming relationships

A great deal of research in gerontology has focused upon the social relationships of older people. Most of this work continues to be quantitative in its orientation. Disengagement theory, for example, led researchers to count the number of relationships lost due to aging (Cumming & Henry, 1961); opponents of this perspective (e.g., the activity theorist, Maddox, 1963) counted, and are still counting, the number of relationships added or maintained in later life. This latter, more popular, perspective has promoted work on social support: who do older people have in their social networks to call upon for emotional support and tangible assistance? (e.g., Martin Matthews, 1991).

While this work is useful, it does not address the issue of *how* important relationships are added to an older person's social world. In particular, we know very little about how peer relationships are developed in later life. Do old and young adults have the same criteria for close friendships? One study by Blieszner (1989) suggests that they do. Using an exchange perspective developed by Foa and Foa (1974), they examined the friendships of older women. Central to this perspective is the idea that all interpersonal encounters are based on mutually rewarding exchanges of love, status, information, services, goods, and money. If perceptions of the need for a resource and the ability to provide it are shared by members of a dyad, then the relationship will, over time, grow in intimacy. Blieszner's (1989) data on members of a newly established retirement community supported these ideas, leading her to conclude that the old conceptualize friendship in much the same way as the young.

Studies of friendship styles carried out by Matthews (1983; 1986) also support this view. Matthews found that some old people reported always having been "acquisitive" about friends. Others seemed to be more solitary, rarely having made friends (the "independents") or not replacing the few that they had made early in their adult lives (the "discerning"). It appears that whatever constructs about friendship guided these people when young continued to affect their relationships when old. Similar continuity was found in a study of never-married older people (Norris, 1990). These singles reported a cognitive strategy for independent living that influenced the development of peer relationships when young. Good friends were selected to provide opportunities for shared activities, and did not threaten personal freedom or intrude upon privacy. Consider the comments of three women in their 70s reflecting upon their childhood friendships:

> We used to holiday in groups together. If anyone was too demanding then that friendship tended to taper off.

I can't remember telling anyone everything. I doubt that I did. When I got working, I had a friend and we talked more. We didn't do a lot of blabbing like they seem to these days.

We used to go horse-back riding, swimming together, skating at the reformatory. We had a lot of the same interests. But I'm independent so I'd go my own way if they weren't available (Martin Matthews & Norris, unpublished data).

This approach to friendship – shared interests, but separate lives – seemed to carry over from their childhood years in the never-married. Many reported that they felt their never-married status was a blessing: they could share activities with their friends but still be free to live a fully independent life. The comments of these never-married adults illustrate their love and need for autonomy:

I enjoy a sense of personal autonomy. You don't have to placate somebody or stroke somebody. You don't have to account to someone. I love being alone when I want to be.

I love my independence. I value it so much that if I ever come back into this world, I'll be an only child.

It's nice not to have to be bothered with anybody – freedom to come and go as you like. I can go out with some of my friends.

I couldn't be more pleased with the situation I currently have. My friend is here when I want him to be and gone when I need to be alone (Martin Matthews & Norris, unpublished data).

It could be argued that this group was providing a defensive inter-pretation of their lifestyle in view of the pressures within our society to marry. This seems less likely, however, when another finding of this study, psychological functioning, is considered. Relative to others their age, this group experienced less loneliness and better morale. As well, loneliness and morale were not related to the presence or absence of a confidant. This result is particularly interesting in view of other studies supporting the role of a close relationship in promoting mental health (e.g., Lowenthal, 1968). In one study, in fact, the never-married old were labelled, *a priori*, as suffering from an attachment deficit (Andersson & Stevens, 1993). The self-sufficiency and good mental health of the never-married in the Norris (1990) study, however, provides strong evidence that a close relationship such as marriage is not essential for adaptation to old age.

The persistence of friendship styles and ideals suggests support for an attachment model of social relationships in later life. Even though working models of attachment probably evolve from the parent–child relationship as a result of peer and early family experiences (Tesch, 1989), it is likely that significant elements of early models endure (Cicirelli, 1989). During her interview as part of the never-married study, a 70-year-old women, for example, explained that her early experiences with her father made it difficult to establish a close relationship with other men:

I was never comfortable with men. My father certainly wasn't a role model. You couldn't be close to him (Martin Matthews & Norris, unpublished data).

Recent studies of intergenerational functioning have also found a relationship between adult children's perceptions of their family of origin experience and current psychosocial functioning (Taylor & Norris, 1993; Fine & Norris, 1994). Fine and Norris's study of older parents and their adult child found that the more positively adult children interpreted their early family interactions, the better were their present social encounters with others. Interestingly, the same was true for older parents: positive parenting experiences were related to currently good social functioning. Secure early attachment to offspring seemed indicative of overall healthy functioning later. The Taylor and Norris (1993) study on middle-aged women's experience of their mother's death supported this conclusion. In this research, attachments disrupted by parental abuse had long-lasting effects. In adulthood, almost half of those women with avoidant or ambivalent close relationships reported instances of abuse during childhood; only 10 percent of the women with secure attachment relations did so. Poor models of attachment, and difficulty with the parent–child relationship even after the mother's death, seemed to cause many of these women problems in other significant relationships.

Enduring models of attachment throughout life may also accentuate the increasing selectivity that the old show in choosing social partners (Duff & Hong, 1980; Fredrickson & Carstensen, 1990). Fredrickson and Carstensen (1990) found that older people are less tolerant in their cognitive appraisal of others, preferring to invest time and energy only in those with whom a positive outcome is ensured. They suggest that this may be because experience has taught the old to recognize a potentially rewarding encounter. Presumably, they possess a well-tested working model for potential attachments that helps screen, organize, and analyze relevant social information. Anyone who does not fit this "template" will be excluded from the list of possible social encounters.

Such a strategy may be a double-edged sword. On the negative side, it could lead older people to avoid opportunities for social interaction, restricting the number of possible new relationships (Norris & Tindale, 1993). At a time in the lifespan when social losses such as widowhood and retirement are common, this approach becomes problematic. Fewer individuals are available to provide tangible assistance, moral support, and social stimulation. In the most extreme case, egocentrism can result from the absence of corrective social feedback (Looft, 1972).

On the positive side, in being selective about social encounters, older adults may be showing evidence of "expert performance," rather like that noted by researchers studying non-social behaviors such as typing or chess (Salthouse, 1990). This literature has demonstrated that the old are able to compensate for cognitive declines, such as slower processing of information, through strategies developed after long experience with a task. The older "social expert" has an extensive repertoire of social behaviors accumulated over a lifespan, and knowledge of the appropriate setting for such behaviors (Norris & Rubin, 1984). This may allow quicker and more accurate judgments about the compatibility of another person than would have been the case earlier in life. Such a strategy would conserve energy and save time, both important issues for individuals concerned about the foreshortening of their lifespan (Fredrickson & Carstensen, 1990).

There is no direct support for this concept of expert social performance in later life. As noted in chapter 4, the evidence is mixed concerning the emergence of more sophisticated social thought with age. Nevertheless, the speed with which some older people can form new, intimate relationships is supportive of this view. The research on courtship and remarriage, for example, suggests a much accelerated pace to the building of heterosexual relationships in later life (Bulcroft & O'Connor-Roden, 1986), as well as the greater likelihood that these relationships will be successful than if the partners were younger (Campbell, 1981). Thus, it would seem that older daters can spot a potential mate more quickly, and are more accurate in their judgment that the relationship will work out well. This should alleviate some of the fears of adult children whose parents remarry very quickly after widowhood.

Maintaining relationships

Gerontologists' preoccupation with the *description* of relationships has created a literature of snapshots: surveys capturing single points in the lives of older people to illustrate their ongoing interactions. Thus, we can estimate the size and content of an individuals's social network, but cannot illustrate adequately the processes by which older people maintain significant relationships in their lives. In particular, not enough is known about the factors affecting successful social functioning within existing family relationships and friendships. It is possible, nevertheless, to extrapolate from existing data to examine possible effects of social and individual processes on later-life relationships.

How the old manage family relationships

Security of intergenerational attachments appears to play a major role in promoting positive relationships in later life. There have been no direct, longitudinal investigations of attachment *per se*, but retrospective accounts are supportive of this finding. For example, Fine and Norris (1994) found a relationship between parents' and adult children's perceptions of family closeness early and late in the family life cycle. Similarly, Pratt, Roth, Cohn, Cowan and Cowan (1991) found that there is some evidence for continuity in the transmission of attachment security across three generations. This study also suggests that attachment bonds are mediated by the complexity of reasoning about family relationships.

Cicirelli's (1983; 1990) research on adult children's caregiving relationships with their parents provides further support for the persistence of attachment bonds. This researcher suggests, however, that attachment behaviors change in a fundamental way when a parent becomes frail. Cicirelli maintains that this situation invokes protective behaviors on the part of the child which are a direct result of a secure parent–child relationship. This process seems driven by an underlying mechanism which differs in its expression with age. Young children are motivated by their attachment feelings to seek the proximity of a caregiver in times of stress; adult children are motivated by their protective feelings to provide care for frail parents. Support for this view can be found in Cicirelli's (1983) study which found that attachment feelings towards the parent were a stronger predictor of future caregiving than were feelings of duty and obligation.

A study by Norris and Forbes (1987; Forbes, 1985) identified some of the factors which can produce a successful caregiving experience when attachment feelings are activated. Again, the history of the relationship proved to be extremely important. Drawing on concepts from the family therapy field, these researchers investigated the relationship between frail elders and their family caregivers. When the relationship was overly close, or cohesive, caregivers were impaired in their ability to cope with their relative's needs. Often, they felt guilty, depressed, and physically ill themselves. It appeared that the attachment between parent and child had never fully evolved into a healthy and balanced adult relationship, but instead was characterized by markedly unequal power, usually favoring the older person.

Problems were compounded when the dyad created inflexible rules governing the relationship. This made adapting to changed circumstances difficult and prevented other family members from offering support. From the comments, below, from a daughter, it would seem that protective feelings, once elicited, are not always easy to implement:

> I got Meals-on-Wheels and she cancelled them and I told the Meals-on-Wheels to go ahead anyway and I think that is the only time I ever had a confrontation with my mother. She called me back after that and said, "Who is the boss?" And I said, "Well, I guess I am, but if you don't want to do what I suggest then there is no point trying. You say you want to feel better, but if I suggest things and you don't want to go along with them, then there is nothing I can do." She then got quite huffy and then backed down and the meals came and she gets the Meals-on-Wheels, three days a week. I am not a person who likes conflict and so I was very frustrated (Forbes, 1985, p. 112).

It is not surprising that older families can have difficulty negotiating their relationships as they age. Norms governing family relationships have been established over many years, and may be quite resistant to change. Roberts and Bengtson (1990), for example, recently reworked their theoretical model of intergenerational solidarity to suggest family norms are directly related to affection and contact. Some empirical research, as well, has shown that older adults become upset with children who do not live up to the standards of behavior established for the family (Fisher, Reid & Melendez, 1989; Rook, 1987). In the Fisher et al. (1989) study, older adults were asked about the issues that angered them most in their interactions with family and friends. Overwhelmingly, the most anger was caused by adult children who did not follow familial or societal rules (e.g., being late for an appointment; drunkenness). Perhaps because the old have a great interest, or generational stake, in the future of their family (Bengtson & Kuypers, 1971), they are harsh in their judgment of offspring who appear to threaten that future.

Despite their greater intergenerational stake, older people seem to require little from their adult children. Under normal circumstances, "intimacy at a distance" guides their interactions: older parents enjoy seeing their offspring, but ask for little support from them. In fact, quite the reverse is true, with adult children asking for considerable aid from parents (Norris & Tindale, 1994). If a critical situation arises, however, older people feel that they should be able to draw on a lifetime "support bank" that they have established with their children (Ingersoll-Dayton & Antonucci, 1988). Some research has suggested that older people may feel quite comfortable being overbenefitted by their children (Ingersoll-Dayton & Antonnuci, 1988; Rook, 1987), whereas such inequity in a peer relationship would have serious consequences for feelings of personal self-efficacy (Stoller, 1985).

How the old manage peer relationships

Relationships with peers are critical to the well-being of older people (Adams & Blieszner, 1989). In fact, friendships are more important than relationships with adult children in promoting successful aging (Blau, 1981). Of particular importance are long-term relationships with peers. In Norris's (1990) study of never-married older people, for example, many respondents reported that their closest friendships were, on average, 35 years in duration, and had grown closer over time.

Such findings suggest an attachment to age-mates in later life. These attachments can provide a buffer against some of the stresses and losses related to aging. Even in the absence of the attachment figure, an older person can continue to experience the bond symbolically, invoking memories of shared experiences, interests and values (Cicirelli, 1989). It is likely that encounters, both real and symbolic, promote good cognitive functioning and prevent loneliness.

To maintain these important peer relationships, older adults appear to follow rules of reciprocity which vary according to the type of relationship. Within close relationships, a norm of generalized reciprocity is invoked. This means that repayment is not expected immediately, or could even be passed on to some other needy person in the network

(Jones & Vaughn, 1990). Exchanges with casual friends or acquaintances are typically not desired by older people, but when they do happen, immediate restitution is considered necessary (Wentowski, 1981). As can be seen in the reaction of Mr Elder, a 70-year-old "junk dealer," to help from casual acquaintances, it is important that others in his network follow the same rules:

> Mr Elder uses the immediate exchange strategy to maintain distance from others and maximize his personal autonomy. He does not own a car and is regularly given rides to local flea markets by Mr Jones. As repayment, Mr Elder calculates a fixed percentage of his daily profits and pays Mr Jones at the end of each day. He allows no outstanding debts to obligate him to others. Mr Jones was sick for a while, and [the researcher] drove Mr Elder to the market a few times. Not as yet understanding the significance of repayments, [she] refused money for the rides, arguing that [she] was making the trip anyway. In spite of the fact that he desperately desired the rides, Mr Elder soon stopped accepting them (Wentowski, 1981, p. 607).

Findings from Wentowski's (1981) anthropological study of peer relationships in later life suggest that older people keep accurate mental records of each other's performance in the role of "helper." Their evaluations are remarkably consistent with Lerner's (1981) ideas about entitlement. Casual friends, those involved in unit or non-unit relationships, who do not measure up are dropped quickly; intimates, those in identity relationships, are excused unless their violations are extreme.

Gender differences in managing relationships

There is evidence that women and men differ in their approach to relationships throughout adulthood and into old age. There appear to be differences in the social cognitive strategies employed by both sexes in managing friendships and family interactions. Women look for "communal" relationships with peers and family characterized by a high degree of intimacy and confiding (Wright, 1989). Because of this, they find their most rewarding friendships are with other women. Cross-sex relationships may provide tangible support but rarely as much intimacy (Rubin, 1985). Men, on the other hand, look for "agentic" relationships with other men characterized by shared activities and interests. Intimacy is sought in cross-sex relationships, particularly with a spouse (Wright, 1989).

These gender differences leave men and women differentially affected by aging. Women's insistence on intimacy and nurturance, combined with social norms, often place them in the role of primary caregiver, first with children, then parents, and finally with an ailing spouse (Baines, Evans, & Neysmith, 1991). Such roles can be burdensome and stressful. Long-standing attachments to other women, however, can provide social support in the face of these stresses as well as other losses such as widowhood (Norris, 1994; Petrowsky, 1976). Men, in contrast, may be more at risk from isolation and loneliness, particularly if widowed (Wright, 1989). They may lack the strategies for establishing and maintaining intimate relationships with peers. Perhaps this is the reason for the high rate of remarriage among widowers – wives provide a buffer between older men and their social world.

Losing relationships

Lowenthal and Haven's (1968) study of well-being in later life demonstrated that having a confidant could be a buffer against some of the stresses of aging. Losing such a close relationship tended to lead to depression. Since then, other researchers have confirmed the importance of an intimate friend to happiness in old age (e.g., Baldassare, Rosenfield, & Rook, 1984; Reisman, 1981). These findings underscore the relationship between social interaction and affect in later life, but a link with cognition seems equally likely. Social–cognitive ability could be adversely affected by losses in later life, as well as providing a means of recovery from these losses. No research has examined these issues directly, but there is suggestive evidence in the theoretical literature and in other studies of social relationships which provides some insight.

Looft (1972) proposed that social isolation could lead to a decline in social cognitive functioning in later life. This decline, he reasoned, would resemble egocentrism. The sociologists, Kuypers and Bengtson (1973), reflecting on the power of negative stereotypes of old age, made a similar point. According to these researchers, some individuals may be predisposed to poor social functioning. This "personality" variable seems equivalent to our conceptualization of social cognitive ability. If such individuals were exposed to negative labels of aging combined with significant social losses, the result would could be social and psychological withdrawal or even breakdown. Perhaps this is what has led to the despair voiced by one new resident of a nursing home:

> I did not want to come here; they sent me here because I was old. Two kids and all those sacrifices. I want to live with my daughter. Thirty years I lived with her, all the work that I did for her and her seven kids and I am here now. I'm lost (Coppola, 1987, p. 63).

What is it about social loss which has such a powerful effect on some older people? One factor is probably the type and strength of the attachment to the lost person, lifestyle, or object. For example, the widows in Sable's (1989) study who were insecurely attached to their parents as children, and subsequently insecurely attached to their husbands, suffered more extreme grief reactions than did those with normal attachment relationships. A similar finding emerged in Taylor and Norris's (1993) study of bereaved daughters. Those who had poor relationships with their mothers had more difficulty coming to terms with the loss. Even when the relationship has been healthy, bereavement can lead to loneliness, especially when older people construct a "lonely" identity for themselves (Wood, 1986). In this situation, an individual may interpret his or her lack of social contact as consistent with having poor social skills or unreliable friends. Internal attributions about incompetence are made which prohibit the establishment of new relationships.

In an interesting analysis of how older people deal with inevitable aging-related losses, Lerner and Gignac (1992) also argue that cognitive processes are extremely important. These authors suggest that through a process which they call "self-role taking," the old learn to appreciate various perspectives on their losses and to understand that each perspective has a different impact on their emotions. For example, an older diabetic who has just had his leg amputated may view the event in several ways, each of which has its own accompanying affect. He could perceive the loss as a disastrous blow to independence and become depressed; he could feel that life had dealt yet another unfair blow and become bitter and resentful; he could perceive the surgery as lifesaving and feel relief and gratitude. Lerner and Gignac suggest that a person in this situation has the choice of which construction he will adopt and which emotions he will experience.

There is as yet no empirical evidence to support Lerner and Gignac's (1992) conceptualization of coping in old age. As well, it is not clear how, and why, self-role taking would be more likely to emerge in the old relative to the young. The authors suggest, however, that the social and personal circumstances of most older people help promote this skill: they have the time and the motivation to reflect upon crises in their lives; they are required by society to relinquish their role as effective actors in the world; they endure inevitable social loss.

Given the normative nature of social loss in later life, it seems likely that old people would take a proactive stance to protecting their well-being and preserving cognitive functioning. Anecdotal evidence suggests that the aged realize their social vulnerability and strive to maintain contact with others. This may be difficult to do in view of the often fierce need for independence that is also expressed (Butler, Lewis, & Sunderland, 1991). Nevertheless, there is some evidence that older people continue to seek out new relationships for as long as they are physically and psychologically able (Matthews, 1983; 1986). Those successful in achieving the delicate balance of attachment and individuation in later life, according to Cohler (1983), have developed a healthy sense of "relational autonomy."

Those older adults unable to compensate for the loss of significant relationships may also defend against loneliness and social cognitive decline through symbolic interactions. Cicirelli (1989), for example, has noted that older people can maintain important attachments to absent siblings by invoking memories of closeness, shared values, goals, and interests. Similarly, widows' grief may be alleviated as they learn to interact, symbolically, with the memory of their spouses (Norris, 1994). What happens is not simple reminiscing, but a cognitive process more consistent with Butler's (1963) notions of life review. Older people use this review to evaluate past experiences and relationships and place them within the broader framework of their whole lives. A successful life review, according to Butler et al. (1991), may lead not only to a sense of well-being, but also to renewed intellectual and creative achievement. Symbolic interaction with the memory of others, then, both seems to exercise social cognitive powers as well as to promote and enhance them.

Tracing the book's themes

The first theme of the book concerns older people's perceptions of changes in their social functioning. In this chapter, we considered how old people successfully form and maintain relationships, as well as recover from their loss when this occurs. We also considered whether these processes change with advancing age. The research indicates, in particular, that older adults value the relationships which they made early in life, and are concerned with the survival of these relationships into old age (Matthews, 1983; 1986). This suggests the persistence of internal working models of attachment, the roots of which may lie in childhood experiences with parents (Main et al., 1985).

It is not at all clear whether the old get "better" at handling their relationships with age (see also chapter 4). Some research suggests that accumulated experience and the presence of post-formal operational reasoning may promote social functioning in later life (Norris & Pratt, 1980). Other work indicates that the old may be excessively simplistic or stereotypic in their approach to relationships (Hess & Tate, 1991). Perhaps the question is not one of quantitative change, but one of qualitative differences in understanding social relationships. The available research indicates that the old follow the same rules as the young in selecting potential social partners (Blieszner, 1989), but that they may apply these rules differently and on a different timetable (Bulcroft & O'Connor-Roden, 1986; Fredrickson & Carstensen, 1990). Older adults' nearness to death and awareness of finitude (Marshall, 1980), for example, could speed the development and course of relationships and highlight concern about rules of equity, reciprocity, and deserving. The young, believing that they have many years to work on their relationships, may take more time and be less concerned about immediate reciprocity (Norris & Tindale, 1994).

A second theme focuses on individual differences in patterns of aging. Research on friendship suggests that variation in older adults' patterns of social interaction may reflect life-long individual differences (see Tesch's, 1989, review). The never-married in Norris's (1990) study, for example, reported that they had been "loners" from childhood. Such findings point to the enduring influence of individual differences in personality, social skill, and cognitive models of attachment.

It is also clear that early influences are not the only influences (Baltes, Reese, & Lipsett, 1980). With age, events and experiences collect, creating greater heterogeneity late in life than at any other period in the life cycle (Maddox & Douglas, 1974). It is important, then, to recognize the role of normative events, such as grandparenthood, and non-normative events, such as caring for an Alzheimer's patient, on social abilities and preferences. The former situation may expand an individual's social world and provide opportunities for interaction and cognitive stimulation; the latter situation may restrict opportunities to interact with others and limit the exercise of social skills.

As we have seen, other individual differences may have an equally powerful impact on social functioning. Some of these relate to structural factors such as gender and social class; others are related to physical and psychological health. Women may possess the skills necessary to recover from social losses by substituting new relationships, whereas men may become isolated due to weaker social skills (Wright, 1989). Poor physical health may limit mobility and therefore social opportunities; deteriorating cognitive capacity may interfere with or prohibit social discourse (Norris & Rubin, 1984).

Finally, the third theme of the book is also the central question of this chapter. How are social encounters and social cognitions interrelated? To date, most research has focused on the role of social interaction in promoting life satisfaction (e.g., Kozma, Stones, & McNeil, 1991). Typically, variables such as activity, health status and living arrangements are considered. More explanatory power would be added to these investigations by examining the role of social–cognitive processes. The research reviewed in this chapter indicates that older adults are active participants in the construction of their social worlds. The way in which they understand relationships is a likely mediator between social behavior and psychological well-being.

Understanding Mrs McIvor

Even though existing research leaves many issues unexplored, it still provides some insights into the social world of people like Mrs McIvor. This older woman's positive approach to her relationships can be linked to three specific features of her life: secure attachment, the use of well-established rules, and structural variables such as gender and family composition.

Mrs McIvor's comments about her parent–child relationships suggest the transmission of security down through several generations. She described the strict, but loving, environment of her childhood, and her efforts to create a similar environment for her children, and her children's children. The security of her attachment was played out both in symbolic fashion with memories of her parents, and her children as youngsters, as well as in her current relationships with grandchildren.

Mrs McIvor's use of rules for social functioning was also clear in her account of her life. These seemed so well established that she was not conscious of them until we asked her to examine them directly. In the short quotation which began this chapter, we can see two rules for

child-rearing: one general – instill a sense of morality in your children
– and one specific – kids come before housework. Later, when discussing her friendships, she revealed guidelines on handling friends which
are consistent with the literature: old friends should be cherished, but
opportunities for new relationships welcomed as well. This strategy has
kept her social network large, diversified, and satisfying.

Even with secure attachments and successful social strategies, old
people may still be disadvantaged in later life. Mrs McIvor was fortunate in that structural features of her life helped to facilitate her social
functioning. Her gender increased the likelihood that intimate relationships would be available to her, and that she would learn how to manage them. Her comfortable income insured that basic needs would be
met, with resources left over to enhance her social life. She was not
widowed, had a good relationship with her husband, and had, in fact,
suffered few bereavements. The addition of grandchildren addressed
the generational stake which she had in her family. Her observations on
this event provide a powerful statement about Mrs McIvor's approach
to life and some of the significant issues in this chapter, in particular the
pervasive influence of secure family attachments:

Was there something special about your first grandchild?

That shouldn't be, but there it is, and I don't know what it is. I
remember the very first day I went in there after he came home
and I put my hand in the crib and touched him and his fingers
curled around and I can feel that yet. He's eight years old, but I
can remember that like it was yesterday. I certainly love the rest
every bit as much but whatever it is about that . . . then my son
came in and I was almost weeping and he laughed and I think that
he realized how I felt. Adam is a very tender-hearted soul (Norris
& Tari, unpublished data).

6

Thinking about Society

I grew up in a very political home where politics was discussed morning, noon and night so I suppose that lay latent within me, but in [this city], in municipal politics, I came upon it by accident. A group of women were bad mouthing [the city] and I resented it and I was surprised at myself for resenting it and so I said well, if that's the case then why don't you do something about it. So I began monitoring City Council and I became hooked.

It's important to have other interests too. Golf contributes to my physical well-being. I can walk along with the sun on my shoulders and the extraordinary beauty of the course puts things into perspective. I think because politicians love to be loved they spend a lot of time chasing their own tails and I think it is doubly important that they have time to sort things out as to what is important and what isn't. You know it's really not one of my major goals in life to win a popularity contest (Mrs McKillop, age 65, a veteran city councillor for 16 years; Norris, unpublished data).

Urie Bronfenbrenner (1979), in an attempt to characterize the multiple levels of socialization influences on development, has sketched a model of four "nested" social contexts for the individual (see figure 6.1). Bronfenbrenner terms the immediate contexts of face-to-face interaction and social influence "microsystems." In adulthood, these are probably represented most centrally by family, friends, and work. The church is also a significant microsystem for many older adults, as we discuss below. This is surrounded by the "mesosystem," which describes the links among these microsystems and how they interact. All of this is embedded in what Bronfenbrenner labels the "exosystem," which includes the neighborhood, community, and institutional settings of the individual's local society. Finally, this is in turn encapsulated within the

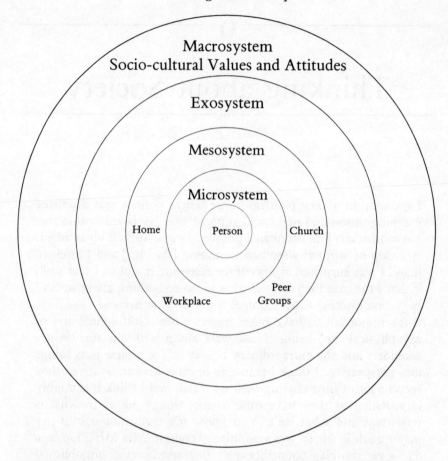

Figure 6.1 Bronfenbrenner's ecological model of socialization, adapted to adults
The ecological system: microsystem refers to relations between the child and the
immediate environment; mesosystem refers to the network of interrelationships of
settings in the child's immediate environment; exosystem refers to social settings
that affect the child but do not directly impinge upon him or her; and macrosystem
refers to the attitudes, mores, beliefs, and ideologies of the culture.

"macrosystem" of values and cultural norms that characterize the wider
society in which the individual lives.

The present chapter aims to review the aging individual's thinking
about, involvement in, and reactions to, some of these increasingly
widening contexts, from the microsystems of work and church through
the exosystem contexts of community and politics. Mrs McKillop's
comments, above, reveal something of these interacting influences on

her social–psychological functioning. She was deeply affected by her family's interest in politics, the attitudes of some of her peers towards the city where she lives, and her perceptions of the nature of politicians (reflecting the influence of experiences in several microsystems). She was able to create a balance among these various microsystems of her life (the mesosystem), thus making politics a viable lifestyle for her. She also has a strong commitment to her community (the exosystem), and she fulfils this commitment through involvement in politics (reflecting the macrosystem of values within her society).

We first discuss these interacting influences through our four theoretical approaches to thinking about social groups and institutions across the adult lifespan. Following this, we review the research evidence on the transition from the work setting to retirement in later adulthood, norms regarding the timing of later-life disengagement from this important role, and gender and ethnic variations in these patterns.

Next, we discuss the topic of neighborhood and community involvement in adulthood. Here we adopt a focus on such involvement as exemplifying "generativity," that is, sustained commitment and engagement as teacher, mentor, carer and helper for other generations and for the wider community. Again, issues of both engagement in and timing of these roles in adulthood are considered.

We then discuss the involvement of older adults in the domain of religion, both in public, formal ways, and in private religious activities. We focus particularly on the meaning and implications of religion for how older adults understand and evaluate their lives. Finally, we consider political thinking and participation in later adulthood, utilizing this topic area to discuss general issues of attitude development and change across the adult lifespan. The chapter concludes, as usual, with a discussion of the book's three themes.

Theoretical frameworks for societal involvement and aging

The **psychometric** approach has played a major role in the development of a construct of great importance in social psychology, the concept of "attitude" (e.g., Olson & Zanna, 1993). Attitudes are generally conceptualized as evaluations of some entity or idea, with affective, cognitive, and behavioral components that may be more or less tightly interrelated (e.g., Olson & Zanna, 1993; Oskamp, 1991). Attitudes thus represent a critical mediating variable, a way of conceptualizing how people's reactions to their experiences influence their actions and behaviors, and a number of models of this process have been presented (e.g., Olson and Zanna, 1993).

The most widely used technique for measurement of attitudes is that developed by Rensis Likert in the 1930s (Oskamp, 1991). This approach relies on a quantitative scaling of the degree or intensity of a respondent's agreement with a statement, as rated on a dimensional scale of positivity–negativity. A relatively elaborate psychometric procedure is required to construct and validate scales based on sets of these individual items, in order to measure individuals' underlying attitudes in both a reliable and valid way (Oskamp, 1991). The assessment of attitudes is clearly a major way in which the psychometric perspective has contributed to the study of social opinions across the lifespan. In the present chapter, we discuss attitudes in adulthood in more detail in the section on politics below, though attitudes are a central construct in most of the topic areas discussed throughout the book.

The basic theme of the **information-processing** perspective, that cognitive skills and resources may be reduced in later adulthood, has implications both for basic social–cognitive processing and for social role maintenance (e.g., meeting workplace demands; Park, 1992). Over the years, for example, industrial psychologists and gerontologists have been concerned with aging workers' ability to maintain optimal performance at work, and to adapt to the changing demands of the workplace (McFarland, 1956; Murrell & Griew, 1965; Schludermann, Schludermann, Merryman, & Brown, 1983; Salthouse, 1990). Later in this chapter, within the context of a discussion of retirement, we will turn our attention to some recent research on work demands and performance in older adults.

The **developmental** perspective has contributed important conceptions with respect to research on adults' societal engagement as well. Particularly noteworthy here is the theorizing of Erik Erikson (e.g., 1950). Erikson proposed three adult stages of psychosocial development (as part of his eight-stage scheme of development across the lifespan). The first of these stages focuses on the development of intimacy, and its prototype is the formation of committed couple relationships in early adulthood. Following this stage, the seventh stage in Erikson's scheme (characteristic of the midlife period) focuses on the "crisis" of generativity, the formation of a capacity to be useful to others in society, and, in particular, other generations. The prototype here is caring for one's own children, but Erikson's conception goes well beyond this particular instantiation to a concern with being responsible for others in a productive way (Wrightsman, 1988).

As do all of Erikson's stages, this stage has a danger point, the negative resolution of "stagnation" or self-absorption (Erikson, 1950). A successful resolution of this period of development permits the individual to move forward into the final stage of "ego integrity." Erikson's conception of generativity has obvious implications for the adult individual's role in his or her wider social world, and we discuss some recent work on this construct in the section on community engagement below.

A second conception of some interest from the developmental perspective is the work of James Fowler (e.g., 1981) on stages of faith. Fowler's stages are derived from the ideas of Kohlberg (e.g., 1976) regarding moral development. He sees the individual progressing across the lifespan from an "intuitive–projective" faith in early childhood, based in projections from interactions with caretaking adults, to the highest levels of "paradoxical–consolidative" and "universalizing" faiths, attained only by a small minority of adults. These levels are based in the sequence of Piagetian stages of knowing, and represent alternative ways of knowing and being. Because of this, they represent a developmental progression in how the individual experiences both the divine, and the religious institutions, such as the church, in which he or she participates. This conception is discussed in relation to aging in the section on religion below.

A third important conception from the developmental perspective is the work of Neugarten and her colleagues on the "social clock" (e.g., Neugarten & Hagestadt, 1976). The social clock refers to a kind of timetable by which the individual assesses his or her progress through the life course. Neugarten argues that this timetable is derived from the individual's sense of several aspects of time: life time based on biological development, social time based on the timing of normative roles in the individual's society, and historical time based in the wider, marker events of one's particular generation (e.g., Neugarten & Datan, 1973). The normative expectations that individuals hold for the timing of life transitions and events like marriage or retirement can have a marked impact on how they experience their own life course. For example, Ravenna Helson and her colleagues have shown how congruence with the "feminine social clock" has a strong impact on women's feelings about their lives and careers in middle adulthood (e.g., Helson, Mitchell, & Moane, 1984). In the present chapter, we discuss these timing issues with respect to the transition to retirement.

The **social–psychological** perspective has been particularly influential recently in guiding research on the ways in which people "make meaning" out of social and interpersonal experience. Such meaning-making is viewed in this perspective as a process of abstracting essential, simplifying qualities or structures from complex experience (Fiske, 1993). Fiske suggests that there are three major abstractions that are important in perceiving others: traits, stereotypes, and stories. As we said in chapter 4, stereotypes can be considered as distinctive, frequently visually-based, elaborated categories that carry broad predictive expectancies about how another, as an exemplar of a group, will interact. Gender, age, and race are "core" categories that form the bases for stereotypes, though subtypes within these categories are likely the usual level at which people think about others (e.g., "the sweet old grandmother" versus "the crabby old neighbour;" Fiske, 1993).

As noted, Fiske (1993) also suggests that narrative processes are important in the representation of social experience. As described in chapter 3, they are certainly important in people's construction of a coherent self and its experiences through time as well. McAdams and his colleagues have been interested in "life stories" and their impact for some time (e.g., McAdams, 1985). Recently, he has turned his attention to the role of such narrative representations of personal meaning in relation to generativity, as we discuss in the section on community involvement below.

Societal involvement, satisfaction, and aging: the evidence

Work and the transition to retirement

Well, the biggest thing in my life where I had to decide and analyze was to decide to retire. I started teaching at the age of 20. In those days you were through early and I had my degree, and I worked fairly hard and, by the time I was 60, I had 40 years of teaching in and could collect my maximum pension for that time, and I thought, well there must be another way to live besides this job I'm doing. I was vice-principal in a high school. So I dithered about it for a year . . . And I wrote my friend who had been my minister. With my own thoughts and some advice from him I just sort of jotted down the pros and cons and in the end I decided to retire. I did all my worrying before and once I did it, I didn't regret it. The real conflict was will I miss it? It was hard work but I felt very important. That was foolish of course but I felt that I was needed and while I wasn't doing a spectacular job, it was a good, reliable, sensible job . . . I felt that my life might get very meaningless if I had no job, and that I had no excuse to retire . . . Now, I just think about it and how silly I was to debate so long . . . (Ms Townsend, a woman in her mid-70s; Pratt, unpublished data, 1993).

Ms Townsend's comments illustrate some of the important issues of work and retirement in later life. Work for the adult can be a source of both personal fulfilment and the economic means to a lifestyle. Retirement involves changes in both of these (as well as in other factors such as social relationships). Because of this, retirement is a significant event and life transition for many older adults. The timing of this transition can have implications for later-life experience and development as well.

Modernization theory presumes that retirement is an imposed status in modern society, due to changes in labor force participation and needs based on industrialization and the movement of work out of the home, and that retirement was not a typical pattern in traditional societies. It appears, however, that retirement may have been desired, but not achieved, by elderly people in the historical past when their financial circumstances were poor (e.g., Quadagno, 1982). Evidence from eighteenth- and nineteenth-century New England, for example, shows that older adults were typically forced into working in part-time, lower-status occupations (e.g., mowing grass, hauling grain) due to financial necessity, since adequate resources were usually not available for retirement (Demos, 1978).

In the twentieth century, mandatory retirement has been rationalized as a means of handling the supposed inevitable deterioration in older adults' ability to work. Some have argued, however, that the real reason for national retirement policies is as it was in the past: that is, to manage the size and cost of the labor supply (Tindale, 1991). There is little evidence that older workers are less able to handle most jobs than their younger counterparts (e.g., Park, 1992; Stagner, 1985). In fact, when decrements with age have been reported in work performance, they are often associated with ratings made by judges, rather than with more objective indicators (Waldman & Aviolo, 1986).

There is reason to be concerned about the possibility of "ageist" bias in such ratings in both research and practice (see chapter 4). As Tindale

(1991) has noted in the Canadian context, even the Canadian Supreme Court decision upholding mandatory retirement is a form of age discrimination. The Court's sweeping conclusion that "older doctors are less able to contribute to hospitals' sophisticated practice" (Tindale, 1991, p. 22) has little empirical support. Nevertheless, as Park (1992) argues, it is possible that greater difficulties for older adults can be expected specifically in "transitional" work conditions, where the aging worker must learn to deal with new information or procedures, rather than in "maintenance" situations, where the worker relies on familiar skills. This distinction deserves further careful research.

What is known about work satisfaction and work commitment across the adult lifespan, in contrast to the evidence on work performance? Generally, older workers report more job satisfaction and contentment than younger workers, although this pattern may be somewhat U-shaped, with the lowest points in the 30s (e.g., Warr, 1992). Presumably, the youngest workers become less satisfied with their work as its novelty wears off by their late 20s and 30s. The satisfaction of older workers, however, seems to increase gradually, and this effect is not entirely accounted for by job characteristics or job position, work values, or other demographic factors (Warr, 1992). Since the studies to date are cross-sectional, there may be both cohort factors and selective attrition factors that influence this finding. For example, those older adults who were most dissatisfied with their work may have already left the workforce (Warr, 1992). Longitudinal analysis of the same panel of workers over time is needed to disentangle these issues.

There is some evidence that commitment to work may decline as people approach retirement age (Warr, 1992), and most older employees seem to anticipate retirement as a positive and desirable status (e.g., Goudy, 1981). Nevertheless, this pattern of results may be affected by the perceived intrinsic rewards of working. One study (Norris, 1993) investigated the reasons given by professionals over the age of 65 (physicians, engineers, architects, and senior managers) for remaining in the work force or deciding to retire. All these individuals worked at careers not governed by mandatory retirement. Norris (1993) found that regardless of retirement status, all of her sample were psychologically well-functioning and in reported good health. Retirees and workers could be distinguished, however, by their beliefs about work. Even though all described successful and satisfying careers, those still working emphasized the importance of their jobs in promoting physical and mental functioning. Those who had chosen to retire believed that work might not be conducive to healthy aging.

How do older adults react to retirement? As Ms Townsend suggests, work is a source of income in our society, and can also be a central source of intrinsic satisfaction and a sense of purpose. How people respond to leaving work naturally depends a good deal on what it has meant to them over the life course. Research has investigated effects of retirement on both physical and mental health, on morale, and on social participation (e.g., Atchley, 1985). For the most part, the evidence suggests few overall effects of retirement on individuals for each of these dimensions. For example, Ekerdt, Baden, Bossé, and Dibbs (1983) showed that there were no overall differences in health over time between those men who retired in a large longitudinal sample and those who did not, when pre-retirement health status was controlled in this longitudinal study. Similarly, there is no evidence of consistent overall effects of retirement on individuals' subsequent life satisfaction (Norris, 1993; Palmore et al., 1985).

Atchley (1985) has suggested that people do adjust to retirement in predictable ways. His stage conceptualization proposes a honeymoon period often characterized by intense activity, a phase of disenchantment, followed by a reorientation phase which involves stock-taking of oneself and one's situation, and finally, a mature retirement routine. There is some empirical support for this phase model (Ekerdt et al., 1985), but there is also considerable controversy about whether such "phases" are identifiable (Schulz & Ewen, 1988). It seems likely that any such phases that may broadly characterize adult life transitions will be highly variable compared with those of childhood, and dependent on a variety of social–contextual and personal factors (e.g., Cowan, 1991).

One of these moderating factors is likely to be perceived social support. Longitudinal research on a large sample of men from the greater Boston area (the Boston Normative Aging Study or NAS) indicated that retirees reported quantitatively less overall support for the discussion of personal problems than those remaining employed, though an apparent "compensatory" increase in *satisfaction* with non-work social supports for the retirees was also indicated (Bosse', Aldwin, Levenson, & Workman-Daniels, 1990). Retirement thus clearly entailed some disruption of the friendship and social support network associated with the workplace for these men, as well as a tendency to perceive this disruption as replaced.

Another important factor in adaptation to retirement may be its normative timing. Bossé, Aldwin, Levenson, and Ekerdt (1987) found that those men in the NAS study who retired "off-time," either earlier or later than peers retiring "on-time" at 62 to 65, showed higher levels of psychological distress. The symptom checklist used in this study measures problems such as depression, anxiety, phobias, hostility and paranoid ideas. Since this finding is only correlational, we cannot be sure of the meaning of this relation between mental health and retirement timing. Perhaps, however, early retirees feel somewhat "out of step" with their peers, and this may be upsetting, as Bossé et al. (1987) suggest. Like Ms Townsend, they may feel somewhat "guilty" for violating the typical age norms.

It is also possible that "early" retirees are actually the middle-aged unemployed, laid off, for example, in a company's attempt to remain viable in the sluggish economy of the late twentieth century (Lindsay, 1987; Osberg, 1988). These "discouraged workers" are not likely to adapt well to retirement because of their poor financial situation (Diamond & Hausman, 1984; Tindale, 1991). In contrast, late retirees may have stayed on as long as possible, and been distressed when they finally did have to retire because of their strong investment in the work role (Bossé et al., 1987).

Another complicating factor when examining the normative timing of retirement is the definition of retirement itself. Much of the literature has treated the event as a one-time crisis (McDonald & Wanner, 1990; Norris, 1993). It has become increasingly clear to many researchers, however, that retirement is often a graduated process. Whenever possible, workers may gradually decrease their hours or alter their responsibilities before permanently leaving the workforce (Tindale, 1991). Even more variability is introduced when we consider the career path of many women. Female workers have probably moved in and out of the full-time work force throughout their lives as a consequence of family responsibilities. Their ideas about work and the timing of retirement may be very different from those of men.

Despite probable differences in patterns of work and retirement, few researchers have concerned themselves with gender issues. As Calasanti (1993) has recently noted from a feminist perspective, large-scale studies of retirement in North America, such as the NAS just discussed, have generally excluded women, due to assumptions about the lesser importance of retirement in their lives. As well, research and theorizing have typically asked how women's experiences are different from those of men, utilizing a "male model" of retirement (Calasanti, 1993). Based on these admittedly biased models, there is some agreement that the same factors that predict men's retirement satisfaction also predict that of women (e.g., Seccombe & Lee, 1986).

Retirement, however, may not *mean* the same thing to women and men. In Calasanti's own interviews with white working-class men and women, she reports that both sexes defined retirement as a time when life becomes "freer" and less constrained. But for women, stopping work in the labor force often meant simply having more freedom to structure their "second shift" – domestic labor in the home (e.g., Hochschild & Machung, 1989; Szinovacz, 1989), and women were often puzzled about how to discuss their domestic work in talking about retirement issues. Just as women's greater domestic responsibilities shape their experiences of earlier life transitions, such as parenthood (e.g., Cowan & Cowan, 1992; Hochschild & Machung, 1989), they also have an impact on the perceptions of work and retirement. It is interesting to note that when asked to talk about her career, a retired physician in fact reflected upon her struggle to maintain a balance between work and family, despite the views of her co-workers:

> [My supervisor] was very keen on us young doctors and insisted that our work wasn't enough for us and that we should join different groups [like] the Art Gallery. She felt that we needed a lot of different activities to broaden us a little bit and to make us interesting people and to enjoy our own life. I didn't feel that I needed too many of these things because I had three children and my life was broad enough! (Norris, unpublished data).

We clearly need to conceptualize career and employment issues more "socially," in terms of gender roles and relations in the wider context of the family (Calasanti, 1993).

Gibson (e.g., 1987, 1991) has discussed ethnic variations in how retirement is viewed as well. In her research on older black Americans, she has shown that perceptions of being retired are consistently related to past work histories. Those older African-American individuals who had experienced a relatively continuous pattern of employment in their earlier lives were much more likely to see themselves as "retired" than were those African-Americans (an unfortunately substantial group in this culture) who had had a more discontinuous and marginal pattern of employment. Not surprisingly, this latter group of older adults seemed to see their current status as marginal and ambiguous, and as providing an uncertain contrast with their past work history (Gibson, 1987).

Canadian researchers have also been concerned about the influence of ethnicity on retirement. As McDonald and Wanner (1990) have pointed out, the Canadian government has consistently encouraged ethnic diversity and multiculturalism within the population; nevertheless, income security programs rarely offer the same protection for recent immigrants during old age as they do for native-born Canadians. This is especially true for older workers from Third World countries. Census data reported by McDonald and Wanner indicate that considerably more men of African, Asian and Latin-American origins continue to work past the normal retirement age than do their Canadian- and European-born peers. When we consider that only 30 percent of the first group who do retire receive retirement benefits, versus 86 percent of the second, the reason for some new Canadians remaining longer in the workforce becomes clear.

Community and generativity in adulthood

When Mike worked for some time in the US Appalachian south many years ago, he was struck both by the level of deprivation of many of the older (and younger) rural poor, and by the extent of the support network of relatives and neighbors who shared resources and provided assistance for these individuals. This was the late 1960s, and many of these families and individuals lived without electricity or even indoor plumbing. For example, one family (of 11) coped with a frankly psychotic child on their own, partly because of limited resources in the community to assist them. Yet this family was fiercely proud of their independence, and the traditions of neighborliness and helping had to respect these feelings, while still providing some much-needed support.

What is known systematically about the factors that affect older adults' feelings about their neighborhoods and communities? Lawton (1980, p. 34) found that both younger and older adults reported that the most important dimensions of their ideal community, in order, were: 1) good quality services, (e.g., schools, medical care facilities, shopping), 2) relational attributes (e.g., being near friends, having a voice in community affairs), and 3) personal development attributes (e.g., recreation, clubs, entertainment). The general importance of both resources and relationship attributes may well account for the evidence that older people's life satisfaction in urban versus rural communities of residence does not seem to differ systematically (Lawton, 1980). While services, income and health care are all "lower" on average in rural areas, social interaction with friends and neighbors seems to be higher in rural and small-town settings, as noted for the Appalachian communities mentioned above. These two attributes may thus offset each other to some extent in their impact on life satisfaction as studied in different community settings. As well, anxiety about personal safety and fear of crime is also a central factor in lowered satisfaction for many elderly in higher-risk urban areas (e.g., Lawton, 1980).

What is known about levels of commitment and involvement in the community across the adult lifespan? In *Habits of the heart*, Robert Bellah and his colleagues (1985) report the results of an analysis of American society based on a series of interviews with adults from a wide range of backgrounds. Bellah et al. suggest that American society is particularly conflicted by a strong emphasis on individualism and self-reliance, in competition with a characteristic penchant to "get involved" and to be committed socially. Bellah et al. trace the complexities of this conflict across many domains, including both family and public life. They argue that Americans' language and ways of thinking about social commitments have become clouded and difficult over the past 200 years, as a radical individualism has transformed and eroded many aspects of the founding "biblical" and "republican" traditions which stressed citizen participation (Bellah et al., 1985). Certainly elements of this conflict between independence and involvement were apparent in the Appalachian setting mentioned above.

Bellah et al.'s (1985) description of Americans' struggle with these issues, and their limited means for expressing them, rings true. What these authors do not discuss in their broad, sociological portrait of contemporary American life is the possibility that there may be meaningful life cycle variations in propensities toward commitment and involvement in the wider community. The ideas of Erik Erikson (e.g., 1950) provide a framework for thinking about adult developmental variations in what he termed "generativity," as we noted in the introduction to this chapter. Bellah et al.'s observations on the pervasiveness of this generativity theme in modern North American culture surely do not mean that such developmental trends and variations are irrelevant.

Consider the dilemma reported by Ms James, a 74-year-old woman, as a illustration of some issues of generative involvement in the life of the community by an older person:

> The situation is that I just heard last night about a child who is probably being abused by his single-parent father. The father is evidently trying to evade the authorities. He's moved without telling them where he has moved to, and I know where he is . . . I have thought of going to the school that the child attends and letting them do it. They could also make sure if the child is being abused, and they'll know how undernourished he is . . . I know

that I should report it to the Children's Aid. At the same time, I know too that I should talk to him (the father) as well. And yet there's the temptation there that it would be a lot simpler just to report him and not get involved. It would be a lot easier to avoid that and yet I think he has a right to know . . . It's a moral problem as far as I'm concerned. He's another human being. He's a very unattractive, shifty character. I'd rather not have him angry at me. But if I were in his place, I would want to be told what was happening . . . (Ms James; Pratt, unpublished data).

Is Ms James unusual in her continuing engagement in later life in such issues of concern about her neighbor and his son? In some recent research, McAdams and his colleagues have described research on a model of generativity and its development over the life course (McAdams & de St Aubin, 1992; McAdams, de St Aubin, & Logan, 1993). They view generativity as an interaction between cultural demand and inner desire, leading to concern for the next generation and commitment and actions to express this concern. In their studies, they developed a scale to measure this concern, the Loyola Generativity Scale, which includes items such as "I have a responsibility to improve the neighborhood in which I live," and "I feel as though my contributions will exist after I die." Scores on this scale were considerably higher for a mature adult sample (mean age in the 30s) than a college-age sample, and these scores predicted people's self-reports of generative actions, such as "teaching a skill," "providing constructive criticism," and "performing a community service" (McAdams & de St Aubin, 1992).

In a subsequent lifespan study of adults, McAdams et al. (1993) found that older adults (in their 60s and 70s) were equivalent to midlife adults on generativity scores, whereas both older age groups scored higher overall than young adults. There was some inconsistency depending on the measure used, but generally it appeared that these young-old adults retained a relatively high level of generative commitment in their daily lives, compared to what had been predicted based on Erikson's theory of a special focus on generativity at midlife. Perhaps an older, less engaged, group of seniors might have demonstrated the predicted lower scores, but it seemed clear that younger adults differ from midlife and elderly persons in the substantially lower level of generative focus reported in their lives. McAdams et al. (1993) provided the projects listed by a 68-year-old woman as examples of some the intergenerational commitments involved in generativity: "counsel a daughter who was recently let go from a job due to cutbacks," "help another daughter with her sick child," "help as a volunteer at a non-profit organization," "assist a candidate running for election," "offer financial aid to someone close if needed" (p. 228). What seems striking here is the varied nature of both family and social–community involvement central to this woman's "personal strivings."

Erikson's (1982) notions about generative involvement were clearly based on the prototype of parenting involvement, but go beyond this to discuss involvement with future generations and the community in a broader sense. Though we have primarily discussed this broader community focus in the present chapter, involvement as a parent and grandparent in the family is certainly a central way in which these strivings are expressed as well (see chapter 5).

Aging and religious experience and participation

As our parents and their friends have grown older, the local church has become more and more important in their lives, both for social and religious reasons. Sunday school classes, or visits from members of the congregation, have become more and more eagerly anticipated events. Indeed, the pews of most North American churches are full of gray-haired heads. Partly, this is a phenomenon of the aging of the population as a whole, of course, but partly, it seems likely that older adults are particularly heavily involved in organized religion (Ainlay, Singleton, & Swigert, 1992; Bibby, 1987). In surveys, nearly half of all those over 75 in the USA report that they belong to a church (Atchley, 1991), and many older people hold church positions of responsibility. In this section, we will document what is known about the meaning and place of the institutions of religion and the church in the lives of older adults, and then discuss evidence on the impact of religiosity on older people's well-being. Finally, we consider evidence on gender and ethnic differences in religious experiences.

Recent investigations of religion and aging have argued that it is critical to make distinctions among a number of different dimensions of religiosity (e.g., Koenig, Kvale, & Ferrel, 1988; Krause, 1993). One area concerns "public" religion, both the outer practices and the inner belief structures associated with formal religious participation, such as attendance at church functions, or the orthodoxy of one's religious attachment to a particular religious body's doctrine or belief system (e.g., Hunsberger, 1985). A second area focuses on "personal" religion, including actual behaviors such as home prayer, and the inner dimensions of religious faith and its personal meanings for the individual. In both the public and private spheres of religion, then, it seems useful to distinguish between a person's outward activities, and his or her inner orientations (cf. Moberg, 1970).

Participation in formal religious bodies and services appears to be somewhat higher in older adults up to age 75, than in younger adults below 40 (Bibby, 1993; Cox & Hammonds, 1988). Approximately 80 percent of older American adults report having attended services in the last year in these survey data, compared with about 70 percent of younger adults. Those over the age of 80 show a slightly lower rate of church attendance than those in their 70s, but it seems quite likely that this is related to physical health and functional impairments which hamper the oldest-old in this regard (e.g., Ainlay et al., 1992). In one eight-year longitudinal study, Markides, Levin, and Ray (1987) found that church attendance declined only slightly in a sample of Mexican-Americans and Anglos followed across their 70s, suggesting relative stability in attendance for mature adults into later life. Most findings have been consistent with this, once functional health problems have been controlled for in the older adult populations being studied (e.g., Ainlay et al., 1992).

What about people's beliefs about and commitment to public religious doctrines? Cross-sectional studies have suggested that samples of people over 60 report more belief in God than younger groups (e.g., Riley & Foner, 1968). Belief in immortality is sharply higher in this older age group as well (Cox & Hammonds, 1988). As Cox and Hammonds note, this is obviously a belief with central personal relevance for older adults. Hunsberger's (1985) Christian Orthodoxy Scale measures endorsement of "core" Christian doctrinal items, such as "God exists as: Father, Son, and Holy Spirit." Both Hunsberger (1985) and Pratt et al. (1992) reported cross-sectional evidence that older individuals were more likely than younger or middle-aged adults to endorse these types of items, thus indicating stronger adherence to traditional Christian doctrines (see figure 6.2). Courtenay et al. (1992) also reported greater endorsement of traditional ideology by their oldest groups in their sample of 60-, 80- and 100-year-olds. Overall, then, there is some cross-sectional evidence that older persons and/or generations are somewhat more traditional in their adherence to religious doctrine than younger groups. However, longitudinal studies are needed to understand whether these represent developmental or cohort differences in religious orthodoxy (cf. Cox & Hammonds, 1988).

Evidence with regard to the level of private religious activities is

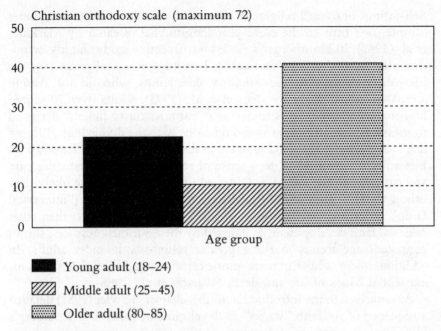

Christian orthodoxy scale (maximum 72)

Age group

■ Young adult (18–24)

▨ Middle adult (25–45)

▦ Older adult (80–85)

Figure 6.2 Level of Christian Orthodoxy by age group
Significant age differences (p < .05); adapted from Pratt et al., 1992

generally consistent with stability into later adulthood, or perhaps a modest increment. Across the age range 65 to 90, Ainlay et al. (1992) reported evidence of a marginal increase in private activities such as prayer and Bible reading, and in the following of religious television and radio programs. In fact, fully 95 percent of elderly Americans report that they engage in prayer (Koenig et al., 1988), leaving little room for further gains! Markides et al. (1987) found the frequency of private prayer remained quite stable over an eight-year period in their longitudinal sample of older individuals. In addition, Koenig and his colleagues (1988) have suggested that such private religious activities reflect, in part, a tendency for older individuals to use them as a coping strategy in dealing with life and health stresses. Courtenay et al. (1992) observed that their centenarians used religious coping activities more than nonreligious coping strategies, whereas their 60-year-olds used nonreligious coping activities more frequently; 80-year-olds were intermediate. As one of their centenarians remarked, "I don't worry about the future; it's in God's hands." (p. 55).

Personal beliefs and faith are the final dimension of religion studied.

Self-ratings of overall religiosity showed modest increments in an older sample over time in the eight-year longitudinal research by Markides et al. (1987). In Hunsberger's (1985) retrospective study, highly ortho-dox older adults recalled themselves becoming more religious over the lifespan, in contrast to less orthodox older adults, who did not. And in a cross-sectional study by Benson et al. (1993), adults over 70 scored higher than all other age groups on a "Faith Maturity Index," designed to measure both attitudes toward relations with the divine (e.g., "Every day I see evidence that God is active in the world") and to relations with humanity (e.g., "I feel a deep sense of responsibility for reducing pain and suffering in the world"). Older adults were much more likely than others to score high on both of these components of faith ("integrated faith," according to Benson et al., 1993). It would seem, then, that personal faith development, as indexed by these various measures, shows consistent age trends marking greater religiosity in older adults. In addition, older adults express more certainty of belief about various existential issues of life and death (Watson et al., 1988).

As described in the introduction to this chapter, Fowler (1981) detailed a sequence of six faith "stages" in development, parallel to Kohlberg's (1969) stages of moral reasoning. Shulik (1979) investigated concep-tions of faith in an older adult sample, using these stages. He reported a modest non-significant trend in his 53- to 87-year-old sample towards higher scores among older adults. Shulik also observed that higher levels in Fowler's system were positively associated with greater "interiority" or "age sense" in older adults, an awareness by the individual of the ways in which he or she is changing personally with age. "Age sense" was higher in the older adults in this sample, and may be part of the process through which the older adult comes to grips with faith issues in his or her own life. As discussed below in chapter 7, Pratt, Diessner et al. (1991) found a similar pattern of relations between age sense and moral development in later adulthood.

Shulik's (1979) work suggested that older adults' perspectives on all aspects of religious life are shaped by their level of faith development in the Fowler system. For example, a stage three (synthetic–conventional level) comment on religious doctrine and belief:

Yes, I believe in the Holy Trinity of Father, Son, and Holy Spirit, even though I can't really describe it to you or explain it.

It makes sense to you?

It isn't a question of its making sense to me. It's the way that it is.

*But did you ever question it or sense some shakiness in your own faith in
it?*

Oh! Heavens, no! What a terrible idea! Why do you even raise the
question? I don't like the thought one bit . . .

Do you feel that God would want everyone to be Catholic?

When I think about that, I think, definitely, yes, that He would be
pleased if all were Catholics (Shulik, 1979, p. 212).

A contrasting perspective on religious authority is offered by another
older adult from a stage five (paradoxical–consolidative faith):

My spiritual journey has involved participation in a number of
different churches and movements . . . But it was the [certain
Protestant denomination] which I respected the most, because they
were quite accepting of the fact that, at a certain point, I had to
leave off associating with them and I had to go away for a time,
for the sake of my own growth and further development . . . They
said that this was something that I had to decide to do for myself
and that they respected my need. And that I could always go back
to them. They never closed off the possibility of further "dialogue"
with them because of this need for some separation (Shulik, 1979,
p. 214).

What is especially noteworthy in contrasting these two comments is
the pervasive difference between the two individuals' attitudes toward
religious doctrine and authority. At stage three, the locus of authority
is clearly external; at stage five, it is within the person herself. One's
relationship, both with the divine and with the church as a mediator of
religious doctrine, cannot fail to be strongly shaped by these different
perspectives. A person's openness to doubting may in fact be a pervasive characteristic of his or her religious orientation and expression
(Hunsberger et al., 1993). Variations in Fowler's faith levels seem likely
to be closely linked to these patterns of tolerance for doubt.

Do those who are more religious enjoy higher levels of life satisfaction in later adulthood? Many studies have examined this proposition,
with quite complicated results overall (e.g., Krause, 1993). A major
reason for this, of course, is the multidimensional nature of religiosity
we have just discussed. It is important to understand the processes by
which aspects of religious experience are linked to life satisfaction. Some

dimensions of religious practices, notably "public" experiences, have important social dimensions for the older person, whereas others do not. Indeed, it does seem as if the level of public religious participation has been consistently positively related to adults' life satisfaction and mental health in several studies, even with level of physical health controlled (e.g., Cox & Hammonds, 1988; Koenig, 1992; Markides et al., 1987). In contrast, private religious activities and self-rated religiosity were not consistent predictors of life satisfaction in the longitudinal study by Markides et al. (see also Koenig, 1992). It seems plausible that the social integration aspects of church participation have particularly important benefits for older adults. As Koenig (1992, p. 180) notes, "involvement in the religious community provides companionship and friends of similar age and interest, a supportive environment to buffer stressful life changes, an atmosphere of acceptance, hope, and forgiveness, a source of practical assistance when needed, and a common world view and philosophy of life." Though more sophisticated work, discriminating among the different dimensions of religiosity and controlling other influences on adjustment is needed, these social dimensions may be central components of the apparent positive effects of religiosity on life adaptation in older adults.

Finally, most of the studies described above have indicated overall gender differences in religiosity in later life, with women tending to score higher on all of the dimensions discussed (e.g., the Faith Maturity Scale, Benson et al., 1993; both public and private religious practices, Koenig et al., 1988, Krause, 1993). There is also some evidence that religiosity is more important in the lives of women than of men with respect to processes of social adaptation (Koenig et al., 1988). Greater religiosity among women was also evident in a sample of older Black Americans (Chatters, Levin, & Taylor, 1992). It seems possible that both women's own childhood socialization patterns, and the relatively greater involvement of mothers in the religious socialization of children (e.g., Chatters et al., 1992; Hunsberger, 1985) play some role in this gender difference that seems to persist into later life.

Less is known about ethnic variations in religious activity and social life in later adulthood, but there is some evidence that religion plays a larger role in the lives of black Americans than in the lives of their Anglo counterparts (e.g., Gallup, 1984). For example, the black church in the southern United States traditionally has been a dominant community institution in many respects. Recent investigations have pointed to the importance of informal social networks, based in the church, in providing support for elderly blacks (e.g., Taylor & Chatters, 1986). It seems certain that similar patterns obtain for older individuals in other groups in North America as well, cutting across denominational lines. As Bellah et al. (1985) point out in their comments on the role of religion in contemporary America, "There are thousands of local churches in the United States, representing an enormous range of variation in doctrine and worship. Yet most define themselves as communities of personal support" (p. 232). Both the public and private aspects of religion surely play a substantial role in the lives of many older North Americans.

Aging and political thinking

Arguing politics over the kitchen table was something of a regular ritual in Mike's family as he grew up. His father, from rural Michigan, has been a life-long Republican. In fact, he may be one of the only people still part of the Herbert Hoover fan club – if only they'd given that guy a chance in 1932, he'd have turned that Depression around! Despite somewhat differing political and economic views, however, Mike and his father have found across the years and the arguments, that on many contemporary issues, they have shared, and continue to share, a good deal of agreement. And sometimes they have been able to change each other's views, in both directions.

What do we know of older adults' political involvement and satisfaction? Older adults remain politically active, and are at least as likely to vote as younger age groups in the Western democracies (see table 6.1, adapted from Edinger, 1985). Older adults also report similar levels of trust and satisfaction with the way that government works in their country to those of younger adults in the same cross-national sample (table 6.1).

While there has been little systematic research on the topic of political thinking across the lifespan, two specific topics regarding political attitudes have been systematically studied in relation to issues of aging. The hypothesis that the *content* of political attitudes becomes more conservative with age has been widely suggested, and has received some research attention (e.g., Glenn, 1974). Second, the related argument that the *structure* of political attitudes is more rigid and less open to change in the elderly has been considered as well (e.g., Sears, 1981).

One of the major questions in testing the "increasing conservatism" hypothesis of aging and politics has, naturally, been the definition of just what conservatism is (e.g., Campbell & Strate, 1981). A range of

Table 6.1 Political attitudes and actions of adult age groups in the United States, West Germany, and Great Britain, 1973–1975

	Age groups in years	United States	West Germany	Great Britain
Say they voted in the last national election (%)	16–20	11.7	15.3	6.5
	21–44	68.0	94.1	68.6
	45–64	80.0	95.6	85.5
	65–	80.4	93.3	85.5
	Total	68.1	89.9	73.3
Say they more or less trust government "to do what is right." (%)	16–20	31.0	44.3	32.4
	21–44	33.6	53.4	39.9
	45–64	37.0	52.6	37.7
	65–	34.0	50.5	49.2
	Total	34.4	52.2	40.3
Say they discuss politics with others (%)	16–20	58.0	48.9	37.7
	21–44	69.9	49.7	50.5
	45–64	67.5	42.1	49.0
	65–	48.7	26.7	37.6
	Total	64.7	43.1	46.6

Adapted from Edinger (1985), table 1, p. 60

measures have been examined in several different studies, including people's self-reports of their personal ideologies as liberal or conservative, their actual party affiliations, their attitudes on specific and general social issues, and their levels of authoritarianism. Most studies have pursued these questions by using panel data from large-scale surveys of different age groups (often over several time periods), thus confounding possible cohort and age differences. Only one study has reported a direct longitudinal investigation of the same individuals' political attitudes across adulthood, the Bennington College Study begun in the late 1930s by Theodore Newcomb, and recently followed up when the Bennington sample women were in their late 60s (Krosnick & Alwin, 1989).

In general, these studies have suggested that the evidence for a turn to the "right" in later life is not very clear or convincing (e.g., Danigelis & Cutler, 1991a). Older people in the United States tend to report themselves as conservative about as frequently as middle-aged persons

(Campbell & Strate, 1981). Moreover, groups of adults in their 50s and older were just as likely to become more liberal in racial tolerance as were younger adults over the period 1960–85 in the USA (Danigelis & Cutler, 1991a). And they were no more likely to become increasingly conservative on law and order issues such as capital punishment over this same time period, where the US societal tide was running in this conservative direction (Danegelis & Cutler, 1991b).

Finally, there are the longitudinal data from the Bennington College Study. The women involved had become markedly more liberal with their exposure to university life in the 1930s at this avowedly liberal institution, and these liberal attitudes appeared to have persisted across the lifespan (Krosnick & Alwin, 1989; Newcomb et al., 1967). Since this is of course a highly select group of individuals, it would be important to have more systematic longitudinal evidence on conservatism in the general population.

There are data available for certain attitude domains, however, that are somewhat contradictory. Particularly with respect to authoritarianism of social and political views, some evidence of increasing conservatism across the adult lifespan has been found (Altemeyer, 1981; Pratt et al., 1993). The oldest adults in the Pratt et al. study, for example, were considerably more likely to agree with statements from Altemeyer's right-wing authoritarianism scale expressing deference to authority and/ or conventionality (e.g., "obedience and respect for authority are the most important virtues that children should learn," Altemeyer, 1988, p. 22, see also chapter 4). In a subsequent, unpublished study, levels of authoritarianism were shown to vary widely among mature adults, and to be linked to perceptions of social support as well as to educational level, so that those elderly persons who felt isolated from others were much more likely to be authoritarian in their belief structures, as were those who were less educated (Pratt et al., 1992, see figure 6.3). And cross-national survey data do in fact show that older adults (over 65) report considerably less discussion of politics with others than do younger cohorts overall (see table 6.1, Edinger, 1985).

These findings suggest the important role of social interaction in later life in mediating "individual" cognitive style differences, in this case, in authoritarianism of political views. However, since these studies were all cross-sectional in nature, cohort or age trends are equally plausible explanations for these observations on authoritarianism. Observations across different cultural settings and political systems would be of value as well, as most of these data are derived from US or Canadian samples.

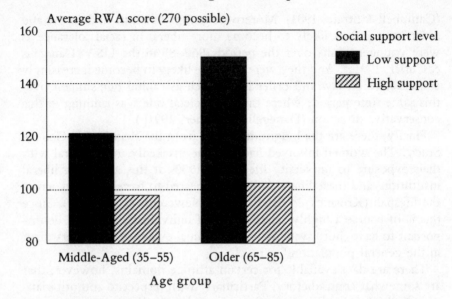

Figure 6.3 Right-wing authoritarianism score by age group and support level, controlled for educational background
Age and social support effects (ps <.05); adapted from Pratt et al., 1992

With regard to the second research question, that of "attitudinal rigidity," several hypotheses have been suggested (Krosnick & Alwin, 1989). One is the "increasing persistence" model, indicating that as adults get older, they gradually show less openness to attitude change, i.e., their attitudes are more likely to persist. A second model, the "impressionable years" hypothesis, suggests that young adults (like the Bennington women described above) are exceptionally likely to show flux in political attitudes, but that after early adulthood, there is little change in susceptibility over the lifespan. In general, the evidence from several recent studies is not supportive of the "increasing rigidity" model of political aging (e.g., Danegelis & Cutler, 1991a; Krosnick & Alwin, 1989; Tyler & Schuller, 1991). Older adults as a group are as likely to show changes in attitudes on various political dimensions as are younger adults. In the Krosnick and Alwin study, younger individuals (18 to 30) were shown to have somewhat less stable political attitudes than others, providing modest support to the "impressionable years" hypothesis mentioned above. However, as Tyler and Schuller (1991) pointed out, it is important to distinguish between having the capacity to change one's thinking and having the opportunity. In their work, older adults who had direct experience with the police or courts in Chicago were shown to be as affected on subsequent attitude measures toward these agencies as were younger adults. However, older adults in general were less likely to have direct encounters with the legal system, and thus, perhaps, less likely to have the opportunity to change. Tyler and Schuller (1991) suggest that their results support a third model, "lifelong openness," with respect to attitude change. They also suggest the importance of specific social experiences in attitude formation and change. As with the data on conservatism, they indicate that age trends may be more associated with changes in social opportunities for the elderly than with any inherently age-linked cognitive shifts.

Overall, then, there is little evidence that older adults in North American cultures are distinctively more conservative in their political outlooks than others, or that they are more rigid and resistant to political attitude change. The specific evidence on authoritarianism of political beliefs requires more research. However, it is clear that there is great individual variability in this tendency in the elderly groups studied, which seems to be associated with educational and social–environmental factors. In principle, as noted by Campbell and Strate (1981), the elderly seem very much a part of the political mainstream in North America.

What is missing in all of this research from the developmental point of view, of course, is a theoretical framework for conceptualizing how political thinking and behavior are organized and constructed across the lifespan. There has been a beginning on such work in childhood and adolescence (e.g., Adelson, 1971), but much more remains to be done. As might be expected, there is evidence that political reasoning and values in younger persons are linked to aspects of the development of stages of moral reasoning, as studied by Kohlberg (e.g., deVries & Walker, 1986; Lonky, Reihman, & Serlin, 1981; Tapp & Kohlberg, 1971). Furthermore, developmental measures of the sophistication of political thinking in adolescence have been found to be linked to differential family socialization experiences (Santolupo & Pratt, in press). However, nothing on the topic of lifespan research on political thinking has been completed from any developmental perspective so far. As stressed in our first theme, understanding how older adults construct and interpret their experiences within a domain is critical. Until such a conception is outlined, and appropriate research is carried out, it will be difficult to say much more in a systematic way with regard to the *meaning* of politics for older adults.

Tracing the book's themes

Our first theme stresses that personal experiences of social systems (ranging from microsystems to macrosystems) can vary over the lifespan, and are actively constructed by the individual involved. For example, as we noted in the discussion of retirement, people's interpretation of this apparently clearly defined status may vary, based on their own past experiences associated with the social categories of gender and ethnicity. Retirement is not the same phenomenon for women in late twentieth-century North America as it is for men, because women's domestic roles and their *understanding* of those roles are different from those of men. Consequently, older women think about retirement status and its meaning differently than do older men (Calasanti, 1993). Men, as well, are redefining retirement as they explore opportunities for flexible work schedules or are forced into the ranks of "discouraged unemployed workers." As another example, the role of the church as a faith "authority" in the lives of adults is likely to be quite different, depending on how the individual understands this issue from the various developmental vantage points defined by Fowler (1981).

As stressed in our second theme, there is wide diversity of adaptation among older adults to the variety of institutional and social roles discussed above. For example, as we discussed, there are gender and ethnic variations in the retirement experience and in the intensity and impact of religious experiences. The spectrum of political beliefs in later adulthood is wide, likely as wide as it is in early adulthood, and it is not diminished by any tendency for the older adult to become more "conservative" in dealing with new institutional experiences. Clearly, diversity is the rule, both in people's experiences and in their reactions to these experiences of societal roles in later life (e.g., Tyler & Schuller, 1991).

Finally, this evidence points once more to how social resources have an impact on the aging individual's thinking, in this case about society. For example, older adults' political attitudes are no more likely to be "rigid" and unchanging than those of younger adults, if they have the relevant new social experiences with the attitude object (Tyler & Schuller, 1991). Older adults, however, are less likely to have such contacts overall, and thus are less likely to have the opportunity to change. Similarly, older adults report less opportunity to discuss political issues with others than do younger adults (Edinger, 1985), and this may be particularly true of those older adults who seem relatively authoritarian in attitudes (Pratt et al., 1992).

Comparison processes with other individuals, in terms of the timing of role transitions like retirement, also appear to influence and shape how older adults understand and experience these transitions. Thus, it seems that social interactions and social reference points are central to the experience of later life societal understanding and involvement, though much more research on this issue is certainly warranted.

Mrs McKillop revisited

We began this chapter with the comments of a veteran city councillor, Mrs McKillop. It is interesting to note that her reflections about her career came within the context of an interview about grandparenthood (Norris & Tari, unpublished data). During her conversation with Joan Norris, this older woman made it clear, in her own way, that the microsystems of her life were fully interactive, making it impossible to separate out one role for examination. This perspective is instructive for researchers who often target one role or relationship out of the context of other significant components of an individual's life. Bronfenbrenner's conceptualization of nested social systems reminds us that a variety of ever-larger social contexts must be considered to understand developmental questions. This perspective is quite consistent with the view that a lifespan developmental conceptualization, which allows for multiple influences and multidirectional change, is the best way to understand social functioning in adulthood.

7

Decision-making, Wisdom, and Moral Judgment

Tell me about a moral dilemma in your own life.

Well a recent moral decision for me was my daughter's choice to leave the public school and take Grade 11 at [a private school] . . . probably a few years ago I would have recommended against going but now I realized that I was sort of in favor of it . . . In the past I had always supported the public school system as being the basis for a good society and everything, and then finding that's true in a general sense but when it comes down to a specific instance you've got one shot at it with yourself or your child so it doesn't matter what your overall principles are, you better do what is right for this particular person at the time . . . Again, I think the public school system should be supported and improved and so on, but that's in a general way. If it's not working you have to deal with it in a specific instance.

Did you consider this a moral problem?

Yes, in a way, because I'm very interested and concerned about society and my own support of certain community structures and everyone's welfare . . . and supporting my daughter's change [of schools] was something I wouldn't have contemplated five or six years ago as even being possible (Mr Little, age 54; Pratt, unpublished data).

Mr Little's reflections on his daughter's needs and his own convictions highlight the topics of this chapter – maturity and social judgment, wisdom, and morality. Everyday social life involves constant instances of making judgments, choices, and decisions regarding appropriate courses of action. Indeed, social cognition can be viewed, in its prag-matic applications, as a form of real-life problem-solving (Luszcz, 1989). Deciding what to do in everyday social contexts inevitably involves consideration of the feelings, thoughts, wishes and plans of others, and of how best to deal with others and the self within this sociocognitive framework. Furthermore, the majority of the everyday life problems that adults of all ages report seem to involve social or interpersonal issues (Hartley, 1989).

This chapter begins with some general comment on recent research on human decision-making and reasoning capabilities and limitations. Then, adult development and change in these skills are considered in the light of our four theoretical orientations. Next, the evidence on variations across adulthood with regard to problem-solving is reviewed. After that, the chapter focuses on one particular topic of recent interest in this general area, the notion of "wisdom" in later life and associated theory and research. The last part of the chapter considers a third cen-tral area of social judgment, the topic of moral reasoning, and its devel-opment in later life.

Everyday decision-making and problem-solving

Background and theories

Much recent research and theorizing has drawn attention to the ways in which everyday reasoning and decision-making does and does not resemble "optimal" models (e.g., Kuhn, 1989; Nisbett & Ross, 1980; Tversky & Kahneman, 1973). Social judgment and inference processes used by the "person on the street" are likely to follow the basic frame-work of "expert" or "scientific" reasoning, but to demonstrate many faulty inferences and the frequent use of inadequate short-cuts or simplified rules that ease the task of problem-solving (e.g., Tversky & Kahneman, 1973). For example, adult "intuitive scientists" often base their social judgments on vivid single-case examples, while ignoring "boring" statistical evidence based on much larger and more representa-tive samples (Nisbett & Ross, 1980).

Nevertheless, despite this widespread evidence of the fallibility and limitations in everyday adult judgment, recent work demonstrates that there *are* progressive developmental trends in the adequacy of such "scientific" reasoning, concerning the relations between theories and evidence (Kuhn, 1989). Mature reasoners, compared with young children, are more likely to keep the boundaries clear between evidence and theory by using their better developed reflective capacities (Kuhn, 1989). In turn, such improvements in formal reasoning skills may aid everyday judgment. As an example, Kuhn, Pennington, and Leadbeater (1983) reported that the quality of jurors' reasoning about evidence in a trial was linked to their levels of reflective reasoning about the relations of facts to theories. Those jurors who recognized the possibility of multiple interpretations of reality were more likely to construct accounts that made reference to, and distinguished, both the facts of the case *and* the testimony of the trial. In contrast, those who admitted to only a single view of "truth" in their responding on standard measures discussed the evidence with little explicit reference to the testimony of different witnesses (Kuhn et al., 1983).

Theoretical frameworks

Some investigations in the **psychometric** tradition have been particularly focused on understanding our everyday language and conceptions of the notion of "wisdom" (Holliday & Chandler, 1986; Sternberg, 1985). Wisdom has been approached variously in these studies, as discussed in a later section of this chapter, but the biblical prototype of wise King Solomon, solving a seemingly insurmountable practical problem in social relations through a grasp of the psychology of human needs and desires, is probably a widely shared example. These studies, using adult populations across the lifespan, indicate that members of our culture share a notion that skills in *practical* problem-solving and judgment may improve into later adulthood.

A contrasting psychometric model of aging and problem-solving performance is represented by the ideas of Denney (1982, 1989). Denney proposes that ability and practice (or "exercise") are fundamental to understanding skilled performance across the lifespan. Optimally exercised ability levels are always higher than unexercised ones. "Practice makes perfect" is the central adage in Denney's framework. In her model, both exercised and unexercised ability levels are presumed to increase up to early adulthood and then to show decline for any skill. However, abilities that are more frequently exercised (for example, practical decision skills such as purchasing items on a budget) will show a slower rate of decline over the later portion of the lifespan, since they approach the optimal level more closely than do less exercised (for example, "academic") problem-solving skills. Furthermore, Denney's model makes a number of suggestions regarding the comparison of practical and laboratory problem-solving tasks across the lifespan that have led to considerable research, some of which is reviewed below.

The **information-processing** models of lifespan development, as noted in chapter 2, have generally viewed aging in terms of the gradual loss of various basic cognitive skills or capacities (e.g., Salthouse, 1988). Such models might be expected to predict declines in complex decision-making performance in later life, to the extent that task performance is dependent on these critical basic processes. Nevertheless, recent formulations have stressed the potential maintenance of complex performance in later life, in specific areas of expertise, through the use of compensatory tradeoffs with other basic skills which may substitute for those areas showing decrements (e.g., Rybash, Hoyer, & Roodin, 1986). Such compensatory mechanisms might be found too in social problem-solving.

A central contemporary approach to moral judgment is the **developmental** stage theory of Lawrence Kohlberg, formulated in the tradition of Piaget's model. Kohlberg (1981, 1984) posits a universal six-stage hierarchy of moral reasoning over the lifespan. This describes developmental movement across three major levels, from a childish morality of external constraint through a level of societal conformity and compliance to an autonomous, internalized level of reasoning from broad, self-chosen principles (see table 7.1). This final, principled level is believed to be rare, even among adults, and is regarded as unlikely to appear until mature adulthood (Kohlberg & Higgins, 1984). Thus, in contrast to the cognitive stages of Piaget, which are believed to be fully attained by late adolescence, Kohlberg (1973) postulates a substantial and even central role for adult development. Both education and experiences of commitment and personal responsibility for one's decisions are thought to play a major role in adult growth. Following in the Piagetian research tradition, Kohlberg studied moral reasoning by means of a semi-structured interview procedure focused around a set of hypothetical dilemmas or stories of moral choice and action. A complex scoring procedure is utilized to assess the reasoning in this interview and assign a stage score, irrespective of the specific position or content of an individual's opinions (Colby & Kohlberg, 1987).

Several closely related positions in this cognitive–developmental approach have focused specifically on adult developmental issues. Gibbs (1979) takes issue with Kohlberg's view of his highest, principled level, arguing that it cannot represent a true "stage" in the Piagetian sense,

Table 7.1 Kohlberg's six stages of moral development

Preconventional level

Stage 1
Punishment and obedience orientation. The physical consequences of an action determine whether it is good or bad. Avoiding punishment and bowing to superior power are valued positively.

Stage 2
Instrumental relativist orientation. Right action consists of behavior that satisfies one's own needs. Human relations are viewed in marketplace terms. Reciprocity occurs, but is seen in a pragmatic way, i.e., "you scratch my back and I'll scratch yours."

Conventional level

Stage 3
Interpersonal concordance (good boy–nice girl) orientation. Good behaviors are those that please or are approved by others. There is much emphasis on conformity and being "nice."

Stage 4
Orientation toward authority ("law and order"). Focus is on authority or rules. It is right to do one's duty, show respect for authority, and maintain the social order.

Postconventional level

Stage 5
Social-contract orientation. This stage has a utilitarian, legalistic tone. Correct behavior is defined in terms of standards agreed upon by society. Awareness of the relativism of personal values and the need for consensus is important.

Stage 6
Universal ethical principle orientation. Morality is defined as a decision of conscience. Ethical principles are self-chosen, based on abstract concepts (e.g., the Golden Rule) rather than concrete rules (e.g., the Ten Commandments).

From R. V. Kail & R. Wicks-Nelson, *Developmental psychology*, Prentice-Hall, 1993, table 11.2.

since it is so rare, even in adult populations. Rather, it is better thought of as an alternative mode of reflection on moral questions and on earlier stages of moral reasoning. These are brought on by the large issues of adulthood and the human condition, such as the inevitability of death. Others have similarly argued that adult development beyond conventional levels of moral reasoning is based on modes of coping with the existential dilemmas of life raised by experiences such as loss of a loved one (Lonky, Kaus, & Roodin, 1984). Adult experiences of commitment and real-life responsibility for one's own decision-making have also been thought to lead to a greater sense of tolerance in moral judgments of others and the self (Murphy & Gilligan, 1980), as illustrated by Mr Little. Collectively then, these theories draw attention to the unique role of experiences that typify mature adulthood in stimulating reflections on the moral judgment process itself.

Another major approach in contemporary moral judgment derives from **social psychology**. This approach attempts to view much of everyday moral action and choice as reflecting the application of broadly shared normative principles which are invoked in various specific social situations (Rest, 1983). Examples of these principles are the norms of "exchange," "reciprocity," or "altruism." For example, the norm of reciprocity obligates one to reciprocate help received from another when appropriate at a later time.

An important issue is the extent to which individuals across the lifespan invoke and adhere to such norms. With respect to aging, Kahana, Midlarsky and Kahana (1987) have argued that adherence to a norm of social responsibility or helpfulness, without immediate motives for self-benefit, may be greater in later life. They base this argument on the importance of the role of "giver" to the elderly, due to its implications of a sense of broad contributions to societal functioning and a continuing sense of self-worth in the later part of the lifespan (cf. the discussion of generativity in chapter 6).

Research on aging and
social problem-solving

Could you tell me about a time when you made an important decision?

Well, I decided that I needed to get a job after my husband died. And I had to have a very big push to decide that . . . It was like I was standing on the edge of the water and didn't want to get my feet wet . . . The conflict was that I had got married in 1941 and my husband died in 1971 and I hadn't, during all those years I had worked at home but not for money. And that's a very big conflict, that's very scary. The immediate push was money because a government check hadn't come through. And another push was I found myself worrying about two of my kids who were out and didn't come home on time. So the combination of the two things pushed me into saying, "Is this what I'm going to do the rest of my life?" So I decided I was going to get myself a job, working in a doctor's office. At the time it was a very good idea for me because it rooted me out of the house and I found I could manage in spite of making a terrible mess of those wretched government forms until I finally got the hang of it . . . Anyway I did manage and I survived and we all survived and the check came in . . . (Mrs Gray, a widow now in her mid-70s; Pratt, unpublished data, 1993).

How do people deal with the decisions and challenges of adult life, such as that described by Mrs Gray? In a series of studies, Denney and her colleagues (e.g., Denney, 1989) investigated age differences in adulthood in various types of problem-solving performance. In general, these studies have suggested that the pattern of age differences varies somewhat by content type. Abstract, formal problems are solved "best" by young adults, as judged by experts unaware of participant age. Middle-aged, and especially elderly, adults perform more poorly on these types of problems (Camp et al., 1989). In contrast, real-life, practical reasoning problems are best solved by middle-aged adults, with older adults still performing more poorly than this group based on expert ratings. This finding seemed to be true even when the content of the problems was adapted to issues that more typically confront the elderly (e.g., retirement issues, taking medications). Older adults were found to be less able to generate safe, effective solutions to such standard "elderly" problems than were middle-aged adults (Denney & Pearce, 1989). However, when solutions to personal, *participant-generated* problems were studied in this paradigm (as opposed to the standardized problems typically used), no age differences were found in expert ratings of solution efficacy (Camp et al., 1989). In general, these patterns in the Denney studies held for both social and non-social types of everyday problems.

In contrast to Denney's findings, studies by Cornelius and colleagues (Cornelius & Caspi, 1987; Cornelius, Kenney, & Caspi, 1989) have suggested that the elderly may not show lower adequacy in the solutions they select for a standard set of daily life problems. In these studies, solutions were presented in a multiple-choice format, with four types of solutions given for each problem. The four types of solutions here involved ways of coping which had been previously described by Folkman et al. (1987): problem-focused, cognitive–analytic, passive–dependent, and avoidant–denial styles. An example of these items for a friendship problem is as follows:

You would like to get some friends to come visit you more often. What would you do?

a) Invite them to your home [problem-focused].
b) Try to figure out why they do not seem to make an effort to visit you [cognitive–analytic].
c) Accept the situation and do nothing [passive–dependent].
d) Do not be overly concerned about it and turn your attention to other things [avoidant–denial] (Cornelius & Caspi, 1987, p. 146).

The four solution types had previously been rated by an independent sample of participants for adequacy in relation to each specific problem studied. Cornelius and Caspi (1987) found that selection of the most effective problem-solving styles showed no differences over the lifespan (average ages 20, 40, and 70) in rated effectiveness of solutions chosen for family and friendship issues. For consumer and work issues, there was a significant increase from young to middle-aged groups, and a non-significant gain between middle age and later adulthood (cf. Hartley, 1989).

Dolen and Bearison (1982) conducted a study of older individuals' interpersonal problem-solving skills, using the Means–End Problem-Solving Test, in which participants are required to generate as many alternative social courses of action as possible to solve a problem (e.g., trouble with a supervisor at work). They showed that scores were equivalent across the age range of 65 to 89 (Dolen & Bearison, 1982). In addition, the researchers found that social problem-solving scores were positively related to the level of social role participation reported by these elders.

In a fascinating study of 165 elders at three age levels (60s, 80s, and 100s), Poon et al. (1992) reported that while all of the standard IQ and memory measures which they administered to these individuals showed substantially lower scores among the oldest groups, performance on their everyday problem-solving measure did not differ across the three ages. Problem-solving was measured in this study by questions (modelled on Denney & Palmer, 1981) about what to do in both social and non-social difficulties (e.g., being awakened by a loud knocking at your door in the middle of the night). This result may suggest that individuals who survive into very late adulthood (clearly a very select group), must be especially competent in critical life skills, despite losses in standard academic performance. Of course, longitudinal studies would be needed to establish this over time. Following people to age 100 would of course be one of the more heroic longitudinal investigations ever

conceived and certainly ever conducted. In any event, the findings raise
questions about Denney's (1989) model of inexorable later-life decline
in all types of problem-solving skills.

Kuhn (1991) reported few age differences across adulthood (from
adolescents to those in their 60s) in the quality of everyday reasoning
about evidence regarding the causes of social phenomena (e.g., causes
of school failure, unemployment). Older adults were as able to provide
evidence, both for their own ideas and for opposing theories about the
causes of these social problems, as were younger adults (though no-
body was too successful at the latter task). Education-related differences
between a college and non-college sample of adults did appear, with the
more highly educated showing greater skills in comprehending evidence and thinking about alternative theories. Kuhn et al. (1983) also
showed no age differences in the quality of 20- to 70-year-olds' trial
reasoning in the jury-simulation study mentioned earlier.

In general, then, the evidence suggests that there are complex patterns
of age differences for different types of real-life decision-making tasks.
A clearer taxonomy of such tasks, which is more theoretically organized and motivated, is probably necessary to understand these complex
variations in performance. For example, Smith and Baltes (1990) asked
people to think aloud as they planned how to deal with standard stories
about work–family conflicts for younger or older adults. Older adults'
social planning was judged less sophisticated than younger and middle-
aged adults for standard life problems for their age range (e.g., retirement), but there were no age group differences in reasoning on
"non-normative" (unusual) problems (e.g., a 60-year-old woman who
must decide whether to help her son with child care or to re-enter the
workforce). The older group's greater experience with a wider range of
life situations might have compensated for any general planning deficits
they had as they worked on these non-normative types of problems.
Smith and Baltes's findings suggest that the normative/non-normative
problem distinction may be useful in examining these issues.

Berg and her colleagues (Berg, Calderone, Strough & Williams, 1993;
Sansone & Berg, 1993) have made two very important points about the
issues of everyday problem-solving and the ways it has been studied to
date. First, people's definitions of the problem are central to understanding their strategy choices, plans, and behaviors in dealing with
real-life difficulties (Sansone & Berg, 1993). Variations in people's goals
in everyday problem-solving situations across the lifespan were documented, and these differences in goals (e.g., competence versus social
relations goals in school-related activities) were reflected in variations in

the activities that problem-solvers engage in (e.g., Leont'ev, 1981). For example, those with competence goals may interact quite differently on a group project than those with social interactional goals. In this research, older adults appeared to have a broader, more individually variable, range of goals that did younger age groups in dealing with everyday problems. We shall have to understand the *meaning* of these problems and activities for adults more clearly to understand developmental differences in problem-solving responses across the lifespan (Sansone & Berg, 1993).

Second, a broader orientation in these studies to the *process* of everyday problem solving is needed (Berg et al., 1993). Most research has focused on what people report that they do in solving a problem that has already occurred. But many other relevant activities also take place in this process, including efforts at prevention of the problem in the first place, and evaluations of the solutions chosen and plans for dealing with the problem if it happens again (Berg et al., 1993).

Berg et al. (1993) showed that age differences across the lifespan were quite variable over these different processes. Older adults were somewhat like younger adolescents in their reported problem solution types (and different from mid-life adults), but they were quite different in their evaluations and plans for future problem-solving than were children. Specifically, they were more likely to report plans to influence others or change the environment, whereas children and young adults were more likely to report plans to change their own behaviors (Berg et al., 1993). Regardless of these specific results, the main point is that a broader focus on the problem-solving process in real-life contexts will be important to understand age differences appropriately.

One interesting and prototypic application of social problem-solving skills in the adult life cycle involves parenting and child-rearing. Experiencing the transition to parenthood provides a rude awakening for many of us in terms of the complexities of these problems (e.g., Cowan & Cowan, 1992). How might young and older adults (e.g., parents and grandparents) differ in their approaches to dealing with child-rearing problems? As suggested by Sansone and Berg (1993), it is important first to understand how adults across the lifespan characterize such problems.

Pratt, Hunsberger, Pancer, Roth, and Santolupo (1993) examined lifespan adult differences in conceptions of parenting and child-rearing issues. They interviewed people about their understanding of the causes of personal parenting issues of their own recollection, a familiar issue of parenting that they knew about but which did not involve them personally (this commonly involved criticisms of a friend's child-rearing), and a hypothetical issue based on a vignette taken from Sameroff and Feil (1985). The hypothetical issue was as follows:

> Mr and Mrs Raymond have two children, Billy who is five and Mary who is three. Billy was a very demanding baby and still asks for a lot of attention from his parents. Billy would get very angry if he didn't get what he wanted from his parents. Lately, Mr and Mrs Raymond have had a lot of money problems because Mr Raymond was laid off from his job. One evening at bedtime Mrs Raymond heard Billy and Mary fighting over a toy. She stormed into the bedroom and began spanking Billy very hard and she wouldn't stop. Mr Raymond had to pull her away from the boy and had a hard time calming her down.

> How would you explain Mrs Raymond's behavior? (Sameroff & Feil, 1985, p. 93).

The level of reasoning about these family and developmental problems and their causes was scored using a stage measure developed by Sameroff and Feil (1985). Results revealed that older adults were less sophisticated in their explanations about the causes of problems in the hypothetical dilemma than were middle-aged and younger adults (Pratt et al., 1993). However, there were no differences between the age groups in stage of thinking regarding the personal and the familiar dilemmas (see figure 7.1).

More educated adults at all ages scored significantly higher in these analyses. As well, adults at all ages who scored higher on Altemeyer's (1988) index of authoritarianism of thinking about social issues were less sophisticated in their reasoning about parenting. Since older adults scored higher on this right-wing authoritarianism (RWA) measure overall, age differences in reasoning on the hypothetical dilemma were non-significant when the effects of authoritarianism were statistically removed. It is also important to note that Pratt et al. (1993) found that maturity of reasoning about parenting issues on these indices was positively related to the quality of actual parenting behavior.

Here's an example of one older adult's (in her sixties) quite sophisticated response to a familiar problem from this interview:

> My sister has a marginally retarded son, he's 20 or so now, but a problem has always been getting him to eat, and she has always

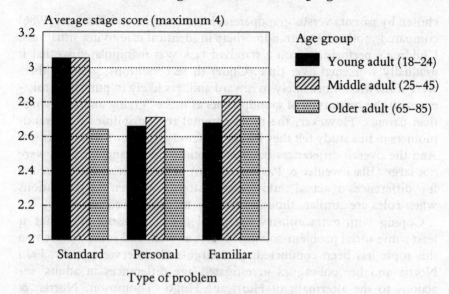

Figure 7.1 Parenting stage score by age and type of problem
Significant age differences for standard dilemma only (p <.05); adapted from Pratt et al., 1993

made a separate dinner for him because he wouldn't eat what the rest of them ate. And I'm sure she knows that she shouldn't be doing this, but it was the short-term solution to the problem, and so she did it. And as a result he's very mixed up. It was frustrating to watch because I could see him becoming a little tyrant, he still is! She still does everything for him.

What do you think produced or caused this problem?

Well I would say it's a whole complex question really because it was a very large family, six children, he was the youngest, and of course they all picked on him, because of his retardation. I suppose then he got a sense of power from controlling his mother, I would say that would be a big factor there. And the father was very unfeeling, very unfeeling. So you see there are lots of factors . . . I think the biggest one is his control of his mother (Pratt et al., unpublished data).

These results suggest that there should be few average differences between parent and grandparent generations in reasoning about actual child-rearing issues. What can be said about the child-rearing solutions chosen by parents versus grandparents? Blackwelder and Passman (1986) compared mothers and grandmothers in identical caregiving situations. Children's performance on a standard task was manipulated so that it gradually worsened over time. Under these conditions, grandmothers were somewhat more likely to reward and less likely to punish, consistent with the stereotype of grandparents as more "giving and forgiving" than parents. However, the more parental responsibilities that grandmothers in this study felt they had in the family, the more they punished. And the overall differences between mothers and grand-mothers were not large (Blackwelder & Passman, 1986). This suggests that there are few differences in actual child-rearing patterns between the generations when roles are similar, though certainly more research is needed.

Coping with extraordinary life problems or stressors likely has at least some social problem-solving aspects as well, and some research on this topic has been conducted. In a large-scale interview study, Fran Norris and her colleagues investigated age differences in adults' reactions to the aftermath of Hurricane Hugo (Thompson, Norris, & Hanacek, 1993). In 1989, this powerful hurricane swept up the southeastern coast of the USA, leaving widespread destruction in its path. Follow-up interviews one to two years after this disaster showed that middle-aged adults (aged 50 to 64) demonstrated much more vulnerability in terms of psychological symptoms like depression and anxiety than either younger adults (18 to 39) or older adults (over 65).

These findings, and others (e.g., Phifer, 1990), were interpreted based on generational differences in "burden." Middle-aged adults feel more parental, filial, financial, and occupational stress prior to disasters than other groups, and such events seem to magnify these stresses (Thompson et al., 1993). Indeed, the middle aged in this study felt that they provided considerably more support than they received, whereas older (and younger) adults felt more balanced in terms of giving and receiving support. In fact, Thompson et al. suggested that older people, given their relative psychological health and apparent capacity to cope, might be a valuable potential resource in such disaster situations that deserves more consideration than it presently receives.

Aging and social problem-solving: a summary

It is not easy to summarize the evidence just reviewed on adults' social reasoning. Clearly older adults sometimes perform less well on these types of tasks than younger groups, but sometimes show equivalent levels of functioning. Problem familiarity seems to be one mediator of these differences; unfamiliar, hypothetical issues tends to be more difficult for older samples than for younger ones. In contrast, as found in the Camp et al. (1989) and Pratt et al. (1993) studies, familiar everyday problems are apparently handled relatively equivalently across middle to later adulthood. As Mr Little's thinking illustrates, older adults' pragmatic social judgment in real-life situations, where they have had the time to understand and apply their knowledge, may be as complex as their younger counterparts, and their principles perhaps better tempered by experience (e.g., Murphy & Gilligan, 1980).

A number of factors have been suggested in this review of the literature which influence age differences in social problem-solving. The clearest findings are with regard to education level; in most studies, those with more formal education tended to perform somewhat better. Given that unselected older populations are routinely less educated than younger adults in our culture, this factor is clearly of pervasive importance in relation to variations in the quality of older adults' reasoning in our current cultural context. The results of the Dolen and Bearison (1982) study suggest that wider levels of social experience might be of importance in facilitating elders' social problem-solving as well. Finally, some evidence for the role of a cognitive-style factor (authoritarianism) in mediating age differences was identified in the Pratt et al. (1993) research on conceptions of parent–child interactions and problems.

It is also noteworthy that these findings are based on objective ratings of problem-solving and decision-making performance by others. When people are asked to report their *own* assessments of their problem-solving skills, older adults seem to be quite clear that their skill levels in practical decision-making (in contrast to more academic intellectual abilities) have increased in later life (Cornelius et al., 1989; Williams et al., 1983). As discussed below, there is a cultural belief in the presence of mature "wisdom" which produces some consensus in surveys of adults in various age groups (e.g., Holliday & Chandler, 1986; Taranto, 1989). To what extent these cultural stereotypes influence personal judgments of one's own competence is unclear as discussed in chapter 4 (see McFarland et al., 1992), but this result is important and deserves further investigation. In what specific ways do older adults feel their decision-making has improved, and why or how do they feel it has done so? Answers to these questions will most certainly involve the domain of social cognition, since older adults particularly focus on gains in social reasoning skills when describing positive changes in their thinking over the lifespan (Willis & Schaie, 1986).

A final question concerns training or other interventions that might have an impact on the quality of such social reasoning in later adulthood. Christoph and Li (1985) have shown that older participants can be trained to perform better on the Means–End Problem-Solving task of Spivack et al. (1976), mentioned above, but this performance gain seemed to have little impact on other measures of functioning in their study. Generalization of training is a crucial issue for any intervention study. As noted, models such as Denney's (1989) suggest that such training may be more difficult with older populations. Given the importance of these issues of later adult potential for growth, more extensive life span research on this question is badly needed.

Research and theory on wisdom

Science tells us what we can know, but what we can know is little, and if we forget how much we cannot know we become insensitive to many things of very great importance ... Uncertainty, in the presence of vivid hopes and fears, is painful, but must be endured if we wish to live without the support of comforting fairy tales. It is not good either to forget the questions that philosophy asks, or to persuade ourselves that we have found indubitable answers to them. To teach how to live without certainty, and yet without being paralysed by hesitation, is perhaps the chief thing that philosophy, in our age, can still do for those who study it ... (Bertrand Russell, *A history of western philosophy*, 1945, p. xiv).

These maxims regarding "wise living" are from a prominent contemporary philosopher, whose life we will discuss in more detail later in the chapter. Wisdom, a topic with roots in ancient philosophical and religious traditions, is currently making a "psychological" comeback in contemporary lifespan development research. A book edited by Robert Sternberg (1990) is an excellent source for the most recent scientific research and theorizing about this venerable, but long-neglected, topic. Its contemporary relevance to lifespan developmental studies lies in the widespread cultural belief in its flowering in later life (e.g., Baltes, 1987).

Western philosophical traditions dating back to the Greeks stress notions of wisdom as involving a "deep" and integrative reflection on knowing, living, and on the self's role in the world. Socrates's injunction to "know thyself" meant to develop the unique powers of the human mind and to use this cognitive power to appropriately order and regulate the diverse components of the psyche (Robinson, 1990). Such understanding of the self (though in radically different terms) is at the root of Eastern wisdom as exemplified by Buddhism as well. The Buddha's last words to his followers reflect this inner- and self-directed search for wisdom: "Be lamps unto yourselves. Betake yourselves to no external refuge. Look not for refuge to anyone beside yourself. Hold fast to the Truth as to a lamp" (Ross, 1980).

The ancient Greeks' notion of wisdom as a "golden mean," a balance or harmony among the various elements of the human psyche, strikes a contemporary chord with respect to various modern conceptions of wisdom in lifespan research as well. Birren and Fisher (1990) noted that different contemporary conceptions of wisdom reflect emphases on one or more of three major dimensions of knowing and living, including cognitive, affective, and conative (action and motivation to act) elements. These authors view wisdom as a multidimensional concept that entails a balance of all three of these elements in harmony. However, various contemporary positions on wisdom and how to study it emphasize one or more of these elements more prominently.

One of the most influential contemporary perspectives on wisdom is that of Baltes and his colleagues (e.g., Baltes & Smith, 1990), mentioned earlier. Their approach emphasizes the cognitive aspects of wisdom, particularly its social cognitive foundations, and draws on a notion of "expertise" of particular interest to information-processing models of cognition. Wisdom is characterized as "expert knowledge involving good judgment and advice in the domain [of] fundamental pragmatics of life" (Baltes & Smith, 1990, p. 95). This approach has led to studies of adults across the lifespan planning or reviewing how important issues in the life course should be dealt with (e.g., family–career issues). "Think aloud" protocols are collected from participants, and then rated for various wisdom-related criteria (as is often done in other studies of expertise in specific problem domains such as chess, e.g., Ericsson & Simon, 1984). Older adults seem to do as well as younger groups on problems specific to their age group, but do not generally show greater expertise than younger adults in these problems (e.g., Smith & Baltes, 1990).

The somewhat exclusive focus on cognitive expertise in Baltes's research program has been criticized by others, however (e.g., Chandler & Holliday, 1990). Chandler points out that this emphasis on a unidimensional notion of domain-specific wisdom may be misguided (despite the scope of the domain "fundamental pragmatics of life"), given the implication of breadth of vision inherent in our everyday, and traditional, conceptions of wisdom:

> The contemporary woods, as everyone knows, are full of technical experts of narrowly specialized skill whom we would never suspect of being wise . . . Imagine your surprise when, upon reaching that Himalayan mountain or that damp cave where truly wise persons are purported to live, you are told that the particular expert on your particular problem in living happens to reside on the next mountain or in the next cave. The obvious reason that you would be taken aback is that wisdom, to the best of our memories, has nothing to do with narrow forms of specialized and restricted expertise and everything to do with a broader form of human understanding capable of cutting across unique particulars in order to arrive at some view that has the widest scope of possible application . . . (Chandler & Holliday, 1990, pp. 133–134).

Chandler's own approach to the wisdom issue draws heavily on research in the psychometric tradition carried out with Holliday (Holliday & Chandler, 1986) which focused on everyday conceptions of what it means to be a "wise" person. Adult raters of all ages tended to agree in this research, apparently reflecting a culturally defined prototype of wisdom. Most importantly, this cultural prototype was seen to be multidimensional in nature, including aspects of both cognitive expertise, social, and affective skills, and "exceptional understanding," for example, seeing issues in a larger context, rather than simply emphasizing expertise in any one domain.

A third contemporary group of researchers on the topic of wisdom draws heavily on the Piagetian tradition of stage theory. However, these scholars emphasize the need to extend Piaget's conception of formal operations as the highest level of adult reasoning, to discover new adult "post-formal" stages (e.g., Arlin, 1990; Kramer, 1990; Labouvie-Vief, 1990). In general, these authors see development beyond adolescence (and its hallmark skills of logical manipulation) to be the attainment of a more integrated perspective in maturity, which combines the use of these abstract reasoning skills with an understanding of the "inner," affective, and subjective self that utilizes them (Labouvie-Vief, 1990). These ideas of individual development as integrating cognitive/objective and affective/subjective modes of knowing have been studied by examining stages in how individuals conceptualize and talk about their own emotional states (e.g., Labouvie-Vief et al., 1989), and studies of how stages in a more interactive and dialectical view of social processes and events develop over adulthood (e.g., Kramer & Woodruff, 1986). There is, so far, only mixed indication that these developments in "wisdom" are directly linked with age in adulthood, however.

Birren and Fisher (1990) summarize these and other perspectives on wisdom research in their integrative chapter, and note the tendency for some approaches to emphasize one or another among the cognitive, affective, and volitional dimensions they stress. Their own preference is to emphasize a sort of "golden mean" notion of balance among all three of these elements in approaching the field of contemporary wisdom research.

A wise person has learned to balance the opposing valences of the three aspects of behavior: cognition, affect, and volition. A wise person weighs the knowns and unknowns, resists overwhelming emotion while maintaining interest, and carefully chooses when and where to take action (Birren & Fisher, 1990, pp. 331–332).

As noted above, this broad conception corresponds well with the traditional approaches of the Greek philosophers. But as Birren and Fisher (1990) note, this field is only now beginning to define itself and its subject matter, and tentativeness in all agendas should surely be the watchword at present.

Research derived from the three perspectives described above has tended to involve either expert analyses of protocols of thinking and problem-solving (e.g., Labouvie-Vief et al., 1989; Smith & Baltes, 1990) or semantic ratings of everyday language terms for "wisdom" by naive raters (e.g., Holliday & Chandler, 1986; Sternberg, 1985). In an effort to integrate these research approaches by investigating everyday conceptions of the *products* of wisdom, Roth, Pratt, Pancer, and Hunsberger (1990) asked groups of raters to read and judge sets of interviews of adults across the lifespan regarding personal moral dilemmas in their own lives on dimensions such "wise," "caring," "just" and "complex thinker." Raters agreed that older adults in these studies were less likely to be complex in their reasoning about these life problems, but they did not judge them to be less (or more) "wise" than other age groups. Examples of protocols from this study of two older adults, the first judged to be not so wise and the second as exemplifying wisdom, are provided below:

Can you tell me about a situation for you where you weren't sure about the right thing to do?

Right up the street there's people have their hedge right out on the sidewalk. And we walk up there a lot and we can't go double file, we have to go single file and the bushes catch in your hair, and I would like to call some department of the city and ask them to do something about it. But I just don't know whether to do that or not. They're neighbors, I don't know them, but they planted this hedge outside the fence and the rainy days, and any time, it's a nuisance and I don't know whether I should call the city or not. I haven't decided, but I think I will. I think people, good citizens, should think of that.

Do you consider this situation to be a moral problem?

No, I think of it as a citizenship problem (Mrs White, an 80-year-old).

Can you describe a situation where you weren't sure about the right thing to do?

I'm thinking of a case where somebody comes to me, not because I'm a [Roman Catholic] priest, but just somebody they know. A young girl is in pregnancy and she's not married and somehow or other she feels that this is a wrong thing, but she is simply explaining to me that they feel that the right thing to do is to terminate this pregnancy. Well, I believe that would not be right, but on the other hand I can see that their view of the situation is such that they believe that they are doing the right thing . . . I think the conflict for me is that I believe that it's morally wrong what they are counselling to themselves and that I would be participating in that to some extent, but on the other side [is] that they are acting in good faith . . . morality is a code of living that is not optional. But on the other hand, it is tempered by the way in which it is assimilated by a person's conscience and this person's conscience says to her that it is perfectly all right to go in some other direction . . . I think when somebody is contemplating an abortion, it is important that they have some kind of counselling as to what would happen to the woman. I think now I would certainly make an effort to get them to go to somebody who would look at it from the viewpoint of the woman herself and give her the options . . .

Do you consider this situation a moral problem?

You mean my action? My system of morality involves me in a rejection of free abortion . . . therefore I should make any effort to keep people from entering into something that is a moral fault from my point of view. And I would presume if they could hear the reasoning, it would be from their point of view, but they would still be free to take their choice (Father Stones, a 71-year-old priest; Roth et al., unpublished data).

As illustrated in Father Stones's protocol above, raters in the Roth et al. study found wisdom closely associated both with cognitive skill in seeing the broad implications of an issue, and with a sense of caring and respect for the perspectives of others and the self. As in the complex frameworks for understanding wisdom suggested above, this notion of a harmonious balance of knowledge, affect, and right action seemed important to raters' judgments. The results of these studies suggest that wisdom is more than simple complexity of problem analysis. Roth et al. (1990) in fact found that ratings of "complexity of thinking" were substantially correlated with objective indices of the complexity of discourse in the interview as measured by the Suedfeld and Tetlock index (Baker-Brown et al., 1992), but that wisdom ratings were not. Thus these results are consistent with the multidimensional picture presented in the other rating studies mentioned above. It would be interesting in future work to pursue the actual criteria that raters use to make their judgments of wisdom in this rating task. At any rate, the conception of "balanced" judgment suggested by Mr Little's recognition of principles within a personal context discussed at the beginning of the chapter also seems to capture something of this view of wisdom.

Moral reasoning and judgment across adulthood

Mr Little's personal dilemma about his daughter's schooling, with which we began this chapter, is first and foremost for him a *moral* conflict. Such decisions involve making judgments about the "rightness" or "wrongness" of courses of action in particular situations, in other words, the evaluation of actions and choices. Of course, actions can be evaluated on the basis of many types of standards (there's only one "right way" to volley well in tennis), but here we are concerned with evaluation on the basis of the implications for people's rights and welfare (e.g., Turiel, 1983).

Rest (1983) has proposed a model of moral thinking that places this topic squarely within a broader decision-making framework. He suggests that moral choice involves four components: gathering information (particularly about the consequences of a situation for all the actors involved), formulating an ideal moral course of action (based on analysis of one's perceived duties and obligations), weighing these ideal moral considerations against other considerations of importance (such as the non-moral needs of the self) to select a course of action, and finally, following through in a consistent fashion with the chosen plan. Rest (1983) notes that there are two major contemporary approaches to understanding the individual's reasoning regarding a moral ideal (the second component of his model): the cognitive–developmental theory of Kohlberg (e.g., 1981, 1984), and the social–normative approaches of social psychology (e.g., Schwartz, 1977).

Aging and moral development: the developmental evidence

Several different types of measure have been commonly used in the developmental tradition of Lawrence Kohlberg to study moral development. This review will first discuss measures of "production" (formulating one's own judgments about moral questions), then measures of preference (choosing among different standard judgments presented), and then measures of moral comprehension (understanding and remembering moral issues).

The most widely used index of moral reasoning production is Kohlberg's stage score, which is based on his six-stage developmental model. A number of studies have investigated age differences during adulthood in average scores on Kohlberg's Moral Judgment Interview (MJI) which includes sets of hypothetical moral dilemmas regarding issues of fairness and justice (see table 7.1).

Considerable evidence indicates that there is progressive development in average stage scores from childhood into middle adulthood (e.g., Kohlberg, 1984), thus supporting the developmental sequence postulates of the theory. Several of these studies have been longitudinal in nature, thereby demonstrating gains in the same individuals' reasoning over time (Colby et al., 1983; Walker, 1989). However, the Walker study did show that the *rate* of increase in moral reasoning over a two-year time period was considerably greater for youngsters than for middle-aged adults.

Cross-sectional research on older adult samples suggests relative *stability* in level of moral reasoning from mid- to later-life. Chap (1986) and White (1988), for example, using dilemmas drawn from or modeled on those of Kohlberg, observed no average differences in stage scores between midlife and older adult samples. However, White did report increasing differences by educational background across the latter part of the lifespan, with more educated older adults scoring higher, and less educated adults showing somewhat lower scores in later adulthood.

Pratt, Golding, and Hunter (1983) and Pratt, Golding, and Kerig (1987), controlling for education, also observed no overall average differences between middle and later adulthood groups on Kohlberg stage scores. However, the highest stages of reasoning were rare in these studies in younger adults (those in their early 20s), and became more common in middle and older adult samples. This seems compatible with Kohlberg's (1973) argument that life experiences in maturity are important in stimulating development to the highest stages in his sequence. In a recent study, Pratt, Diessner, Hunsberger, Pancer, and Savoy (1991) examined age differences between a mid-life (35 to 55) and an older (65 to 85) sample of adults, and also measured several predictor variables that might mediate individual differences in moral stage scores. Results revealed no age differences in average stage scores when education level was controlled. More sophisticated levels of perspective-taking were positively linked to moral stage level in this study, as was more recognition of changes with aging in the self (a psychological "age sense" variable originally studied by Shulik, 1979).

Pratt, Hunsberger, Pancer, and Roth (1992) recently reported on longitudinal age trends in an older adult sample, a study comparable to Walker's (1989) longitudinal research for childhood and middle-aged samples. This was a five-year follow-up study of 50 mature adults using the standard Kohlberg dilemmas. No significant longitudinal trends were found over this five-year time period, either for the middle-aged (35 to 55) or elderly (65 to 85) groups overall, with educational background controlled. However, those participants who perceived themselves to be lower in levels of social support from others showed significant declines in reasoning, whereas those who saw themselves as high in support showed modest, but non-significant, evidence of gains (see figure 7.2). Thus, this study seems consistent with the previous cross-sectional evidence on relative stability over time in moral reasoning into later adulthood overall, but suggests that social interaction and

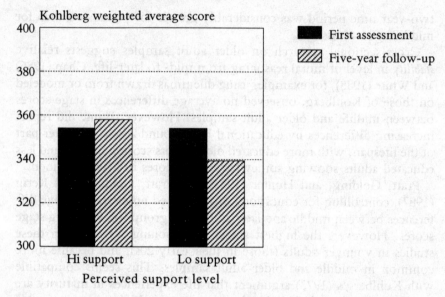

Figure 7.2 Average moral stage score by time and perceived social support level
Controlled for educational background

support may be critical in moderating these change processes in later life.

Kohlberg's stage scores have also been applied to the reasoning produced regarding real-life dilemmas in some recent studies. Several studies have shown that adults' scores from standard MJI dilemmas, and from real-life dilemmas reported by the same participants, were related (e.g., Pratt et al., 1991; Walker, deVries, & Trevethan, 1987). Recent cross-sectional studies using the Kohlberg stage scoring on real-life dilemmas provided by midlife and elderly adults show no average differences across these age groups with educational background controlled (Pratt, Diessner et al., 1987; Pratt, Diessner et al., 1991). An example of a personal moral problem recalled by a 73-year-old woman was:

> What happened was our daughter opened our home to a teenager who had run away from home and had been apprehended and was on probation. And so she just felt that if somebody had done that to her own daughter she would have been happy herself. And so what do you do? Our best intentions often fall short and yet this one little item in the whole process, you don't say, well it was a

useless thing for her to do. Perhaps this girl couldn't have been trusted and maybe you shouldn't even have allowed her into your home, but you can't think in those terms. You see the person and you're trying to be helpful and looking back, maybe when she's ten or fifteen years wiser she can look back and say "Well, all right, somebody did care." And so this is my thing that in all of these issues that caring people have to be there, regardless, and this is the sadness of our penal system because it just throws people into a situation which isn't helpful (Pratt, unpublished data, 1991, scored at Kohlberg stage three/four).

In the Pratt, Diessner et al. (1991) study, real-life moral stage level was positively related to perspective-taking levels, to educational background, and to greater "age sense," but not to rated health, life satisfaction, or social role engagement levels. In Pratt et al.'s (1992) longitudinal study of moral reasoning across mature adulthood, there was no significant evidence for change in Kohlberg stage scores for real-life dilemmas over a five-year period, though the patterns actually suggested some trend toward gains. Education level was a significant moderator of these trends, with those with higher education levels showing more evidence of gains than those with lower levels of education. Given current interests in reasoning and decision-making in everyday life, more work on real-life stage measures of moral judgment is needed (e.g., Krebs et al., 1991). Such work will also help to establish the relevance of Kohlberg's stages for studying people's actual moral reasoning, an issue of great importance to the theory (Walker et al., 1987).

Another type of measure of moral judgment within the Kohlberg paradigm is based on *preferences* for standard statements of moral reasoning framed at differing stage levels according to the theory. This index, the Defining Issues Test (DIT) developed by James Rest (1979), has been widely used as an objective assessment of moral reasoning, and is moderately positively related to Kohlberg's stage scores (Rest, 1983). Nevertheless, these two types of measure are clearly focused on somewhat distinct notions – patterns of preference for standard statements versus actual production of moral reasoning. The most commonly used measure from the DIT is the P score, an assessment of preference for the highest level, principled (Kohlberg stages five and six) statements in thinking about standard moral dilemmas.

A review of studies of age differences in later adulthood on the P score index revealed cross-sectional research only. These studies suggest few age differences across much of adulthood in average P score, with

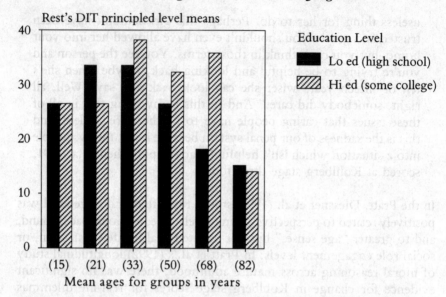

Figure 7.3   Moral judgment stage preference scores by age and educational background
Adapted from Pratt et al., 1988

educational effects removed (e.g., Lonky, Kaus, & Roodin, 1984; Pratt et al., 1983). However, lower preferences for principled moral reasoning may characterize those in later adulthood (specifically those over age 75; Pratt, Golding, Hunter, & Norris, 1988). These age differences appeared to vary with educational background as well. Those without a university education showed lower P scores in middle and late adulthood than did younger adults, whereas those with a university education showed no differences across adulthood until after age 75, when P scores were lower than those for younger groups (see figure 7.3).

The research of Lonky et al. (1984) was especially interesting in terms of factors mediating these moral preference scores in a mature sample (age 20 to 78). These authors showed that distinct patterns of coping with existential issues and personal losses characterized those who selected higher versus lower proportions of principled reasoning on the DIT. Those high on the P score from the DIT were also higher on use of "problem-focused," generally more adaptive, coping in dealing with losses, and on "openness to experience," a variable that measures the tendency to seek out challenges and to have a broad range of interests. While these correlational relations cannot tell us directly about causality, the pattern suggests the hypothesis that individual coping styles may shape the ways in which adult experiences affect moral development. Those with more adaptive, open styles may deal with stressful life problems (e.g., loss of a spouse) in ways that foster more growth in moral reasoning across adulthood.

The MJI and the DIT are the major assessment procedures used within the Kohlberg paradigm. However, a few alternative assessment measures have been investigated as well. Specifically, comprehension measures on the Kohlberg dilemmas (asking people to restate the issues in their own terms) have been explored in one study, revealing some differences across adulthood (Pratt, Golding, Hunter, & Norris, 1988). Older adults in this study were much more likely to reinterpret or reframe the dilemma issues, rather than simply to restate them (as did younger adults). Older adults typically viewed the dilemmas in more general terms. For example, a doctor's dilemma about whether to commit euthanasia was often viewed as a "societal" problem by older adults, concerning the way in which doctors' roles conflict with cultural norms regarding euthanasia. In contrast, younger groups typically described it as a "personal" dilemma for the specific characters involved. The oldest adults also showed less interest in being provided with more information regarding the specific details of dilemmas (Pratt, Golding, Hunter, & Norris, 1988).

These findings suggest a possible compensatory strategy by older adults to focus more on the larger issues represented by the particular problem exemplar, and to choose to avoid details which may be complex or difficult to process or remember. Thus, these results for moral comprehension in the adult years may indicate that moral issues are dealt with differently by older adults. Further investigation of this finding regarding moral comprehension and its implications for reasoning is needed. If older adults are actually representing moral dilemmas differently than younger adults, the outcomes of their deliberations may be influenced in ways not yet understood.

Another issue is the consistency, within the Kohlberg paradigm, between moral reasoning and actual behavior. There is some evidence from young adult studies that those using higher levels of moral reasoning tend to behave in ways more consistent with their principles than those reasoning at lower levels. For example, soldiers appealing to principled-level reasoning were reported to be more likely to resist demands for illegitimate behavior, such as participation in massacres of innocent civilians in the Vietnam conflict (Kohlberg & Candee, 1984). However, to date there has been no research reported on such reasoning-behavior consistency for older adults. To the extent that older adults might be less susceptible to some of the social pressures of earlier life that might lead younger persons to behave differently than they actually believe, it would clearly be of interest to examine this question across adulthood.

There has been considerable intervention research aimed at stimulating the development of moral reasoning in childhood and adolescence. For example, studies of school programs (e.g., Higgins et al., 1984) and of prison programs (e.g., Jennings, Kilkenny & Kohlberg, 1987) have been conducted within the Kohlberg framework. These studies have generally shown that opportunities for responsible perspective-taking in real-life moral situations, for example, in democratic school governance settings, have important beneficial effects on moral development through the Kohlberg stages (Higgins et al., 1984). Despite the interest in the general topic of the plasticity of cognitive functioning in later adulthood, however, there appears to have been no research on the role of interventions for moral reasoning in older adults.

Research on the Kohlberg measures described above has been criticized by Gilligan (1982) and others as representing a gender-biased approach to moral development. Because Kohlberg's stage sequence and measures were developed on a sample of men (and by male theorists primarily), Gilligan suggested that they might not appropriately capture how women think about issues of moral conflict. At least two major questions have been studied to date on this topic: a) is women's *level* of reasoning scored inappropriately as deficient by the Kohlberg system (e.g., Baumrind, 1986), and b) is women's moral reasoning different in its focus or *orientation* than men's?

The answer to the first question seems to be no. A number of studies using the current scoring systems have shown that women and men tend to score at equivalent levels, when education and occupational variables are controlled (e.g., Walker, 1984; Rest, 1983). The same pattern of no gender differences has generally been observed in studies with later-life populations (Chap, 1986; Pratt, Diessner et al., 1991). However, the answer to the second question is more complex and more interesting. Gilligan (1982) argued that women are more likely to think about moral issues in terms of "care," concerns about preserving and enhancing relationships and welfare (the dilemma presented on pp. 164–165 above is an illustration). Men, in contrast, are more likely to focus on "justice," concerns that revolve around the rights and principles governing social relationships. Gilligan's book was entitled *In a different voice*, and she suggested in it that Kohlberg's system is centered on justice, and thus fails to adequately "hear" the care voice so important to women's thinking.

What is the evidence on this second point? Several studies have documented that women in adulthood are more likely than men to frame real-life moral dilemmas in care terms, though the evidence for younger children and adolescents is not consistent (e.g., Gilligan & Atanucci, 1988; Pratt, Golding, Hunter, & Sampson, 1988; Pratt et al., 1990; Walker et al., 1987). In general, however, this sex difference does not extend to responding to Kohlberg's *standard* dilemmas (e.g., Walker et al., 1987). It appears in several studies that women are more likely than men to choose to discuss a real-life problem involving close personal relationships if asked for a moral dilemma (Pratt et al., 1990; Skoe & Diessner, in press; Walker et al., 1987). When this type of problem is chosen, care reasoning is more likely to be used by both sexes. Thus, women's greater use of care thinking is likely accounted for by their greater tendency to talk about this sort of personal relationship problem in discussions of real-life moral issues. Both men and women seem to have both "care" and "justice" orientations available, and both sexes draw on these different types when appropriate.

The fact that women turn to this type of thinking more than men in everyday life may well be of significance, however. Gilligan (1982) also suggested that such care thinking shows developmental patterns, just as the justice thinking studied by Kohlberg. Eva Skoe has developed a measure of stages of care reasoning, using several standard dilemmas of care, such as the following:

> Betty, in her late thirties, has been married to Erik for several years. They have two children, eight and ten years old. Throughout the marriage, Betty has been at home, looking after the house and children. For the last few years Betty has felt increasingly unhappy in the marriage relationship. She finds her husband demanding, self-centred and insensitive as well as uninterested in her needs and feelings. Betty has several times tried to communicate her unhappiness and frustration to her husband, but he continually ignores and rejects her attempts. Betty has become very attracted to another man, Steven, a single teacher. Recently, Steven has asked Betty for a more intimate, committed relationship.

> What do you think Betty should do? Why? (Skoe, 1993, p. 5).

At the lowest level in Skoe's hierarchy, the respondent is concerned with "survival," and focuses solely on the needs of the protagonist (in this case, Betty). At the second level, the person sees issues in traditional care terms, and argues for self-sacrifice and the need to preserve relationships at all costs. Only at the highest (level three) stage in Skoe's hierarchy, can the respondent consider both the needs of self and other in an integrated fashion, attempting to balance both.

These stage levels of care reasoning do not differ for males and females in Skoe's late adolescent and young adult groups (e.g., Skoe & Diessner, in press; Skoe & Marcia, 1991). However, identity development in women is much more strongly related to stage of care reasoning than it is in men (Skoe & Marcia, 1991). This finding suggests that care reasoning may play a more central, self-defining function in the lives of women.

What do we know about care reasoning in older adults? Curror, Skoe, and Pratt (1994) have documented some cross-sectional evidence that stages of care reasoning are significantly higher for women than men in mature adulthood. It is unclear whether this represents a developmental or a cohort effect, but if it is developmental, it may be that women's persistent tendency to utilize care thinking more often than men in adulthood eventually leads them to reason at higher levels in this hierarchy. A longitudinal study would be important to test this speculation. At any rate, the research has shown that care concerns are important in the reasoning of both women and men across the lifespan. It certainly validates Gilligan's (1982) attention to this moral "voice," if not always her claims of strong gender differences.

Moral norms in later adulthood: the evidence

There has been little work on age differences in adulthood in endorsement or application of the various social–normative models which play a role in moral contexts (Kahana, Midlarsky, & Kahana, 1987). It has been argued that the norm of altruism may be more widespread in later life, and there is one study regarding specific behaviors that is consistent with this (Midlarsky and Hannah, 1989). When the costs of donating were carefully equated between age groups, Midlarsky showed that older adults were more ready to show helpful donation behaviors to those in need than were younger groups. It thus seems possible that altruism as a norm (as well as a behavior) is more salient for older populations. Since this was a cross-sectional study, however, it seems just as likely that such differences are due to cohort factors. Perhaps those of earlier generations are more likely to feel altruistic in such potential helping situations than are more recent generations. Certainly, further research is needed on age differences in adherence to such social–moral norms.

The central issue of what norms are applicable and invoked in understanding personal problems may also vary across the generations. Karuza, Zevon, Gleason, Karuza, & Nash (1990) found that elderly adults (both in recipient and helping roles) were more likely than younger adults to prefer a "medical" orientation to coping with problems, which minimizes the responsibility of the individual for either the causes of a problem or its solution. Younger adults preferred a "moral" orientation, which emphasizes personal responsibility for both cause and solution. This suggests that there may be general age or cohort differences in how the norms involved in helping and coping are preferentially invoked, and that the experience of and reaction to helping relationships may be somewhat distinct across the generations.

One practical topic of relevance here is the issue of care-taking for dependent elderly persons. When older persons are perceived to be in need of assistance in their decision-making, ethical conflicts between the norms of "caring" and fairness in granting personal autonomy may be raised (e.g., Cicirelli, 1990). For example, an older adult's opportunity to exercise personal control and choice may be sacrificed because of concern about welfare, when others paternalistically take control of her decision-making without her consent or request. Cicirelli (1990, p. 460) found that adherence to a belief in paternalism (e.g., "It is all right for the adult child to force an elderly parent to agree to a financial arrangement that is for the older person's own good, even when the parent has decided against it") was primarily predicted by negative attitudes regarding older persons, both among elderly women themselves and among their adult daughters. Interestingly, elderly mothers were much more accepting of paternalistic statements than were their daughters, suggesting that generational factors in ideological traditionalism may play a large role in accounting for the acceptance of such norms.

Summary of research on moral judgment and aging

A brief summary of this evidence on aging and moral development may be helpful at this point. Evidence from the cognitive–developmental perspective, though largely cross-sectional to date, seems to indicate some consensus that the average stage level of moral reasoning shows stability across middle to later adulthood (in contrast to the evidence for progressive growth in earlier life). However, there are some tentative indications that older adults may be thinking about standard hypothetical dilemmas in a somewhat different fashion than are younger adults. Furthermore, a number of variables seem to predict differences in levels of moral judgment in later adulthood, notably including education level, social support and role-taking skills, as well as personality variables characterizing a psychological "openness" and "sensitivity" to change and novelty (Lonky et al., 1984; Pratt, Diessner et al., 1991). Finally, there is some indication that older adults may show greater adherence to a norm of altruistic helping. Given this evidence, there is certainly reason to believe that many older adults may have much to contribute in the area of ethical decision-making as advisors and guides to others.

Tracing the book's themes

Our first theme concerns the possibility of changes across adulthood and later life in personal orientations to the tasks of decision-making and moral judgment. The review of the literature showed that there is a distinction to be made between practical, real-life problem-solving and more "academic" tasks and problems. Older adults may show less evidence of decline or difficulty in their performance on everyday tasks. Most everyday life problems reported by adults are interpersonal in nature, and as people grow older they seem increasingly to invest their sense of personal competence in this "social" problem-solving domain (Willis & Schaie, 1986). Furthermore, the results of Pratt, Golding, Hunter, and Norris (1988) in the domain of moral judgment, and Sansone and Berg (1993) in real-life problem-solving, indicate that there may be age differences over adulthood in ways of interpreting and representing social problems and dilemmas, and that it will be crucial to understand these differences in studying age trends.

A second theme focuses on the role of individual differences and diversity in later life. Considerable evidence in both the social and moral realms of decision-making is consistent with the notion that some individuals maintain or even enhance their skills in these areas in later life. These individual differences can be predicted from certain experiential and personal factors. The pervasive relation of educational level with performance on most of these tasks suggests that educational attainment plays an important role across the adult lifespan. Some findings (Pratt, Golding, Hunter, and Norris, 1988; Pratt et al., 1992; White, 1988) suggest that education may influence the maintenance of reasoning skills on "formal" moral judgment tasks in later life, possibly through the effects of more extensive practice of these skills by elders with greater levels of education (Denney, 1989).

Not surprisingly, the ease of considering others' perspectives also seems to be positively related to social decision-making performance in older adults. This is consistent with findings for children and young adults as well (Walker, 1988). Given the apparent variations in perspective-taking skills with social experience in later adulthood that were discussed in chapter 4, this finding suggests that there may be many benefits to encouraging greater social contacts for older persons, who often tend to become isolated in our culture (Dolen & Bearison, 1982). Finally, a number of findings suggest that some important cognitive style variations in later life are predictors of higher levels of social reasoning skills, notably authoritarianism versus openness to experiences and aspects of change in the self. The parallel findings with such variables over a number of studies indicate that they deserve careful investigation, preferably in a longitudinal study which could follow their role in relation to changes in sociocognitive proficiencies over time. It would also be of great interest to study the personal and environmental factors influencing differences in such cognitive dispositions. Perhaps diversity of social experience might be one.

A third theme focuses directly on the role of social-contextual support for cognitive processes in later life. There has been some recent interest in both peer and parent – child dialogue and discussion processes in moral development in the earlier part of the lifespan (e.g., Berkowitz & Oser, 1985; Walker & Taylor, 1991), as well as research on peer collaboration effects on problem-solving performance (e.g., Azmitia, 1988). However, there has been little work on this issue in later life. The study of real-life dialogues around moral questions across the adult lifespan should be of considerable interest. Meacham and Emont (1989) have argued that social dialogue and context are critical in real-life problem-solving, but have been largely ignored to date in experimental studies of "problem-solving" in the laboratory. It seems quite reasonable that these contextual factors play an important role across the adult lifespan. Our findings that older adults who perceive themselves to have more extensive social supports are more likely to maintain their levels of moral reasoning over time are consistent with this point (Pratt et al., 1992).

A biographical illustration of some of these points may be provided by the long life and work of the great contemporary British philosopher, Bertrand Russell, cited earlier in the section on wisdom. Born into a rather eccentric family of the British nobility, Russell was reared by his very religious grandparents. He early began to have severe religious doubts, and became determined to be as skeptical as possible regarding the scope and limits of human knowledge. After enrolling in Trinity College at Cambridge, Russell was quickly recognized as an outstanding student with a great breadth of interests. His major early work in philosophy, done in his 30s, was a massive treatise with his former tutor, Alfred North Whitehead, *Principia Mathematica*, an attempt to derive all of mathematics from a small set of logical principles. This was followed by much influential work, in which he analyzed ordinary language usage down to its minimum philosophical implications.

Russell was always passionately interested in and committed to political issues and causes, and he was imprisoned as a pacifist during World War I, while in his 40s. Gradually, his political and social interests came to be more and more central in his work and writing as well, and his interest in analytic philosophy declined. He wrote a wide-ranging and influential history of philosophy in his early 70s, *A history of western philosophy*, in which he took pains to analyze the social and political influences on the thought of the great philosophers from the ancient Greeks onward. In his 80s and 90s (Russell lived to be 97), his writing and political actions demonstrated an extended and impressive commitment to nuclear disarmament. During the last years of his life, he published his three-volume *Autobiography*, a lively account of his life and work.

Russell's interests and his scholarship, though always wide-ranging, thus demonstrated a gradual transition in maturity from his early adulthood focus on mathematical and logical analysis to a much greater interest in the social and historical issues of philosophical and political life. In this, his development seems to mirror some of the transitions suggested above, including the sense of an increasing social focus and competence in the thinking and problem-solving of elders, and the growing interest among older adults in broad integrative themes rather than in detailed problem analysis. Whether he was wise, or moral, or made good personal decisions, surely depends on the vantage point from which his life and work are ultimately viewed. That he was one of the extraordinary persons of this century, there can be no doubt.

Understanding Mr Little and Father Stones

The moral dilemma of Mr Little, with which we began, and that of Father Stones, rated by others as particularly "wise" in his judgments, also provide some illustration of the central features of adult development as discussed in this chapter. Both men stressed the complexity of maintaining one's commitment to general principles or values, in the face of real-life circumstances which call for the tempering of those principles. The mature adult is increasingly faced with this contradiction between the general and the particular case, through experiences of commitment and responsibility (e.g., Kohlberg, 1973). Keeping both his daughter's needs *and* his personal principles in view creates a value tradeoff which makes for Mr Little's subtle, but complex views on his dilemma (e.g., Tetlock, 1986), but also makes mature adult advice and decision-making such a potentially valuable cultural resource.

Reliance on principles of justice, tempered by compassion and caring, as illustrated by Father Stones's advice about abortion, also looks like the "balanced" conception of wisdom that seems to appeal to many in this emerging field of study (Birren & Fisher, 1990). And some sort of integration of these principles of fairness and compassion seems to be an emerging ideal in moral reasoning development as well (e.g., Gilligan, 1982; Kohlberg, 1984). As Mr Little himself feels, this sort of integration depends on experience and maturity as a responsible adult, and it may become particularly evident in one's thinking about the social world, as many older adults seem to believe. Whether it continues to develop or be maintained into late adulthood is a matter for further study. But perhaps Mr Little should have the last word:

What does morality mean to you?

I think morality is a sort of standard by which one operates, a set of principles, I guess. And I don't necessarily mean those principles are obtained daily or anything like that. But they do change occasionally and they do evolve, and so on, while still remaining pretty stable over time (Pratt, unpublished data).

8

Communication:
Social Cognition in Action

Susan Black is an 84-year-old woman in a residential facility. She is somewhat disabled physically, but has a lively wit and a great interest in her surroundings. Mrs French, a matronly woman in her mid-50s, comes by to check on her. "Hi, sweetie! Let's eat all our yummy lunch!" Many of Susan's caretakers use a form of "baby talk" like this when addressing her. Like others of the staff, Mrs French feels that Susan is beginning to go downhill. She seems to talk less to staff members, and Susan herself is starting to feel that her communication skills may be poorer than they were. She is more and more hesitant to initiate conversations with the staff. As Susan stares at the television screen this afternoon, she wishes that there was somebody with whom she could have a rip-roaring discussion about her serious interest in politics.

Simplified speech directed toward young children is a well-known phenomenon in our culture (e.g., Snow, 1980). Such talk (sometimes termed "motherese") is clearly linked to children's limited comprehension skills and probably fills important language learning functions (e.g., Reich, 1986). Such simplified talk is used with pets (Warren-Leubecker & Bohannon, 1989), retarded adults (Pratt, Bumstead, & Raynes, 1976), and with elders too (Caporael, Lukaszewski, & Culbertson, 1983). However, these "elderspeak" simplifications (shorter and simpler sentences, more directive and controlling statements, "cute" intonation patterns) can be experienced as demeaning by elderly recipients, though they can convey warmth and caring as well (Caporael et al., 1983; Ryan, Giles, Bartolucci, & Henwood, 1986). Apparently, such speech patterns are associated with a stereotype of elderly language incompetence which can have an impact on social communication processes, and may be part of a complex set of views of the elderly person as less capable and child-like, both by those who address her, and perhaps by the elder herself (Rubin & Brown, 1975; Ryan et al., 1986).

To what extent are such language stereotypes about the elderly justified? Are they supported by evidence of declining language comprehension capacities in older adults? In this chapter, the evidence on the comprehension of various language structures by older adults is reviewed. This evidence bears directly on the topic of the appropriateness of special adaptations and simplifications by speakers to the elderly. Such adaptations are one way in which social cognition plays a role in regulating elders' communicative exchanges.

In addition to the question of language comprehension in later adulthood, the complementary issues of language production and social cognition are also considered. Do older adults show poorer skills in communicating fluently? Is their talk more difficult to understand than that of younger adults? To what extent are difficulties in social cognition responsible for any such age differences? For example, the elderly storyteller, repeating the same episodes for the umpteenth time to a listener, could be an example of a failure to monitor audience knowledge appropriately. On the other hand, a number of writers have argued that older adults may show especially good skills in narrating to listeners (e.g., Mergler & Goldstein, 1983). Certainly this view of the elder as narrative resource prevails in many non-literate cultures (e.g., Obler, 1989).

The present chapter begins with a brief overview of the issues of communication and social cognition and then discusses the general theoretical frameworks introduced earlier in relation to communication processes across the lifespan. Next, the research evidence on both language comprehension and production in later adulthood is summarized, and its implications are discussed.

Communication and social cognition

Communication is a supremely social and dialogical process. Even when one communicates *intra*personally, with oneself, as in verbal planning or thinking, the developmental roots of this process are social (Vygotsky, 1978). According to Vygotsky, verbal thought develops as the child appropriates the dialogic forms of conversation for use in telling herself what to do.

The links between communication and social cognition are multiple and complex; each influences the other dynamically. As noted, the proto-type of communication is the dialogue, in which two people alternately fill the roles of speaker and listener. Such roles are intimately dependent on social–cognitive skills. The speaker must consider the knowledge, background and attitude of the listener in shaping a "message" – con-sider the salesperson's differing "pitches" to different customers, for example. The listener must use his knowledge of the speaker and his social context to construct or "read" a meaning for the message ("Will that old clunker really be a great town car like this car salesman claims?"). And these intricate conversational processes typically extend over periods of time and changing interpretations of the situation and dialogue by both partners. Communication is truly social thinking in action.

Just as social interpretations play a central role in influencing commun-ication processes, so does communication influence social interpretation and perception in these ongoing interactions. For example, older adults' instructions on how to do a simple task may be viewed as less adequate than those of younger adults by listeners, even when the instructions are identical in content (Ryan & Laurie, 1990). And older speakers them-selves may be perceived as less competent in these situations. Appar-ently age-linked "stereotypes" about abilities are often shaped or elicited by communication factors such as speech rate, tone, and voice quality (Ryan, 1992).

Communication can certainly be viewed as describing both intra-personal "talk to oneself," as well as organizational and even cultural levels of interaction (e.g., the use of media such as television). However, the present review concentrates on the prototypic two-way speaker–listener conversation situation. It is also the case that communication processes can and do centrally involve non-verbal channels and symbols such as gesture (Ryan, 1992). However, the present chapter focuses on linguistic interchange. There is limited evidence to date on non-verbal communication in later adulthood, an important area for future work (Ryan, 1992).

Those who study language and its development over the lifespan typically begin by noting its rule-governed nature. Unlike the "speech" of parrots, human language systems are "generative," meaning that knowledge of rules provides the possibility of continuously producing and comprehending novel utterances which have never been encoun-tered before (Brown, 1973). Four major classes of language rules are important in both speaking and comprehending utterances (e.g., Reich, 1986). *Phonological rules* describe how the sounds of a language are pro-duced and assembled into words. *Semantic rules* deal with underlying meanings or concepts and how these are linked to the language symbols of words. *Syntactic rules*, or grammars, focus on the organization of words into complete sentences or utterances in orderly ways specified by the particular language (e.g., "See the dog" versus "Dog the see"). Finally, *pragmatic rules* specify how an utterance should be used or interpreted in the social context. For example, "Could you pass the milk?" looks like a question about one's abilities, but of course is really an indirect, polite request. The right answer in our culture to such a question requires recognizing this non-literal interpretation and acting on it, rather than responding to the literal form.

A key feature of language systems is their hierarchical nature. Everyday talk can be analyzed into smaller and smaller "chunks" or subparts – from conversations extended over long periods between individuals, to single "speeches" or "texts" by one person, to sentences which compose these texts, to words and phrases that are elements of the sentences, and finally to sound units or "phonemes" (Reich, 1986). Of course, such decomposition is an artificial analytic tool that allows the linguist to focus on particular aspects of the rule systems of language out of their natural contexts, and one must never lose sight of the place of these subsystems in the larger whole. The same sound, for example, can be heard differently depending on its context within the sentence or utterance (e.g., Warren & Warren, 1970). Nevertheless, this hierarchical property does provide a useful frame for reviewing the evidence on aging and linguistic communication, and so in the review that follows below, increasingly extended language features, from sounds to conversations, are discussed.

Theoretical frameworks

Conceptions of aging in the **psychometric** tradition have focused on the central distinction between "fluid" and "crystallized" abilities (e.g., Horn, 1982b). Fluid abilities in this conception represent capacities to process novel information, and are assumed to be relatively independent of previous experience. These types of ability exhibit marked declines as adults age (Horn, 1982a). In contrast, crystallized abilities represent the "residue" of earlier processing, in terms of specific skills dependent on the quality and quantity of past experience (Salthouse, 1987). These types of skill tend to be stable or to show increments into late adulthood. In general, the types of assessment of communication skills included in standard batteries of adult ability in the psychometric tradition tend to fall in the category of crystallized abilities, particularly the widely used measures of vocabulary knowledge. The focus on such evidence in the psychometric literature has contributed to the view in this tradition that language skills remain stable into the later adulthood years (in contrast to losses in other skills areas).

In the **information-processing** model, aging is typically viewed as accompanied by losses in various basic cognitive skills. Recent research suggests that short-term or "working" memory capacity, in particular, is important for aspects of extended language processing (Baddeley, Logie, Nimmo-Smith, & Brereton, 1985), and age decrements in such capacities are expected to have implications for communication processes (e.g., Kemper, 1988). An alternative formulation of this processing resource framework focuses on speed of mental operations. Older persons are found to carry out many cognitive tasks at a slower rate than younger individuals (e.g., Salthouse, 1991), and this too might predict more difficulties in language performance (e.g., Hunt, 1978). However, though both of these accounts seem to suggest increased difficulties in communication by older adults, there is considerable disagreement about how any such basic capacities enter into actual language performance (e.g., Light, 1991). Furthermore, it may well be that various compensatory processes operate to reduce the impact of such cognitive changes in later life. For example, older adults' greater familiarity with different speaking styles (Obler, 1989) may give them more flexibility in selecting appropriate conversational alternatives while using less conscious "effort."

In the Piagetian **developmental** tradition, research on communication has focused on the individual's capacity to consider the perspective or viewpoint of the partner (Piaget, 1926). Both speakers and listeners sometimes seem guilty of "egocentrism," which Piaget described in this context as the failure to take account of the other's communicative needs. For example, young listeners often behave as if they have understood what has been said to them, even if the message is deliberately ambiguous, and fail to give appropriate feedback to the speaker regarding their obvious uncertainty (Flavell, 1985; Pratt & Bates, 1982). As noted in chapter 4, there is substantial evidence that older adults may be more at risk for the problem of failing to consider the perspective of others, and one might expect that this sociocognitive "deficit" could manifest itself in communication difficulties (e.g., Rubin, 1974).

Kemper (1992) has recently reviewed the evidence on aging and language. She notes some suggestions that later-life language use follows patterns of regression that mirror (inversely) the acquisition of language skills by children. For example, Emery (1985) has claimed that "the data show an inverse relationship between the ontogenesis of complex linguistic forms and linguistic deterioration, i.e., the more complex, the later to develop, the earlier to deteriorate" (p. 34). Underlying such descriptions of language regression are models (such as Piaget's) that emphasize that cognitive development in large part determines language development (Kemper, 1992). Loss of higher levels of cognitive capacities in normal aging or in dementia is linked directly to language deterioration in these models (e.g., Emery, 1985).

In contrast, other models of the relation between language and cognition reject any such straightforward dependency between these domains. For example, Fodor (1982) argues that language is one of a set of mental "modules" that are quite independent of one another. In support of this "autonomous language" position, aphasic disorders, which represent language loss associated with various neurologically-based conditions (e.g., strokes, brain injuries), are often quite specific and do not involve impairment of cognitive capacities. Thus, to date there is little agreement about the general relation between language and cognitive development, leading to a variety of formulations of this issue in the study of development (Kemper, 1992).

The **social psychology** perspective has had the most impact on research regarding communication *to* older persons. It has been suggested that various cues of age (e.g., white hair, frailty) can evoke a "schema" or standard routine for conversation with older persons which includes some or all of the speech modifications discussed above (Ryan & Cole, 1990). Such communicative stereotyping by a speaker might lead to inappropriate "accommodation" to the presumed needs of the older person for louder or simpler speech. Such overaccommodation then may have a negative impact on the elder's own sense of skill, and, ultimately, on the older adult's actual cognitive capacities (e.g., Kemper, 1992).

The research evidence on language and aging

Phonology and language sounds

Mike's parents have a very close friend, Bill, from childhood, who has grown increasingly deaf over the last few years. Now in his early 80s, he is often reluctant to wear his hearing aid. Getting a phone call from him is a pretty challenging situation, and you can never really tell whether he has understood that he was supposed to meet you at the golf course at 9:00 a.m., until you get there and look around for him! These kinds of communication breakdown, as a regular occurrence, must make Bill's life more than a bit difficult. Nevertheless, he remains cheerful and positive in the face of it all, with a busy social life that sometimes involves some fairly confused friends.

The evidence regarding the comprehension of language sounds across adulthood generally suggests that healthy older adults do as well as younger groups on such tasks under optimum conditions (Emery, 1986). However, one serious issue in elderly populations concerns the role of sensory impairment, as suggested by Bill's example. Both hearing and visual impairment increase sharply in later adulthood. For example, about 40 percent of the non-institutionalized North American elderly over 75 years of age have a significant hearing loss (Slawinsky et al., 1993). Such sensory handicapping conditions can have a marked negative impact on communication. In contrast to Bill, many of these individuals may withdraw, and may be mistakenly viewed by others as "cognitively impaired" (Bayles & Kaszniak, 1987). As well, even individuals without "clinical" impairments tend to show some loss of auditory sensitivity (Corso, 1977). Speech that is rapid or distorted in any way (for example, by background noise) is more difficult for the elderly person to comprehend (Stine, Wingfield, & Poon, 1989). However, older adults seem to use their "top–down" or higher-level linguistic knowledge of what is to be expected in an ordinary conversational situation to help them interpret speech in many situations (Stine et al., 1989). Such higher-level expectancies may ameliorate potential impairments in older adults' speech perceptions in everyday speech contexts.

Listeners are able to distinguish speakers' ages reliably on the basis of voice quality alone (e.g., Ryan & Capadano, 1978). There are a number of physiological changes in the speech apparatus which accompany aging, as well as changes in rate and clarity of speech, which may be the basis for this identification (Ramig, 1986). Thus, the production of speech sounds in the elderly is somewhat distinctive, particularly for those in poor physiological condition (Ramig, 1986). However, there is little evidence that this seriously impairs a listener's comprehension of older adult speakers. On the other hand, there is considerable evidence that younger listeners judge those speakers with "older" voice characteristics to be less competent, probably because of stereotypic expectancies about aging (e.g., Ryan & Laurie, 1990).

Vocabulary and word use

Mike's mother, a school teacher all of her adult life, has always loved to do the "It Pays to Increase Your Word Power" pages in the *Reader's Digest*. Anyone who has worked on these knows that they are really quite challenging for the most part (we won't comment on the rest of the *Reader's Digest*'s social and political analysis). Into her late 70s, she could always give the rest of us a very good run for our money on these word power tests.

There is extensive evidence from psychometric testing regarding age differences in vocabulary knowledge in adulthood. In general, cross-sectional evidence suggests that vocabulary knowledge remains stable or even increases into later adulthood, particularly among those whose occupations encourage continued high levels of literary exposure, such as teachers like Mike's mother (Obler, 1989; Salthouse, 1987). Longitudinal evidence also indicates little loss of standard vocabulary knowledge, at least until very late adulthood (Schaie, 1983). These findings of little or no adult age decline in listening vocabulary competence suggest that there is little basis for vocabulary simplification when speaking to healthy older adults.

However, evidence on word production across adulthood shows somewhat more indication of problems among older speakers. For example, Bowles and Poon (1985) found that older adults had more trouble identifying a word (e.g., "unicorn") when given its definition than did younger adults. Tests of word fluency, measuring the number of instances of a category that can be retrieved over a relatively brief period of time, clearly show poorer performance in elderly persons (Salthouse, 1988). Of course, difficulties in word-finding are pronounced and characteristic in adults with clinical disorders such as Alzheimer's disease (Huff, 1988). However, these results suggest that some difficulties in word retrieval appear in healthy older adults as well. Interestingly, older adults report more problems than younger adults in word and name retrieval in everyday life (Burke & Harrold, 1988). "Tip-of-the-tongue" experiences, when the person feels that he or she knows the word but cannot retrieve it, were more likely to occur in the older group that these investigators studied, and were particularly more likely to involve common names for objects (e.g., "silo").

These word retrieval problems are usually temporary, and frequently are resolved without effort by the elderly, as the word simply "pops" into mind later on (Burke & Harrold, 1988). However, even temporary word retrieval problems are likely to create greater difficulties for the production of fluent and intelligible messages by older speakers. One aspect of accommodation to the listener relies on the selection of appropriate alternative descriptors of information, depending on listener knowledge ("that man" versus "my cousin George," Clark & Clark, 1977). To the extent that such alternatives are less quickly or reliably available to older speakers, they may have greater difficulty accommodating their discourse appropriately to the listener (e.g., Pratt, Boyes, Robins, & Manchester, 1989). For example, Pratt et al. found that older adults had greater difficulty retrieving the names of characters in a story when retelling it, and tended to produce rather complicated alternative labels (e.g., "the young lad that was steering" rather than "Ross"). These alternatives were frequently insufficiently distinctive, producing confusion for the listener as to which person was being described in the elder's story retelling.

Phrases – the example of reference

One phrase-level structure that has been studied in the elderly is anaphoric reference, the use of pronouns or other substitute terms to stand for a previous noun phrase. For instance, in the sentences "Ralph came to visit for a week. He went home yesterday," the pronoun "he" refers back to the noun "Ralph," and serves to tie the two sentences into a meaningful whole. Such "cohesive" phrases are termed anaphoric when they refer the reader or listener back to a preceding element in the discourse, and they play a crucial role in the organization of sentences into meaningful "texts" (Halliday & Hasan, 1976).

Cohen (1988) noted that older readers of texts more often attribute characteristics and actions to the wrong people. Such problems may indicate that the interpretation of referential phrases in these texts is more difficult for older adults. It appears that older readers and listeners find it more difficult than young adults to comprehend linking pronouns, but only when the pronoun and its preceding referent are widely separated by intervening sentences (Light & Albertson, 1988; Light & Capps, 1986). Presumably this is due to greater limitations in older adults' capacities to keep previous information actively in mind as they proceed through a text, perhaps due to greater processing resource limitations.

Similarly, Pratt et al. (1989) found that older adults *produced* more pronoun ambiguities or anomalies when retelling difficult stories than did young or middle-aged adults (e.g., "Bob and John came. Later *he* went home."). These data are illustrated in figure 8.1.

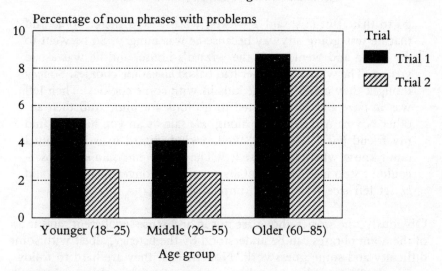

Percentage of noun phrases with problems

Figure 8.1   Age differences in referential error rates in two trials of story retellings
Older group significantly higher than both younger groups (ps < .05); adapted from Pratt et al., 1989

Here are two example stories told by older adults in that study, which illustrate some of the types of pronoun and referring problems which occurred:

> Two girls were visiting the zoo. And they met *the friends.* Mary and Susan met *Betty.* And one of them had a broken foot. So they had to go slowly so that *she* could keep up with *her.* And they decided to visit the lion's cage. And they met *the girl* [NB actually Betty!] that was the zookeeper, and she was just about ready to feed the lion. So they thought they'd watch. And Betty was the name of the girl that left the cage door open. And the lion, it was a mother lion, and she was a bit ferocious. And the lion got out. Two of the girls were able to run away, but Susan was a little slower on account of the cast on her foot, and she was left behind. So one of the girls came back and took her crutch and fended off the lion. And that was it, I guess (Pratt et al., unpublished data).

> Well, one day two boys went sailing. Their names were Jeff and Ross. It was a nice day and they decided to go out, and Ross was to do the steering. They found an island, and they said well they'd

go to that. But *they* said a wicked wizard lived there. So *he* said that he was going anyway because *he* was hungry. So he went to the island and went up to the wizard's house, and he was a bad wizard. The wizard's brother had baked *him* some cookies. So *they* thought they could take the kids in with some cookies. Then Jeff was in *there* and Ross wanted to go look for him. And then another boy named Bill came along. *He* said "Can you help me find my friend Jeff?" *He* said, "Well, a kind wizard lives here, but I don't know where his house is." They *the wizard* said *he* – Ross – couldn't stop his magic. But *my* magic is stronger than *yours*, and *he* set Jeff free (Pratt et al., unpublished data).

Obviously, the stories above are not in any sense incoherent, and most of the noun phrases can be understood by the listener, albeit with some difficulty and some guesswork. Nonetheless, they are hard to follow, and in the Pratt et al. study, the incidence of referential errors in retelling stories such as these was greater for those with smaller working memory capacities at all three age levels. Moreover, older adults had lower average scores on a standard working memory span task than did other adult groups, statistically accounting for their greater average level of referential problems.

Studies in the referential communication situation, a controlled laboratory task where a speaker must produce a description of a particular object so that the listener can pick it out from a set of similar objects, have also shown poorer quality descriptions by older adults (those in their 70s and 80s), compared to college students (Rubin, 1974). The problems of younger children in this task have frequently been attributed, at least partially, to failures to adequately consider the perspective of the listener (Flavell, 1985). Similarly, older adults in the referential task may have had more difficulty in keeping the listener's confusing alternative choices in mind when specifying the correct object. However, Pratt et al. (1989) found that elderly storytellers were as likely as other age groups to spontaneously correct their referential difficulties (e.g., "he – Ross" in the second story example above), suggesting that they were actively monitoring their quality of referencing from the listener's point of view, and not showing "egocentric" inabilities (cf. Zabrucky, Moore, & Schultz, 1987).

In a somewhat different type of analysis, Kemper, Kynette, and Norman (1992) showed that the overall use of anaphoric reference in stories told by older (70 to 89 year olds) adults was considerably lower than that of college students and of those in their 60s. This lower use of anaphora was correlated with smaller working memory spans in the older adults (Kemper et al., 1992). Several other types of cohesion (e.g., conjunction words that join two sentences together such as "but") were also less frequent in elderly storytelling (cf. Heller, Dobbs, & Rule, 1987).

Thus, some older adults may have more trouble with the management of such phrase-level organizing components in texts. Such problems can be expected to influence the quality of both comprehension and production in communicative interchanges to some degree. Parallel types of referring difficulties have been shown to be much more severe for those elderly diagnosed as exhibiting dementias (Bayles & Kaszniak, 1987). However, older adults with greater cognitive processing resources available do not seem to show evidence of such impairment, so there is apparently no reason to automatically expect such difficulties with older communication partners.

Sentence comprehension and production

The topics of sentence comprehension and production lead naturally to the domain of syntax or grammar, those language rules concerned with the organization of words into sentences. Studies focused on sentence comprehension have all been cross-sectional in nature to date. Feier and Gerstman (1980) studied sentence comprehension in young, middle-aged, and elderly adults, by asking individuals to enact complex sentences using objects provided to them (e.g., "The giraffe that bumped into the cow kicked the hippo"). Error rates were low and relatively comparable across the younger age groups (up to age 70). However, the oldest sample (those 74 to 80) made considerably more comprehension errors (cf. Emery, 1986). Those with lower immediate or working memory scores on a digit span measure did not perform as well on these tasks; nor did those with lower levels of education.

Similarly, research by Kemper (1986) shows that older adults (aged 70 to 89) have difficulty imitating sentences with long, embedded clauses, particularly those that begin sentences (e.g., "What I took out of the oven interested my grandchildren"). Dependent clauses require more maintenance and reorganization in working memory to grasp the overall sentence meaning when in initial rather than final position. The difficulties of some older adults in these tasks may in fact be brought about by diminished working memory resources. In support of this, Kemper (1988) in another study reported that an index of working memory capacity was correlated with these imitative skills in older adults. In this study, there was no evidence of impairment in processing such sentences for those in their 50s and 60s. However, those in their 70s, and particularly those in their 80s, had trouble imitating such sentences correctly.

Overall then, there is some evidence that older adults, particularly those over 75, show modest impairments in the comprehension of syntactically complex sentences. This may be directly linked to changes with age in working memory capacity. However, these impairments are most notable for constructions which are quite difficult and uncommon in everyday speech (Kemper, 1988). There is little indication that such problems significantly disrupt comprehension of everyday conversation. Indeed, older adults typically do not complain of comprehension problems in everyday language situations (Burke & Harrold, 1988), in contrast to their frequent concerns over word-finding difficulties. Thus, the present evidence probably provides little support for speakers engaging in syntactic simplification processes when addressing healthy elders, except under the most extreme circumstances, such as very complex or technical communications.

Work by Kemper (e.g., 1988) on sentence production has shown that older adults have greater difficulty than younger groups with sentences which contain complex clause structures. For example, understanding the sentence, "The tree the brown bird the cat chased climbed fell" involves maintaining and organizing in memory the connections between several noun phrases ("the brown bird") and their associated verb phrases ("climbed"). As the reader will likely note, these are difficult sentences to comprehend, because they require maintenance of several partially assembled clauses in memory as one reads from left to right to "parse" or divide the sentence appropriately for understanding. In one of Kemper's (1987) studies, diaries of life experiences kept by a number of adults over a period of 50 to 60 years were analyzed for longitudinal changes in the types of sentences used. Use of various complex clauses declined quite regularly after age 40, though sentence length itself did not. These changes in the syntax of written diary entries may result from increasing working memory limitations as people age, which selectively impair the production of difficult types of sentence constructions. Similar problems were linked to changes in working memory capacities over time in another longitudinal study (Kemper, Kynette, & Norman, 1992). Bromley (1991) has reported quite similar findings in a cross-sectional study of written self-descriptions by adults across the lifespan.

Thus, it seems that working memory limitations may play a role in the difficulties that older adults sometimes experience with complex sentence structures. Note, however, that these are best thought of as "performance" limitations in communication. There is no indication that older adults have relative difficulties in language "competence" at this level. For example, older adults can *recognize* ungrammatical sentences as well as younger adults if not overtaxed by memory or attention factors (Kemper et al., 1992). Thus, older adults' syntactic difficulties are not evidence of some "child-like" regression to lower levels of language knowledge. It is also important to recognize that constructions involving extremely difficult syntax are not commonly chosen for use by any age group in everyday language or writing. Current indications are that there is a small degree of impairment in sentence production in healthy, intact elders, which may be compensated for by use of alternative structures (Kemper et al., 1992). As well, there is no consistent evidence that dysfluencies or sentence fragments, which might be confusing for the listener, increase for older adults (Kemper, 1988). Finally, it is important to note that there is a great deal of variability in the extent to which these problems occur among healthy elders, as shown by the variations in this age group associated with processing resources such as working memory measures in several studies.

An intriguing, but neglected, issue concerns second language acquisition in later adulthood (Kemper, 1992). The age of immigration to the United States for Chinese- and Korean-speaking children and adults was strongly related to their eventual level of mastery of English grammatical forms (Johnson & Newport, 1989). Johnson and Newport examined a number of hypotheses to explain these patterns, and concluded that the most plausible was that there is a "critical period" in childhood for first language acquisition, based on neurological maturation, which influences the capacity for second language acquisition as well. This is a somewhat discouraging prospect for those of us still struggling with our pidgin German in midlife!

Certainly there are many other possible interpretations for these phenomena than a childhood critical period for language learning (Kemper, 1992). More research on the role and influence of social, cultural, and personal resources in second-language learning is certainly needed, though the most obvious of these factors were controlled in the Johnson and Newport study. One interesting question that has not been studied systematically to date concerns the extent to which such second language acquisition capacities may be affected in later maturity. Analyses of language learning in adulthood have not focused on possible differences among older versus younger adults, for example (Kemper, 1992). It may be that various cognitive and attentional changes in later life affect such second language learning processes, just as they appear to have a modest effect on first language competence.

Tran (1990) noted that many older Vietnamese immigrants do not have a good command of English, and wondered if they were "too old" to learn. This is an important practical issue for immigrant adult populations who must deal with the demands of a new society in a new language, and it deserves further careful study (Kemper, 1992). Certainly a lack of fluency in one's adopted language might have quite negative consequences for behavior from the perspective of speech accommodation theory (e.g., Wood & Ryan, 1991). Mike's wife's family is Korean, and the temptation to address less fluent family members in very minimal and simplified English is sometimes overwhelming (it may be appropriate as well at times, of course). Informal inquiries suggest that the self-image of older, less fluent immigrants may also be hindered by their perceptions of their difficulties in such conversations, leading perhaps to more avoidance and lessened opportunities for learning.

Narrative comprehension and production

When Mike was a youngster, the father of some neighbors across the street, a man in his 80s who lived with them, was a frequent visitor at Mike's house. His parents used to cringe sometimes when they saw "Gramps" coming, knowing they were in for a round of stories from his childhood, told for the umpteenth time, regardless of how busy they were with their own work. Gramps probably had trouble getting anyone at his house to listen any more! The world of the late nineteenth century which those stories evoked was fascinating to hear about, though they were a little repetitive after a while (however, as a child, Mike didn't have to be polite and stay to listen all the way through).

Narratives are one important type of larger, multisentence discourse form that play a central role in everyday life and thought (Bruner, 1986). Research on narrative skills across adulthood tends to support the common notion that this may be an area of considerable strength for older adults. Stories within Western cultures tend to follow a prototypic organizational format, with certain types of information appearing in standard sections of the story (e.g., setting, problem or complication, attempt, resolution). Considerable evidence indicates that a psychologically meaningful standard "schema" for story organization is learned by young children, and guides both the comprehension and telling of stories by older children and adults (Mandler, 1984; Peterson & McCabe, 1983). Expectations regarding this standard story structure are widely shared within the culture. A novel such as Faulkner's *The sound and the fury*, for example, which violates standard orientation sequences by beginning with a description of a golf game by a mentally-handicapped observer, can be difficult to follow (though interesting and attention-grabbing because of this). Such deviations from standard organization are generally signalled by the author, so that the listener can adjust expectations appropriately.

Many studies of adult age differences in the comprehension and recall of narratives have been completed in recent years, and in general, the evidence suggests that older adults recall somewhat fewer details of stories (Hultsch & Dixon, 1984). Older adults' recall, however, follows the same pattern of organization as does that of younger adults (Spilich, 1983), with more essential parts of the story recalled better than less essential details by all age groups. It should be noted, however, that elderly persons with severe patterns of memory deficit, show actual breakdowns in these typical patterns of recall (Cohen, 1988; Spilich, 1983).

More educated and verbally skilled older adults seem to perform relatively better in such narrative comprehension tasks than do their less educated or skilled counterparts (e.g., Hartley, 1988; Hultsch & Dixon, 1984). Meyer (1987) argues that more verbally skilled older adults can do as well in text recall as younger adults, if explicitly instructed to focus on the essential parts of the text (cf. Smith et al., 1983). However, when instructed to focus on details, older adults seem more likely than younger adults to lose the higher-level aspects of the message (Meyer, 1987). Meyer suggests that this is due to lower working memory capacity in older adults, which means that they must "sacrifice" either lower-level detail or higher-order material, relative to the recall of younger adults. Meyer and her colleagues (Meyer, Young, & Bartlett, 1989) have provided some evidence that adults across the lifespan can be trained by quite simple techniques to recall prose more effectively, however.

Some cognitive psychologists have speculated that older adults may spontaneously approach such tasks as the comprehension and recall of a narrative in different ways than do younger adults. Mergler and Goldstein (1983) argue that older adults, specialized for transmitting knowledge to younger generations, may be more likely to recode story information into more integrative cultural forms such as metaphor or morals, in order to retell it. Younger adults, more specialized for receiving and storing information, will utilize a more literal style of remembering and retelling (Mergler & Goldstein, 1983). Smith et al. (1983) found that older adults were more likely than were young adults to provide interest-catching "additions" in their recall of standard stories, particularly if they recalled them well. Adams and her colleagues (1990) report some support for this view in a study of elders and college students. They found that elders recalled standard stories in less literal forms than the college group. Similarly, Gould, Trevithick, and Dixon (1991) reported that older adults included more evaluative and interpretive comments than did young adults when asked to recall a story. If this is correct, then some part of the loss of detail in elderly story comprehension and recall may be accounted for by these age differences in the approach to the recall and retelling task, though Gould et al. found little support for this interpretation in their data.

Several recent studies have examined the use of narrative structures in story *production* by adults of different ages. Kemper, Rash, Kynette, and Norman (1990) found that older adults' personal narratives about their lives are judged to be of better quality than those of college students. As well, the narrative structures used by older adults (those in their 70s and 80s) in these stories were more complex. In fact, this complexity accounted for the higher ratings of quality for elders (Kemper et al., 1990).

Similarly, Pratt and Robins (1991) found that raters judged older adults' personal narratives to be more effective than those of college students (and non-significantly better than middle-aged adults' stories). In this study, older adults were found to tell narratives that followed a standard evaluative commentary on events more faithfully than younger tellers (termed "high-point" structure, Labov & Waletzsky, 1967). Labov and Waletzsky's pattern, shown in the following examples by a rising story line, building up to a high point, followed by a resolution, seems to make the story more engaging for a listener. The more positive ratings for elders' stories were explained by their more consistent use of such prototypic narrative structures.

Here are two examples of the stories told by older adults in the Pratt and Robins' (1991) study:

Last Sunday night I was out for dinner and I came home and had a phone call. I was asked to look up something in the paper, which I didn't have, so I went next door. As I stepped out of my unit door you would never guess what was right in front of me:

a snake on the carpet! Now I do get quite excited when I see a snake. It was having a nap and we live in a security building, so things are still very much up in the air as to how that snake ever got there, and it's still quite a concern of mine! I go to bed each night with the door stuffed with a towel (Pratt & Robins, unpublished data, 1991).

I remember one summer at the cottage, I was walking on the beach with Nancy, my little granddaughter who was only about three at the time. She wasn't very big. And we had a very happy time, talking and walking and watching the sunset. Finally the sun sank into the water in all its glory and so I said, "Well come on Nancy, it's time to go back and get to bed." And Nancy kept pulling back and pulling back. She didn't want to come up to the cottage. And I said, "What's the matter, Nancy? What are you waiting for?" And she said, "Well, I'm just waiting to see the steam come up out of the lake." From where the sun had gone in, I guess. So I finally made her understand the sun was a lot farther away than that and there would be no steam. And then she came up to the cottage and happily went to bed (Pratt and Robins, unpublished data).

Thus, in several recent studies, older adults have been found to utilize the larger "macrostructures" of the narrative style in more effective ways than younger adults. In addition, in the Kemper et al. (1990) study, greater use of such complex story structures was accompanied by lesser use of complex lower level grammatical structures (such as subordinate clauses and anaphora) as discussed above for older adults. This suggests that older adults may trade off their resources by investing in higher-order complexity at the expense of complicated syntax at the clause or sentence level (Kemper et al., 1990). Regardless, these findings support the notion that narrative is an important area where older adults may continue to develop their language skills in complex ways (Mergler & Goldstein, 1983).

Interestingly, Mergler, Fanst, and Goldstein (1985) reported that older adults who read stories out loud were more successful in increasing listener recall of story content than were younger adults. Again, this suggests that elders may be especially skillful in this narrative genre. And finally, it looks as if the culture thinks this is so as well! In a recently completed study, Ryan, Kwong-See, Meneer, and Trovato (1992) found that people's general expectancies of language decline in

Figure 8.2 At the Old Spiders' Home; cartoon by Gary Larson, © Farside, 1987

later life were reversed for the specific item of "telling interesting stories," for which older adults were expected to do better than their younger counterparts.

Since all of these studies were cross-sectional in nature, it remains possible that cohort differences may account for these patterns. Perhaps storytelling practice and interest was simply higher in a generation raised without electronic media, for example. However, Kemper (1990) reports a similar age-related gain in narrative structural complexity in her longitudinal study of adults' written diaries (see figure 8.2). Thus, a developmental rather than a cohort interpretation of this finding may be appropriate.

In a series of interesting studies, Peter Suedfeld and his colleagues have studied the influence of a number of individual and situational factors on the complexity of written discourse over the lifespan (e.g., Porter & Suedfeld, 1981; Suedfeld & Piedrahita, 1984). These archival studies have focused on the personal correspondence of a number of public figures (e.g., novelists, politicians) in Western culture in the last centuries. In general, these time-series studies have shown that the conceptual or semantic "complexity" underlying such written discourse is relatively independent of age into late adulthood in these select samples. However, semantic complexity is strongly negatively related to both personal and sociocultural stressors (such as physical illness, economic stresses, or war).

Suedfeld and Piedrahita (1984) further showed that the phenomenon of "terminal drop" could be identified in the personal correspondence of the public figures they studied (e.g., Riegel & Riegel, 1972). Specifically, those individuals who would die within the next two to three years showed substantial declines in the complexity of their correspondence, independent of actual age. Some other recent research indicates that vocabulary loss on standard tests may be a particularly good predictor of imminent death (White & Cunningham, 1988). Generally, these findings suggest the importance of pursuing the impact of various health and social factors on individual differences in communicative competence and sophistication in later adulthood (cf. Ryan, 1992).

Overall, the results of this section indicate that the narrative resources of older adults may be a special form of strength that can serve to interrupt the negative accommodation cycle suggested above in analyses of communication to the elderly. Unfortunately, the emphasis on this traditionally valued cultural skill of oral storytelling may be declining as a whole in modern culture (Pratt & Robins, 1991), with the greater availability and emphasis on mass media in North American society.

Conversational comprehension and production

Much of everyday social communication involves conversational dialogues about everything from cabbages to kings. But there has been very little attention to how older persons participate in such interactions (Boden & Bielby, 1986). In one study, Kausler and Hakami (1983) found that older adults had more difficulty than younger adults in recalling the topics of conversations they had had a few minutes previously with an experimenter. However, older adults were as likely as younger groups to *recognize* when a topic had been previously discussed.

This seems quite important in terms of avoiding conversational problems such as repeating oneself tiresomely ("I guess I told you that story earlier?"). Mike's neighbor, Gramps, may have known that he had told his stories before, but just needed the conversational contact that they could provide.

Sociolinguistic studies of patterns of conversational rule-following have revealed a high level of sophistication in the social rules that people follow in organizing turn-taking, question and answer sequences, or interruptions (e.g., Reich, 1986). Boden and Bielby (1983) found that older persons were as skillful as younger adults in using the range of these pragmatic social rules in a "get-acquainted" session with a peer, and the conversational rule structures used by both age groups were generally parallel. However, the content of conversations was not (Boden & Bielby, 1983). The older group was much more likely to use shared past experiences (e.g., the First World War) as resources to establish some sense of "common identity," a central process in such encounters between strangers. Thus, far from being an example of dysfunctional "rambling," use of the past was an integral and effective part of the present conversational process in these elderly conversants.

Another question regarding pragmatic rules in conversation concerns appropriate, "polite" forms of address in everyday social encounters and conversations (Wood & Ryan, 1991). Calling someone by his or her first name, rather than last name or title, signals several things in conversational context. As Wood and Ryan argue, such choices can be understood as reflecting both a dimension of status, and a dimension of solidarity or intimacy. By addressing her charge as "Mrs Black," rather than as "Susan," our care-taker, Mrs French, would perhaps signal a sense of respect, but also convey a sense of distance. Elderly individuals in such dependency situations may be especially likely to be addressed in less respectful ways in intergenerational conversation. But we know little about how such usage "feels" to the older individuals involved (Wood & Ryan, 1991). Using brief standardized vignettes, Kennaley, Pratt, and Ryan (1994) have found that caretakers at residential facilities for the elderly judged patronizing speech by nurses to be disrespectful primarily when the resident in the vignette had made some efforts to resist patronization previously in the conversation. If the resident acquiesced to staff control, patronizing remarks by the nurse ("Now, now, dearie, I'm sure we'll feel better if we go") are not viewed as disrespectful. In contrast, the elders themselves felt that such remarks by the nurse were patronizing if the vignette resident had been acquiescent, but were quite appropriate if the resident had been resisting!

Clearly, staff and residents had very different perceptions of how these brief conversations should have unfolded. More research is needed to understand the basis of these differing perceptions. As well, these findings indicate that views of the pragmatics of these conversations are complex and dynamic, dependent on the interplay of both partners across the interaction.

A particularly interesting area of research on adult age differences in conversation is the topic of life reminiscence (e.g., Butler, 1963). Butler suggested that reminiscence about earlier life events could serve a positive function in achieving a sense of integrity in old age, following some of the ideas of Erikson (1950) about the importance of a coherent sense of self in later life. However, reviews of the research on this topic suggest that the frequency of such reminiscences in conversation with others is inconsistently related to elderly adults' life adjustment (e.g., David, 1990; Wong & Watt, 1991). Wong and Watt showed that certain types of reminiscence were associated with greater life satisfaction in older adults, particularly those they termed "integrative" and "instrumental." Recall of past plans and goal achievements and relating these to present difficulties was particularly associated with positive adaptation (the instrumental category) in their study. Other types of reminiscence were unrelated or even negatively related to life adaptation, notably "obsessive" descriptions of events associated with guilt over past behavior. Thus, the narrative phenomenon of reminiscence deserves further study to understand its complex role in later life. It might be particularly interesting to attempt to influence the occurrence of positive forms of reminiscence in conversational settings to test these effects more directly.

Gould & Dixon (1993) have recently reported that older adult couples organized the telling of "vacation stories" differently than did younger couples. The older couples showed a more extensive, and more balanced use of monologues by each partner in the course of retelling their vacations, with each person telling some of his or her "own" part of the story. In contrast, younger adults showed less of this extended turn-taking style. Overall, then, the small amount of research to date on conversation in later adulthood seems to indicate considerable sophistication in the organization of these social language structures by older adults. However, more comparative and longitudinal work is needed.

One finding which has been reported several times in the literature is that older adults tend to be more talkative than middle-aged populations in narrations, conversations and descriptions (e.g., Obler, 1980). In a recent study, Gold, Andres, Arbuckle, and Schwartzman (1988) examined the nature of such verbosity in an older adult group. They found consistent patterns of individual differences in the extent of talkativeness across several distinct linguistic tasks. It is sometimes argued that such "over-talking" by the elderly may be linked with loneliness and a lack of social contacts. This seemed true for Mike's neighbor, Gramps. This was not the case in the Gold et al. (1988) study overall, however, where it was observed that more talkative individuals reported more social contacts than did others.

Of course, we don't know what these contacts were like, and there was some indication that more loquacious elders were less concerned about their "social presentation" to others in the Gold et al. study. This finding sounds somewhat parallel to the Piagetian notions of "egocentrism," i.e., a failure to consider sufficiently the other's point of view. At any rate, it has been suggested also that declining social contacts and increasing isolation in later adulthood may negatively influence individuals' communication skills (Norris & Rubin, 1984). This is frequently reported in the specific case of elders with a sensory impairment such as a hearing loss (Bayles & Kaszniak, 1987). More systematic research on individual background factors, such as frequency and type of social contacts, relevant to adult conversational styles and skills is needed.

A summary of research on communication and aging

This review of the evidence regarding both language comprehension and production in later adulthood has examined these processes at increasingly extended and complex language levels, from sounds to conversations. In general, the evidence on comprehension indicates that older adults show increasing impairment in relation to the representation of the meaning of language structures as these become more extended and complex (Emery, 1985). While sound discrimination and word comprehension are not impaired in healthy elders, at least into late adulthood, sentence and discourse comprehension seem more likely to be disrupted, or at least somewhat taxed. This is particularly true for the over-75 population.

The most plausible explanation of these problems is the limitations imposed by working memory resource losses among older adults (Cohen, 1988; Kemper, 1992). Nevertheless, there are many results which do not fit this model (e.g., Hartley, 1988), and more detailed study of how working memory processes enter into language comprehension at these various levels is needed. Furthermore, there is no indication that the processes involved in language comprehension themselves operate differently in non-dementing older adults (Cohen, 1988). These findings of comprehension problems seem to refer mainly to performance difficulties imposed by resource limitations in the use of language competence under demanding conditions, such as very complex or rapid speech. There is little systematic evidence to support the claims of Emery (1985) that older adults show some sort of "regression" to earlier linguistic levels (Kemper, 1992).

Despite the evidence that complex comprehension skills may be somewhat affected by memory resource limitations in older adults, there is also evidence that compensatory mechanisms operate to counteract these problems in everyday situations (Stine et al., 1989). Older persons do not report difficulties in speech comprehension for the most part, and there is generally little evidence that special semantic or syntactic adaptations (such as are used in "elderspeak") are necessary for communication with healthy older adults.

A range of experiential factors may be implicated in predicting language comprehension in older persons, including education level, and social and occupational experiences. Not surprisingly, for example, vocabulary is better retained by those whose experiences or preferences lead them to read more in adulthood (Salthouse, 1987). Of course, sensory impairment is an especially compelling problem for many older adults, though it has not been discussed here in detail.

When one turns to language production, the evidence is a bit different. Older adults seem to show more difficulties in the use of lower-level language structures (words, phrases), but are able to manage higher-level structures (narratives, conversations) as effectively as, if not better than, younger adults. Older persons report word-finding problems in everyday life more frequently than younger groups, and exhibit more difficulty in managing referential phrases in everyday discourse. Again, these problems are increasingly common in later old age, and appear in a more severe form in patterns of linguistic deficit in disorders of aging such as Alzheimer's disease (Bayles & Kazniak, 1987).

Research by Kemper (1988) and Pratt et al. (1989) shows that difficulties in these "lower-level" language processes in adulthood are associated with limitations in working memory capacity (cf. Cohen, 1988). However, both authors have also shown that elders can demonstrate better utilization of "top-level" discourse structures (narrative in particular) than younger adults. Work by Kemper et al. (1990) shows that older adults apparently compensate for the use of more sophisticated, high-level narrative structures by sacrificing complexity in the lower-level cohesion devices that they use. Thus, narrative skill may represent a domain of communicative "expertise" in later adulthood, as recognized in many traditional cultures (Mergler & Goldstein, 1983; Obler, 1989). One aspect of this narrative skill may be a more "engaging" adaptation to the listener's or reader's interests (e.g., Pratt & Robins, 1991). Just how this is achieved is not yet clear, but more extensive and sophisticated study of this skill, preferably using a longitudinal study, should contribute to contemporary theories of expertise and compensation in lifespan development (e.g., Rybash et al., 1986; Baltes, 1987; Backmann & Dixon, 1992).

An illustration of some of the features of lifespan language development is provided by the work of the influential turn-of-the-century novelist, Henry James. The progression of James's work is often regarded as epitomizing the transition to the modern "stream of consciousness" novel (Crews, 1957). His early novels, written while he was in his thirties, were "realist" in tone, with dense description of the lives and social mores of expatriate North Americans in Europe. Detailed character exposition serves as the focus of this early work, as James was never very interested in plot. By his late fifties and sixties, James's style and storytelling has become much more allegorical. The focus of these late novels, such as *The Wings of the dove* and *The golden bowl*, is on the wider society and the philosophical and moral issues raised within the context of the characters' lives. James uses different characters' conflicting perspectives to trace the working out of these broader themes. This "inner" focus made James's work a true forerunner of the writing of the twentieth century by Joyce and others. Thus, James's writing style showed an increasing emphasis on elaborate pattern and structuring as he grew older (Storr, 1988).

In these transitions in the course of James's work, one can see some of the features of lifespan language development suggested, particularly the movement from the early detailed and dense description of individuals' lives to the broader, allegorical, but structurally complex storytelling of the later period. Actually, an increasing focus on the wider philosophical implications of one's work in later life is not uncharacteristic of the writings of many artists and scholars, as we noted in chapter 4.

Tracing the book's themes

Recall that the first theme of the book concerns the role of lifespan differences in purposes and goals in generating differences in performance between age groups. Some of the work reviewed above suggests that this may be a factor, at least in some of the standard observations of communicative differences across adulthood. For example, older adults may use a less literal type of recall in retelling stories, being more interested in embellishing presentations at the expense of detail (Gould, Trevithick, & Dixon, 1991; Smith et al., 1983). Older adults may also use different social strategies in everyday communication situations (Ryan, 1992). For example, Norris and Rubin (1984) suggest that older persons' ideas of friendship may be somewhat different from those of younger persons, and thereby guide their communicative interactions with potential partners differentially. Elders may prefer similar others, and be less willing to engage with partners different from them, because they look for "lower cost" relationships to fill social needs due to their own diminished resources (Norris & Rubin, 1984). In general, more attention to this function question in research on age differences in communication and language use is needed.

Our second theme highlights the role of individual variability in age-linked differences in communication in later adulthood. Here there is much evidence pointing to the specific role of information-processing resource limitations in later adulthood (e.g., Cohen, 1988). In a number of the studies reviewed above, age differences in communication have been accounted for by changes in such memory measures, indicating that those elders with well-preserved working memory capacities function as well as younger individuals. Moreover, some evidence suggests that older adults may compensate for capacity declines by differential investment in other aspects of communication, where they may show special expertise (e.g., Kemper, 1990).

A number of more "distal" influences on the variability in communication skills in later adulthood have also been suggested, including differences in education level, health, and perhaps language history (see Ryan, 1992). More research on these variables is clearly needed. Of particular importance is the role of social expectancies in the communication situation, a variable that is linked to our third theme, the role of social support for cognition across the lifespan. As Ryan (1992) and others have shown, the social expectancies of interactants play a decisive role in the communication process. Older adults are sometimes expected to be less effective communicators by their partners, and this negative stereotype, if activated, may have an important effect on the elderly person's own performance expectations. Such expectancies can lead to a "negative spiral" of diminishing opportunities for communication practice on the part of the elder, and to overprotective and even patronizing behaviors on the part of the care-taker, as in the case of

Susan Black. The fact that such a negative cycle can occur suggests, however, that a positive feedback system of appropriate social support and stimulation may also be possible as a desirable alternative (Ryan, 1991).

Susan Black: the issues reconsidered

Returning to Susan Black, introduced at the beginning of the chapter, it is important to keep in mind each of our themes. As the second theme stresses, there is great individual variability, both in whether older persons need any sort of speech accommodation from others at all and in how older persons react to such communicative modifications addressed to them by others. Ryan and Cole (1990) report that a group of younger, more active community-dwelling elders were not pleased with accommodative, slower and simpler speech used by a younger care-taker. However, an older, institutionalized group of elders actually preferred speech by the care-taker which was slower and simpler. These results emphasize again the central theme that older persons are not a monolithic group, and that Susan Black's needs may be very different than those of her neighbour down the hall.

Consistent with our first theme, much more work is needed on the actual social perceptions of older persons in various communicative situations in order to address these very important issues, which have clear implications for practice (Ryan & Cole, 1990). If the staff were talking to Susan Black about these issues, rather than simply assuming their standard personas, they might have a better chance of finding out how she actually feels.

Finally, the role of social expectancies by communication partners in shaping the process of interaction is clearly illustrated by the conversation of Mrs French and Susan Black. But, as we noted above, self-fulfilling prophecies do not have to be negative. Maybe someone will still have that political chat with our Ms Black, and learn that it is worthwhile coming back for more.

9

Conclusions

I did my master's in Medieval Philosophy, but I didn't have money for a PhD and they were more interested in people with PhDs as lecturers in philosophy. So, I went to see the managing director of the Canadian National Institute for the Blind. He said, "Well, you have a lot of background, but you don't have any experience." The first thing they gave me was night shift, running a cafeteria. CNIB has always been in the business of industrial catering.

So, anyway the war was on then. They gave me the cafeteria in [a large appliance manufacturing plant]. They were turning out, not washing machines and dryers, but guns and marine equipment . . . [The factory] ran 24 hours a day, seven days a week. They had a huge staff. There I had a staff of 27 people. I didn't enjoy it at all. I found it very difficult to ask people to do things, especially in that muddle of people, where they would prefer to go stand in the washroom and smoke, instead of cleaning off the trays or getting the desserts ready or whatever it was. It was different from a university background where you are doing what others tell you.

. . . So then, through the years, I built the PR Department of [the organization I worked with before retirement]. When I left about a year and a half ago, I had a staff of six at the national level and the Ontario division had a staff of four and all the other divisions had public relations people. So, from a staff of myself and one secretary, I built this thing right across the company.

I really didn't want to retire. So, I thought, well, I have a fair number of contacts and I am a member of the PR society. So, I would open a business which I run out of the house . . . Now I have to sell my services along with all the other PR consultants in town. This is something new to learn, but I haven't struggled with it (Mr Patterson, a 67-year-old visually handicapped retired public relations director; Norris, unpublished data).

These comments are from an interview with Mr Patterson about his work history: what kinds of job had he been involved in? What had he enjoyed about each one and what had been problematic? What were the reasons behind any job changes? As we skip from his description of his earliest job to that of his later career in public relations, we can see remarkable changes. These changes reflect not just differences in job description, but attest to personal growth and insight on the part of this older worker. Of particular interest in view of this book's focus is that Mr Patterson revealed evidence of changing social understanding across his adult years. He reported that as a young adult, with a graduate degree in a rather esoteric specialty, he felt overwhelmed when required to supervise cafeteria staff. Later in the interview, he recalled his success as a mature adult in managing people as a public relations director. In addition, he mentioned that he welcomed new challenges to his "people skills" in his retirement years as he started a consulting business.

In this concluding chapter, we want to use Mr Patterson's comments and insights, and the issue of retirement which they dramatize, to summarize and consider both the research and policy implications of the work we have reviewed. We will first comment on the implications we see for future research in the social psychology of aging. Then we turn to policy and practice matters, focusing our discussion on the issues surrounding retirement, but raising general issues that extend beyond that specific topic for those who work with and for older adults in a variety of contexts. Finally, poised as we are on the cusp of the millenium as writers nearing the twenty-first century (thus establishing our own context), we cannot resist some speculative comments about what the future may bring for the social psychology of aging.

Implications for research

The book's themes

Three themes integrate the research reviewed in this book. The first is the need to understand and interpret social performance within a lifespan developmental and adaptational framework. We must realize that the goals, purposes and cognitive frameworks of older adults may be quite different from those of younger adults. This suggests that a social task will not have the same meaning, or solution, for someone currently 80 years old as it does for someone now 20 years old. Mr Patterson, for example, clearly felt that as a young adult he did not handle supervisory positions with comfort or skill. At the time of the interview, however, he cited many instances where he managed his staff, the bureaucracy, and the media with great ease and apparent skill. Thus, it should give us pause if we were to detect "poorer" performance from Mr Patterson relative to a younger man in a simulated management situation. Some weight must also be given to his own view of change in social skill.

Involving older adults as co-researchers rather than as "subjects" in studies of social cognition, requires researchers to exercise some perspective-taking of their own. The evidence from many studies discussed in this book suggests that older adults perform more competently when the task is relevant to themselves or to their age mates. Nevertheless, abstract, hypothetical tasks designed by young researchers continue to dominate the field. Some of these, most notably those focusing on decision-making, wisdom, and moral judgment, have used situations involving older targets. It would be interesting to see what procedural changes might be made by older adults if they were allowed to critique the tasks before completing them, or to create others which seemed more relevant. Indeed, in one of our own investigations we found suggestive evidence that older participants might have interpreted a standard moral problem-solving task differently than did their younger counterparts (Pratt, Golding, Hunter, & Norris, 1988; see chapter 7).

The small body of work on self-narratives holds promising possibilities, as well, if we are concerned about individuals' own appraisal of their abilities. The stories told by young and older adults are clearly different in their content. It remains to be explored whether they are different in their structure and complexity as well. Both Kemper (1992) and Pratt and Robins (1991) have found interesting age differences in the structure of self-narratives of adults (see chapter 8). In these studies, adults seem to preserve and even enhance their storytelling into later life on some dimensions.

Narratives provide an important, but neglected, qualitative mode for investigating people's own representations of their lives and experience (e.g., Bruner, 1986). If we can understand age or cohort differences in people's narratives about their lives, such qualitative modes could then be compared with, and perhaps integrated into, the more traditional tasks and quantitative methods for studying later-life social experience more commonly in use. More generally, we wish here to emphasize the importance of developing rigorous qualitative approaches to the study of aging and social psychology, particularly for the perspectives these can provide on the points of view of older persons themselves.

The second theme of this book is the importance of individual differences in social cognitive processes and social behavior as adults age. Researchers are still inclined to carry out cross-sectional studies comparing the performance of young and old adults, despite the fact that age, in an of itself, is not an explanatory variable. We have seen that such comparisons often lead to conclusions that the old are less capable than the young. Such simplistic contrasts ignore the large variability present in older populations on any characteristic. Thus, if Mr Patterson were part of a study on perceived control, for example, the researchers would be likely to conclude that, on average, he and his age mates felt less in control of their lives than did young or middle-aged adults. It is just as likely, however, that due to large within-group differences there would be some older respondents who felt much more personal control than any of the younger participants. One of these people would likely be Mr Patterson, a man who has triumphed over his visual handicap, achieved a graduate degree and experienced a successful career.

It is fairly simple for researchers to detect within-group as well as between-group variability when examining age differences in social performance or behavior. An example here might be variations in the pattern of social perspective-taking skills and their relation to empathic communication processes (see chapter 4). What remains more challenging is to explain such individual differences. Nevertheless, a lifespan developmental framework can be useful. This approach proposes that development occurs as the result of a strong interaction among three factors: biological, psychological, and social. We can see clearly, from Mr Patterson's narrative, the influence of each of these. His vision problems, present at birth, have provided a powerful biological influence on achievement. This influence is not independent of psychological factors such as personality or intelligence, however, nor of social factors such as formal and informal support. Mr Patterson's intellectual ability, tenaciousness, and support from his family and the Canadian National Institute for the Blind, have all led to the kind of success which might not have been possible if any one factor was missing. Although it makes their studies more complicated, researchers must consider the interaction of factors such as these in producing apparent "age" differences in social behavior and performance.

The third theme of this book involves the role of social-interactional factors in cognitive performance. Many researchers have accepted the view that competence is inherent within the person, and have de-emphasized the importance of the social context. This approach seems misguided when children are studied (e.g., Vygotsky, 1978), and problematic as well when older adults, with rich and varied life experiences, are concerned (e.g., Dixon, 1992). For example, the influence of both macro and micro social factors on social–cognitive performance can be seen clearly in Mr Patterson's self-narrative. On a macro level, the historical effects of the Great Depression and World War I are obvious when we consider his work history. Because of a poor economy, Mr Patterson was never able to complete his graduate education and become a university professor. Instead, he was thrown into the role of manager, a role made more likely because of a manufacturing boom brought about by the war. On a micro level, advice and support from friends, family and authority figures directed this man into a career he had never intended as a young adult. These social factors have influenced the self-concept and social–cognitive abilities that Mr Patterson has constructed and internalized over his lifespan.

The challenge for cognitive researchers is to determine the influence that mundane, as well as extraordinary, social events have upon social cognition. The use of everyday, relevant, tasks in laboratory settings seems to be a step in the right direction. Asking an older adult about a moral dilemma with which she, herself, struggled seems likely to elicit a different response than if a standard moral dilemma is presented (chapter 7). Such methods, as this, however, still do not address the broader context of social experience, including the influence of societal change, and how it becomes internalized over the years. An interesting question, for example, is how the many "possible selves" created by changing social and dispositional influences merge as a unified whole in later life (see chapter 3). Nothing short of process research, which explicitly conceptualizes competence and performance as "located" in a shared, wider environment, will do to examine this question (Dixon, 1992; Meacham & Emont, 1989). Of course, such research will broadly need to emphasize a longitudinal approach in helping us to understand the role of social context in the patterns of adult social development.

The theories

In chapter 3, we noted that researchers have not agreed on the cognitive processes involved in managing possible selves. In other chapters, we noted similar disagreement over the processes involved in other abilities such as competent communication, decision-making, and relationship formation. The major reason for such diversity of opinion appears to be the absence of any unifying theoretical framework when considering social cognition over the lifespan. Instead, four theoretical approaches have guided the selection of research questions and methods and the interpretation of findings. The **psychometric** approach stresses the importance of precisely defining and measuring social processes and variables. The **information-processing** approach encourages researchers to consider both cognitive structures (e.g., memory storage systems) and processes (e.g., retrieval of specific memories). The **developmental** approach focuses on the stages encountered by individuals as they attempt to make meaning out of their world. **Social–psychological** approaches have stressed the importance of understanding how a person perceives and thinks about the social world in understanding specific responses and behaviors.

As we have shown throughout the book, the phenomena on which each study has focused have had a powerful influence on the choice of theoretical framework to be employed. Some examples: a psychometric perspective has been used mostly by those looking at life satisfaction, an information-processing approach has influenced those interested in meta-memory, a developmental approach has been used primarily by those studying moral reasoning, and a social–psychological perspective has been employed by those examining self-efficacy and coping.

At this point in the study of social development in adulthood, it is impossible to select any one of these approaches as "best" or even most promising in a broad, programmatic sense. We appear to be in a pre-paradigmatic stage within adult social psychology, when many competing views vie for support. Researchers need to accumulate more information, both descriptive and explanatory, before larger connections can become clear. At this point, however, it is important for researchers to use *some* theoretical or conceptual framework to guide their hypotheses and interpretation. We must at least move beyond the *a*theoretical "stage" of research in this field. Otherwise, our understanding of the social processes and behaviors observed will be limited to description, and not even description of any particular value in the larger scientific enterprise. Who cares (in a research sense) if older adults attend church services more or less often than the young (chapter 6)? What is important for a social psychology of aging is the *meaning* of this behavior in the social and personal lives of older adults, and the network of factors in which this activity is embedded. We hope that the systematization of topics and approaches suggested throughout this book will be helpful in encouraging this process of theoretical growth. As we also point out below, some of the broad assumptions that characterize the lifespan developmental orientation described in chapter 2 seem to be well-suited to framing the issues and pursuing further theoretical specificity within this field.

Implications for policy and practice

Mr Patterson noted that he did not want to leave his job as public relations director when he reached the age for mandatory retirement within his organization. He stated that many retired people feel useless and abandoned and used the story of a neighbor who was soon to retire to illustrate his point:

> You know, this chap across here will be retiring next January. I was talking to him the night before last. He is saying already that people aren't paying any attention to him anymore. He says, "You know, they used to worry if you were ten minutes late. Now you can come in anytime and nobody knows whether I am there or not. The phone doesn't ring. I find myself taking extra long lunches. Nobody bothers. Already the tide has sort of turned. They are looking at my successor." And I have been told this story in the last little while by four competent fellows. They are all saying the same thing. It's unfortunate (Norris, unpublished data).

It *is* unfortunate for competent older workers that mandatory retirement policies still exist in some countries (Tindale, 1991). The research discussed in this book supports the view that the decision to retire should be voluntary. There is no research evidence that older workers, inevitably, become poorer workers, i.e., less intelligent, motivated, or competent (see chapter 6). Instead, there is considerable variability in performance among and within individuals at any point in the life span. It is true that mean differences between age groups on standardized measures of abilities like decision-making may show the old to be disadvantaged. Nevertheless, it is important to consider three issues related to the themes of this book before concluding that an older worker must be forcibly retired.

First, is the task given to an older worker the most appropriate, given individual experiences, employment history and motivation? Workers are typically reassigned to other jobs based on their supervisor's needs, rather than their own needs and aspirations. Perhaps a 60-year-old employee in an insurance firm, for example, would be better placed in a supervisory position where he could use accumulated social skills, rather than at a computer keyboard where rapid reaction time may be the criterion of job success. More broadly, our first theme stresses that decision-making, service provision and all the associated issues of social policy regarding older adults would be markedly enhanced and well-served by our paying more, and more explicit, attention to the views of older adults *themselves*. As recipients or "beneficiaries" of these social policies or services, they can contribute a unique and critical perspective: their own. As central stakeholders in this decision process, they deserve no less (e.g., Pancer & Westhues, 1989).

Second, have individual differences among workers been acknow-ledged? While it is true, for example, that some workers may experience decline in their abilities, many others do not. Still others have learned to compensate for losses through the acquisition of expert knowledge and strategies (e.g., Dixon, 1992). For example, suppose a public relations director such as Mr Patterson were to experience some decline in the ability to process both spoken and written communication quickly and efficiently. It is likely that because of his extensive experience in hearing and reading similar information throughout his career, there will be no obvious change in his ability to function on the job. Indeed, because of acquired expertise, his analysis of information, in any form, may be quicker and more accurate in later life. More generally, policies and service delivery at all levels must be appropriate to the individual person, and his or her unique qualities and contexts. Discriminatory practices based on superficial charateristics such as age can have no place in a just and caring society, and they clearly are offered no support by our analysis of the literature on adult social development.

Third, the social context of work must also be considered. Does an older female worker, for example, appear lacking in the assertiveness which management requires in its sales people? This may not mean that this employee has lost the drive to produce and succeed. Instead, both birth cohort and gender-role socialization may be interacting to produce a less aggressive style than that of younger men in the same department. This does not necessarily mean that her job performance will be poor, but rather that her style is different. More broadly, the research evidence we have reviewed has pointed repeatedly to the critical role played by social context and social–interactional opportunities in the maintenance (and perhaps in some cases, enhancement) of functioning by the older individual. These findings are supported from a variety of perspectives, and likely operate through a range of mechanisms. But they clearly indicate the potential risks and hazards for society of any strategy, such as mandatory retirement, which artibrarily imposes diminished social and personal opportunities for the older individual and tends to weaken the chances for intergenerational communication.

Returning to Mr Patterson, one cannot fail to be impressed with his resourcefulness and continuing potential. Looking only at a worker's superficial qualities, whether these are chronological age, sex, physical ability, minority status, is clearly misleading when we wish to judge competence. As at all other points in a worker's career, employers must give careful thought to performance reviews based on reasonable performance indicators. The research discussed in this book suggests that these reviews should evaluate many areas of competency, be sensitive to the worker's understanding of changing abilities, needs, and goals, recognize his or her unique qualities and adaptations in the work setting, and consider carefully the social context of performance demands in these evaluations. To do any less risks wasting the valuable and unique resources that older persons may provide to our society as a whole.

Aging into the twenty-first century

Almost all of the research discussed in this book was carried out during the latter half of this century. Thus, it is important to remember that the results of these studies should be interpreted within that social and historical context. Will we see changes in the social functioning of older adults when we move into the twenty-first century?

Three major population factors may change the portrait of elderly people in our societies in the future. Each of these has the potential to alter the kind of research carried out and the results obtained. First, it is predicted that both the absolute numbers of older people in the population, and the proportion of old versus young individuals, will continue to increase until about the middle of the next century. This process of population aging is the logical result of declining fertility, a process that accompanies modernization. As infant mortality rates fall because of better nutrition, housing, and health care, families begin to have fewer children, confident that their children will live to maturity. Canada began this demographic transition (Novak, 1993) slightly behind the

USA. As the process nears completion, however, the effect of blended social and economic systems between the two countries will diminish the difference. When countries reach the point where 10 percent or more of their population are over age 60, they are considered "old" by United Nations standards. Thus, in 1980 15.7 percent of the USA and 12.8 percent of Canada's population were over age 60. By 2020 demographers project that the USA will show 22 percent and Canada will be very similar at around 23 percent (United Nations, 1984).

As well as an overall increase in the numbers of elderly people, we can expect to see more of the very old as we move into the next century. The number of women over the age of 90 in Canada, for example, tripled from 1966 to 1986, and the number of similarly aged men doubled. These increases have prompted some researchers to anticipate a population explosion among the oldest old (Stone & Frenken, 1988).

Such demographic change has important implications for psychologists who study older people. Through this book, we have underscored the wide individual variation that is possible in any group of older people. Does it make sense to look for uniform developmental patterns in individuals who vary in age by more than 40 years? Child developmentalists would consider such a suggestion outrageous. Even though adult aging has fewer developmental milestones, it seems just as ridiculous to propose that the old should be considered as a homogeneous group. In the next century, gerontologists will be expected to explore the differences among the old of various ages. There should be sufficient numbers within each age group to make this possible and necessary.

Such population aging will have implications for many of the phenomena discussed in this book. For example, the networks of relationships discussed in chapter 5 will be affected by these changes. Four- and five-generation families will become more common, all other things being equal, and this will certainly increase the potential (if not the reality) of intergenerational contact. Of course, the specific effects of these changes will depend on how families and the larger society utilize these potential new contacts for the very old and the young. As noted in the discussion of age-stereotyping processes in chapter 4, such contacts can result in a wide variety of outcomes, depending on how they are structured and interpreted by those who experience them.

A second interrelated factor, that of health, may also change the face of aging in the twenty-first century. Does the increasing presence of so many very old adults suggest a better functioning, healthier population? If so, the potential for the maintenance and further development of many of the social skills and abilities we have discussed should be increased. For example, the later-life declines in social participation that are observed in some areas strongly influenced by factors of health (e.g., formal religious services or community organizations, see chapter 6) might be further postponed until even later into the lifespan.

This is the implication of the "Compression of Morbidity" hypothesis proposed by Fries (1980). This researcher felt that longer years of life would be associated with better health, relative to previous cohorts, and a briefer period of chronic illness towards the end. Unfortunately, this optimistic prediction does not appear accurate. Because of recent health practices, many members of the youngest old may be healthier and better functioning than in the past (Atchley, 1991). However, more older people are also living longer with significant disability. This suggests that the young-old may be experiencing richer lives with more diverse and rewarding social experiences than in the past, whereas the old-old may be having difficulty maintaining rewarding social encounters. These very old people are likely to spend many of their last years in institutions. This increased number of less healthy old-old persons surely will have an impact in terms of caregiving demands on the family and the social system, as well.

This diversity in healthiness already makes it essential that researchers do not generalize their observations of the social abilities of older people beyond the age group represented in a given study. It also suggests that researchers should direct more effort towards improving the quality of life for the very old and frail. There is growing concern on the part of interest groups about forging "partnerships" (Tindale, 1993); thus, it is likely that older people will insist on being more active participants in this process than has been the case previously. There is nothing in any of the research discussed in this book to suggest that intact older people cannot make sound decisions about their own lives. Indeed, involving older people more in their own care might produce a very different pattern of aging – less emphasis on physical longevity and more concern with the quality of life.

A third factor which should influence how researchers study aging is the changing multicultural face of North America. In Canada, for example, 31 percent of the population reported in the 1991 census ethnic origins other than British or French (the founding European cultures of the country), an increase from the 25 percent figure obtained during the 1986 census (Renaud & Badets, 1993). Indeed in Canada's largest city, Toronto, more than 59 percent of the almost four million residents reported non-British or non-French origins in 1991, up from 45 percent in 1986. Many of these people come from large multigenerational communities of Italian, Portuguese, Greek, Polish, Chinese, South Asian, Filipino, black and Caribbean inhabitants within the city (Renaud & Badets, 1993).

It is difficult to predict patterns of North American immigration into the twenty-first century. Given the current economic and political climate in both the United States and Canada, the large waves of immigration experienced during the latter half of the twentieth century seem less likely for the moment. Nevertheless, it is also unlikely that either country will lose any of its ethnic diversity. Thus, it is very important for researchers looking for aging-related psychological change to do so within the cultural context. For example, as noted in chapter 5, there may be important variations in the ways in which transitional processes such as retirement are constructed in diverse cultural settings. Surprisingly, *less* attention has been paid recently to ethnic variation, according to a report on psychological research with black Americans (Graham, 1992). If researchers hope to make any claims for the generalizability of their findings, then samples composed largely of white, North American-born adults must be expanded to acknowledge and attempt to understand cultural variation. This is particularly important for researchers, such as ourselves, who are concerned with the impact of the social environment on social development in older adults.

A perspective on the social psychology of aging

Changes in the longevity, health and ethnic makeup of a country's people create challenges for researchers. One way to address some of these challenges is to work within a broad theoretical umbrella which acknowledges a variety of contribution to development at both the micro level (between- and within-individual differences) and the macro level (social–historical change). Such an approach also acknowledges that these factors interact, dialectically, such that some, more than others, may be better predictors of growth in a specific instance. Of all the theoretical frameworks discussed in this book, the lifespan developmental model seems best equipped to address such complexities of adult development (e.g., Baltes, 1987; Dixon, 1992). This model takes into account changing individuals within changing social and historical contexts.

In chapter 2, we discussed three of the central dimensions of such a lifespan perspective: multidirectionality of change, the contextualization of adult social developmental processes, and the potential for plasticity of functioning in later life. A brief review of these three dimensions in relation to findings from our empirical chapters provides considerable support for the value of a lifespan orientation in considering adult social development.

Evidence on the multidirectionality of change in later-life social development is certainly abundant in the preceding chapters. Older adults show patterns of both losses and stability in their social lives, and sometimes at least tantalizing evidence for gains as well. For example, though older adults were shown to perceive a declining "future self," compared to younger adults (see chapter 3), they apparently were able also to use a variety of coping skills to consolidate a more integrated and unitary overall sense of self than the young. In chapter 4, we noted that certain "fluid" social–cognitive skills, notably perspective-taking and aspects of social memory, seemed to indicate average declines in later life. However, many other, more "crystallized" aspects of social perception, such as person perception (chapter 4) or stages of moral reasoning or social problem-solving (see chapter 7) seemed to show little evidence of average losses into later adulthood.

In chapter 6 on societal reasoning and involvement, we showed that some average declines in levels of direct participation in later adulthood in religious, political and community involvement were likely to be offset by increasing engagement and personal involvement in faith and religious development, and paralleled by the maintenance of political interests. And similarly, in the domain of social communication skills reviewed in chapter 8, we found that whereas both sentence comprehension and production showed some evidence of declines in later life, these patterns did not seem to interfere with basic conversational processes. And there was even evidence of possible gains in the narrative skills of older adults (e.g., Kemper, 1992). Overall, then, our picture to date of the direction of later-life social development is complex and mixed. Consequently, it demands a complex model to deal with this multidirectionality.

There was also considerable evidence in our review in support of the need to foreground both macro and micro contexts as critical constituents of analyses of later-life social development. Evidence on self-narratives in chapter 3 suggested the role of generational, historical contexts (e.g., the Depression) in the kinds of life-stories and self-stories created by adults in different generations. Similarly, the different life experiences of women may shape somewhat different patterns of control beliefs (chapter 3) or different experiences of social transitions such as retirement (chapter 6) than those for men. A similar pattern of variability for those of different ethnic backgrounds will undoubtedly also be found, as this variable is studied more systematically (see, for example, variations in societal participation in chapter 6).

With regard to the micro-context of lives, we repeatedly found evidence that differences in the social interactional resources and support available to older individuals shaped the patterns of social aging observed, in areas as diverse as coping with relationship losses (chapter 5) and maintenance of social and moral reasoning skills into later adulthood (chapters 4 and 7). And it was also observed that the specific "task" context in which sociocognitive skills were displayed had a substantial effect on how readily they could be utilized. For example, in the areas of eyewitness memory, and of generational stereotyping, individuals seemed to be less prone to errors and biases when considering their same-age peers rather than those from other generations (see chapter 4). All in all, the critical role of context at several levels in understanding the social lives and skills of older adults seems well supported.

Systematic evidence on the capacity for social developmental change in later life is not so readily available. The most convincing evidence for the capacity for such change is response to training interventions (e.g., work on the "testing of limits" by Baltes & Kleigl, 1992), but few studies on social processes in later life have been conducted to date. However, where training interventions have been carried out, there has generally been evidence for plasticity and for the potential for change. For example, older individuals have been found to benefit from training in social memory skills and from brief practice in perspective-taking (chapter 4). In most other areas considered, we do not have systematic evidence on people's potential to respond to deliberate interventions. However, there is considerable evidence that older adults manage to cope effectively with the undeniable losses and insults of aging to their younger selves, and to maintain a healthy sense of life satisfaction and of personal identity (chapter 3). As well, the capacity to compensate for major losses in one's relationships in later life, by seeking out new confidants or social relations, appears to be great for many older individuals, and they may bring, in some ways, more efficient skills to bear on the identification and development of relationships with compatible others (see chapter 5). And there is evidence too that older adults as a group are as likely to show change in political values as do younger individuals when political climates and issues show historical shifts (see chapter 6). All in all, the evidence, while still sketchy, is solidly in favour of considerable capacity for growth and change in many domains of later social and cognitive life.

Our sense, then, is that only such a complex lifespan-oriented framework can provide some guidance and coherence to the diversity of research and evidence on the social–psychological issues we have addressed in this book – topics as broad-ranging as moral development, communication, relationship development, identity and personality. It remains for researchers to continue to strive for this integration of perspectives, theories and evidence as we move into the next century, in order to construct a social psychology of aging which will help us both understand and support effectively the experiences of older adults into the future we all share.

References

Adams, C., Labouvie-Vief, G., Hobart, C. J., & Dorosz, M. (1990). Adult age group differences in story recall style. *Journal of Gerontology: Psychological Sciences, 45*, 17–27.

Adams, R. G., & Blieszner, R. (Eds.). (1989). *Older adult friendship*. Newbury Park, CA: Sage.

Adams-Price, C. (1992). Eyewitness memory and aging: Predictors of accuracy in recall and person recognition. *Psychology and Aging, 7*, 602–608.

Adelson, J. (1971). The political imagination of the young adolescent. *Daedalus, 100*, 1013–1050.

Advisory Committee for the Women and Aging Conferences for the Ethnocultural Communities in Metropolitan Toronto (1993, April). *Shared wisdom, common ground: Conferencing among senior women from ethnic and rural communities in Ontario*. Ottawa: Health and Welfare Canada.

Ainlay, S., Singleton, R., & Swigert, V. (1992). Aging and religious participation: Reconsidering the effects of health. *Journal for the Scientific Study of Religion, 31*, 175–188.

Aldwin, C. M. (1991). Does age affect the stress and coping process? Implications of age differences in perceived control. *Journal of Gerontology, 46*, 174–180.

Altemeyer, R. A. (1981). *Right-wing authoritarianism*. Winnipeg: University of Manitoba Press.

Altemeyer, R. A. (1988). *Enemies of freedom: Understanding right-wing authoritarianism*. San Francisco: Jossey-Bass.

Andersson, L., & Stevens, N. (1993). Associations between early experiences with parents and well-being in old age. *Journal of Gerontology, 48*, 109–116.

Antonucci, T., & Akiyama, H. (1987). Social networks in adult life and a preliminary examination of the convoy model. *Journal of Gerontology, 42*, 519–527.

Arenberg, D. (1988). Analysis and synthesis in problem solving and aging. In M. L. Howe & C. J. Brainerd (Eds.), *Cognitive development in adulthood: Progress in cognitive development research* (pp. 161–183). New York: Springer-Verlag.

Argyle, M., & Henderson, M. (1984). The rules of friendship. *Journal of Social and Personal Relationships, 1*, 211–237.

Arlin, P. K. (1975). Cognitive development in adulthood: A fifth stage? *Developmental Psychology, 11*, 602–606.

Arlin, P. K. (1989). The problem of the problem. In J. D. Sinnott (Ed.), *Everyday problem solving: Theory and applications* (pp. 229–237). New York: Praeger.

Arlin, P. K. (1990). Wisdom: The art of problem finding. In R. Sternberg (Ed.), *Wisdom: Its nature, origins, and development* (pp. 230–243). New York: Cambridge University Press.

Atchley, R. (1985). *Social forces and aging: An introduction to social gerontology.* Belmont, CA: Wadsworth.

Atchley, R. (1991). *Social forces and aging: An introduction to social gerontology.* (6th Ed.) Belmont, CA: Wadsworth.

Atkinson, R. C., & Shiffrin, R. M. (1968). Human memory: A proposed system and its control processes. In K. W. Spence & J. T. Spence (Eds.), *The psychology of learning and motivation: Advances in research and theory* (Vol. 2). New York: Academic Press.

Azmitia, M. (1988). Peer interaction and problem solving: When are two heads better than one? *Child Development, 59*, 87–96.

Backmann, L., & Dixon, R. (1992). Psychological compensation: A theoretical framework. *Psychological Bulletin, 112*, 259–283.

Baddeley, A. D., Logie, R., Nimmo-Smith, I., & Brereton, N. (1985). Components of fluent reading. *Journal of Memory and Language, 24*, 119–131.

Bahrick, H. P., Bahrick, P. O., & Wittlinger, R. P. (1975). Fifty years of memory for names and faces: A cross sectional approach. *Journal of Experimental Psychology: General, 104*, 54–75.

Baines, C., Evans, P., & Neysmith, S. (Eds.). (1991). *Women's caring: Feminist perspectives on social welfare.* Toronto: McClelland and Stewart.

Baker-Brown, G., Ballard, E., Bluck, S., deVries, B., Suedfeld, P., & Tetlock, P. (1992). The conceptual/integrative complexity scoring manual. In C. P. Smith (Ed.), *Motivation and personality: Handbook of thematic content analysis.* (pp. 401–418). Cambridge: Cambridge University Press.

Baldassare, M., Rosenfield, S., & Rook, K. (1984). The types of social relations predicting elderly well-being. *Research on Aging, 6*, 549–559.

Balinsky, B. (1941). An analysis of the mental factors of various age groups from nine to sixty. *Genetic Psychology Monographs, 23*, 191–234.

Baltes, P. B. (1987). Theoretical propositions of life-span developmental psychology: On the dynamics between growth and decline. *Developmental Psychology, 23*, 611–626.

Baltes, P. B., & Kleigl, R. (1992). Further testing of limits of cognitive plasticity: Negative age differences in a mnemonic skill are robust. *Developmental Psychology, 28*, 121–125.

Baltes, P. B., Reese, H. W., & Lipsett, L. P. (1980). Life-span development psychology. *Annual Review of Psychology, 31*, 65–100.

Baltes, P. B., & Smith, J. (1990). Toward a psychology of wisdom and its ontogenesis. In R. J. Sternberg (Ed.), *Wisdom: Its nature, origins, and development*. New York: Cambridge University Press.

Banaji, M., & Crowder, R. (1989). The bankruptcy of everyday memory. *American Psychologist, 44*, 1185–1193.

Banziger, G., & Drevenstedt, J. (1982). Achievement attributions by young and old judges as a function of perceived age of stimulus person. *Journal of Gerontology, 37*, 468–474.

Barenboim, C. (1981). The development of person perception in childhood and adolescence: From behavioral comparisons to psychological constructs to psychological comparisons. *Child Development, 52*, 129–144.

Barresi, C. (1987). Ethnic aging and the life course. In D. Gelfand and C. Barresi (Eds.), *Ethnic dimensions of aging*. New York: Springer.

Bartlett, J. C., & Fulton, A. (1991). Familiarity and face recognition: The factor of age. *Memory & Cognition, 19*, 229–238.

Basseches, M. (1986). Comments on social cognition in adulthood: A dialectical perspective. *Educational Gerontology, 12*, 327–334.

Baumrind, D. (1986). Sex differences in moral reasoning: Response to Walker's (1984) conclusion that there are none. *Child Development, 57*, 511–521.

Bayles, K. A., & Kaszniak, A. W. (1987). *Communication and cognition in normal aging and dementia*. Boston: Little, Brown, and Company.

Bellah, R., Madsen, R., Sullivan, W., Swidler, A., & Tipten, S. (1985). *Habits of the heart*. Berkeley, CA: University of California Press.

Bem, D. (1967). Self-perception: An alternative interpretation of cognitive dissonance phenomena. *Psychological Review, 74*, 183–200.

Bengtson, V. L., & Kuypers, J. A. (1971). Generational differences and the developmental stake. *Aging and Human Development, 2*, 249–260.

Bengtson, V. L., & Morgan, L. (1983). Ethnicity and aging: A comparison of three ethnic groups. In J. Sokolovsky (Ed.), *Growing old in different societies: Cross-cultural perspectives*. Belmont, CA: Wadsworth.

Bengtson, V. L., Reedy, M. N., & Gordon, C. (1985). Aging and self-conceptions: Personality processes and social contexts. In J. E. Birren & K. W. Schaie (Eds.), *Handbook of the psychology of aging*. New York: Van Nostrand Reinhold.

Benson, P., Donahue, M., & Erickson, J. (1993). The Faith Maturity Scale: Conceptualization, measurement, and empirical validation. *Research in the Social Scientific Study of Religion, 5*, 1–26.

Berg, C., Calderone, K., Strough, J. & Williams, J. (1993, March). *Everyday problem solving: Strategy use and revision across the life span*. Paper presented at the Society for Research in Child Development Meetings, New Orleans.

Bergeman, C. S., Plomin, R., Pedersen, N. L., McClearn, G. E., & Nesselroade, J. R. (1990). Genetic and environmental influences on social support: The Swedish Adoption/Twin Study of Aging. *Journal of Gerontology, 45*, 101–106.

Berger, R. M. & Rose, S. D. (1977). Interpersonal skill training with institutionalized elderly patients. *Journal of Gerontology, 32*, 346–353.

Berkowitz, M. W., & Oser, F. K. (1985). *Moral education: Theory and applications*. Hillsdale, NJ: Erlbaum.

Berry, J. & West, R. L. (1993). Cognitive self-efficacy in relation to personal mastery and goal setting across the life span. *International Journal of Behavioral Development, 16*, 351–379.

Betancourt, H. & Lopez, S. R. (1993). The study of culture, ethnicity, and race in American psychology. *American Psychologist, 48*, 629–637.

Bibby, R. (1987). *Fragmented gods: The poverty and potential of religion in Canada*. Toronto: Irwin.

Bibby, R. (1993). *Unknown gods: The ongoing story of religion in Canada*. Toronto: Stoddart.

Bielby, D. & Papalia, D. (1975). Moral development and perceptual role-taking: Their development and interrelationship across the lifespan. *International Journal of Aging and Human Development, 6*, 293–308.

Birren, J. E., & Fisher, L. (1990). The elements of wisdom: Overview and integration. In R. Sternberg (Ed.), *Wisdom: Its nature, origins, and development* (pp. 317–332). Cambridge: Cambridge University Press.

Blackwelder, D., & Passman, R. (1986). Grandmothers' and mothers' disciplining in three-generational families. *Journal of Personality and Social Psychology, 50*, 80–86.

Blanchard-Fields, F. (1986). Attributional processes in adult development. *Educational Gerontology, 12*, 291–300.

Blanchard-Fields, F. (1989). Post-formal reasoning in a socioemotional context. In M. L. Commons, J. D. Sinnott, F. A. Richards, & C. Armon (Eds.), *Adult development: Vol. 1. Comparisons and applications of developmental models* (pp. 73–93). New York: Praeger.

Blau, Z. (1981). *Aging in a changing society* (2nd ed.). New York: Franklin Watts.

Blieszner, R. (1989). Developmental processes of friendship. In R. G. Adams & R. Blieszner (Eds.), *Older adult friendship* (p. 126). Newbury Park, CA: Sage.

Boden, D., & Bielby, D. D. (1983). The past as resource: A conversational analysis of elderly talk. *Human Development, 26*, 308–319.

Boden, D., & Bielby, D. D. (1986). The way it was: Topical organization in elderly communication. *Language and Communication, 6*, 73–90.

Bossé, R., Aldwin, C., Levenson, M., & Ekerdt, D. (1987). Mental health differences among retirees and workers: Findings from the Normative Aging Study. *Psychology and Aging, 2*, 383–389.

Bossé, R., Aldwin, C., Levenson, M., & Workman-Daniels, K. (1990). Differences in social support among retirees and workers: Findings from the Normative Aging Study. *Psychology and Aging, 5*, 41–47.

Bowlby, J. (1973). *Attachment and loss. Vol. II. Separation, anxiety, and anger*. New York: Basic Books.

Bowles, N. L., & Poon, L. W. (1985). Aging and retrieval of words in semantic memory. *Journal of Gerontology, 40*, 71–77.

Brandstadter, J., Wentura, D., & Greve, W. (1993). Adaptive resources of the aging self: Outlines of an emergent perspective. *International Journal of Behavioral Development, 16*, 323–349.

Brewer, M. B., & Lui, L. (1984). Categorization of the elderly by the elderly. *Personality and Social Psychology Bulletin, 10*, 585–595.

Bromley, D. B. (1991). Written language production over adult life. *Psychology and Aging, 6*, 296–308.

Bronfenbrenner, U. (1979). *The ecology of human development*. Cambridge, MA: Harvard University Press.

Brown, A., & Ferrara, R. (1985). Diagnosing zones of proximal development. In J. Wertsch (Ed.), *Culture, communication, and cognition: Vygotskian perspectives* (pp. 273–305). Cambridge: Cambridge University Press.

Brown, R. W. (1973). *A first language: The early stages*. Cambridge, MA: Harvard University Press.

Brubaker, T., & Michael, C. (1987). Amish families in later life. In D. Gelfand and C. Barresi (Eds.), *Ethnic dimensions of aging*. New York: Springer.

Bruce, P., Coyne, A., & Botwinick, J. (1982). Adult age differences in meta-memory. *Journal of Gerontology, 37*, 354–357.

Bruce, V., & Young, A. (1986). Understanding face recognition. *British Journal of Psychology, 77*, 305–327.

Bruner, J. S. (1985). Vygotsky: A historical and conceptual perspective. In J. Wertsch (Ed.), *Culture, communication, and cognition: Vygotskian perspectives*. Cambridge: Cambridge University Press.

Bruner, J. S. (1986). *Actual minds; possible worlds*. Cambridge, MA: Harvard University Press.

Bulcroft, K., & O'Connor-Roden, M. (1986). Never too late. *Psychology Today*, 66–69.

Burke, D. M., & Harrold, R. M. (1988). Automatic and effortful semantic processes in old age: Experimental and naturalistic approaches. In L. L. Light & D. M. Burke (Eds.), *Language, memory, and aging* (pp. 100–116). Cambridge: Cambridge University Press.

Burt, C. (1937). *The backward child*. London: University of London Press.

Buss, D. (1989). Sex differences in human mate preferences: Evolutionary hypotheses tested in 37 cultures. *Behavioral and Brain Sciences, 12*, 1–14.

Butler, R. N. (1961). The life review: An interpretation of reminiscence in the aged. *Psychiatry, 26*, 65–76.

Butler, R. N. (1963). The facade of chronological age: An interpretative summary. *American Journal of Psychiatry, 119*, 721–728.

Butler, R. N. (1969). Age-ism: Another form of bigotry. *The Gerontologist, 9*, 243–246.

Butler, R. N., Lewis, M., & Sunderland, T. (1991). *Aging and mental health: Positive psychosocial and biomedical approaches* (4th ed.). New York: Merrill.

Calasanti, L. (1993). Bringing in diversity: Toward an inclusive theory of retirement. *Journal of Aging Studies, 7*, 133–150.

Camp, C. J., Doherty, K., Moody-Thomas, S., & Denney, N. W. (1989). Practical problem solving in adults: A comparison of problem types and scoring methods. In J. Sinnott (Ed.), *Everyday problem solving: Theory and applications* (pp. 211–228). New York: Praeger.

Campbell, A. (1981). *The sense of well-being in America: Recent patterns and trends.* New York: McGraw-Hill.

Campbell, J., & Strate, J. (1981). Are old people conservative? *The Gerontologist, 21*, 580–591.

Caporeal, L. R., Lukaszewski, M. P., & Culbertson, G. H. (1983). Secondary baby talk: Judgments by institutionalized elderly and their caregivers. *Journal of Personality and Social Psychology, 44*, 746–754.

Carr, E. G. & Duran, V. M. (1985). Reducing behavior problems through functional communication training. *Journal of Applied Behavior Analysis, 18*, 111–126.

Case, R. (1985). *Intellectual development: Birth to adulthood.* New York: Academic Press.

Case, R. (1992). *The mind's staircase: Exploring the conceptual underpinnings of children's thought and knowledge.* Hillsdale, NJ: Erlbaum.

Caspi, A., & Elder, G. H. (1986). Life satisfaction in old age: Linking social psychology and history. *Psychology and Aging, 1*, 18–26.

Caspi, A., Elder, G. H., & Bem, D. J. (1988). Moving away from the world: Life-course patterns of shy children. *Developmental Psychology, 24*, 824–831.

Cattell, R. B. (1963). Theory of fluid and crystallized intelligence: A critical experiment. *Journal of Educational Psychology, 54*, 1–22.

Cavanaugh, J. (1990). *Adult development and aging.* Belmont, CA: Wadsworth.

Cavanaugh & Green (1990). I believe, therefore I can: Self-efficacy beliefs in memory aging. In E. A. Lovelace (Ed.), *Aging and cognition: Mental processes, self awareness and interventions* (pp. 189–230). North-Holland: Elsevier Science Publishing Co.

Cerella, J. (1990). Aging and information processing rate. In J. E. Birren & K. W. Schaie (Eds.), *Handbook of the psychology of aging* (3rd ed., pp. 201–221). San Diego, CA: Academic Press.

Chandler, M. J. (1975). Relativism and the problem of epistemological loneliness. *Human Development, 18*, 171–180.

Chandler, M. J. (1987). The Othello effect: Essay on the emergence and eclipse of skeptical doubt. *Human Development, 30*, 137–159.

Chandler, M. J., & Holliday, S. G. (1990). Wisdom in a postapocalyptic age. In R. Sternberg (Ed.), *Wisdom: Its nature, origins, and development* (pp. 121–141). Cambridge: Cambridge University Press.

Chap, J. B. (1986). Moral judgment in middle and late adulthood: The effects of age-appropriate moral dilemmas and spontaneous role taking. *International Journal of Aging and Human Development, 22*, 161–171.

Charness, N. (1989). Age and expertise: Responding to Talland's challenge. In L. W. Poon, D. C. Rubin, & B. A. Wilson (Eds.), *Everyday cognition in adulthood and late life* (pp. 437–456). Cambridge: Cambridge University Press.

Chatters, L., Levin, J., & Taylor, R. J. (1992). Antecedents and dimensions of religious involvement among older Black Americans. *Journal of Gerontology: Social Sciences, 47,* S269–S278.

Chudacoff, H. P. (1989). *How old are you? Age consciousness in American culture.* Princeton, NJ: Princeton University Press.

Christoph, D., & Li, A. K. F. (1985). Cognitive versus social rigidity in old age: Implications for therapy. *Canadian Journal on Aging, 4,* 59–65.

Cicirelli, V. G. (1983). Adult children's attachment and helping behavior to elderly parents: A path model. *Journal of Marriage and the Family, 45,* 815–822.

Cicirelli, V. G. (1989). Feelings of attachment to siblings and well-being in later life. *Psychology and Aging, 4,* 211–16.

Cicirelli, V. G. (1990). Relationship of personal-social variables to belief in paternalism in parent caregiving situations. *Psychology and Aging, 5,* 458–466.

Cicirelli, V. G. (1991). Attachment theory in old age: Protection of the attached figure. In K. Pillemer & K. McCartney (Eds.), *Parent-child relations throughout life* (pp. 25–42). Hillsdale, NJ: Erlbaum.

Clark, H. H., & Clark, E. V. (1977). *Psychology and language: An introduction to psycholinguistics.* New York: Harcourt Brace Jovanovich.

Cohen, F., Bearison, D. J., & Muller, C. (1987). Interpersonal understanding in the elderly. *Research on Aging, 9,* 79–100.

Cohen, G. (1988). Age differences in memory for texts: Production deficiency or processing limitations. In L. L. Light & D. M. Burke (Eds.), *Language, memory, and aging* (pp. 171–190). Cambridge: Cambridge University Press.

Cohen, G. (1989). *Memory in the real world.* Hillsdale, NJ: Erlbaum.

Cohen, G., & Faulkner, D. (1986). Memory for proper names: Age differences in retrieval. *British Journal of Developmental Psychology, 4,* 187–197.

Cohen, G., & Faulkner, D. (1989). Age differences in source forgetting: Effects on reality monitoring and eyewitness testimony. *Psychology & Aging, 4,* 10–17.

Cohler, B. J. (1983). Autonomy and interdependence in the family of adulthood. *Gerontologist, 23,* 33–39.

Colby, A., & Kohlberg, L. (1987). *The measurement of moral judgment. Volume 1.* New York: Cambridge University Press.

Colby, A., Kohlberg, L., Gibbs, J., & Lieberman, M. (1983). A longitudinal study of moral development. *Monographs of the Society for Research in Child Development, 49,* (2, Serial No. 206).

Commons, M. L., Richards, F. A., & Armon, C. (1984). *Beyond formal operations: Late adolescent and adult cognitive development.* New York: Praeger.

Connidis, I. A. (1989). *Family ties and aging.* Toronto: Butterworths.

Cool, L. (1987). The effects of social class and ethnicity on the aging process. In P. Silverman (Ed.), *The elderly as modern pioneers.* Bloomington, IN: Indiana University Press.

Coppola, L. A. (1987). *Relocation and the Italian elderly: Transition from community to an institution.* Unpublished master's thesis, University of Guelph.

Cornelius, S. W., & Caspi, A. (1986). Self-perceptions of intellectual control and aging. *Educational Gerontology, 12*, 345–357.

Cornelius, S. W., & Caspi, A. (1987). Everyday problem solving in adulthood and old age. *Psychology and Aging, 2*, 144–153.

Cornelius, S. W., Kenney, S., & Caspi, A. (1989). Academic and everyday intelligence in adulthood: Conceptions of self and ability tests. In J. Sinnott (Ed.), *Everyday problem solving: Theory and applications* (pp. 191–210). New York: Academic Press.

Corso, J. (1977). Auditory perception and communication. In J. E. Birren & K. W. Schaie (Eds.), *Handbook of the psychology of aging* (1st ed., pp. 535–553). New York: Van Nostrand Reinhold.

Costa, P. T., Jr., & McCrae, R. R. (1977–78). Age differences in personality structure revisited: Studies in validity, stability, and change. *International Journal of Aging and Human Development, 8*, 261–275.

Costa, P. T., Jr., & McCrae, R. R. (1988). Personality in adulthood: A six-year longitudinal study of self-reports and spouse rating on the NEO Personality Inventory. *Journal of Personality & Social Psychology, 54*, 853–863.

Costa, P. T., Jr., McCrae, R. R., & Arenberg, D. (1980). Enduring dispositions in adult males. *Journal of Personality & Social Psychology, 38*, 793–800.

Coupland, D. (1991). *Generation X: Tales for an accelerated culture.* New York: St Martin's Press.

Courtenay, B., Poon, L., Martin, P., Clayton, G., & Johnson, M. (1992). Religiosity and adaptation in the oldest-old. *International Journal of Aging and Human Development, 34*, 47–56.

Cowan, C. P., & Cowan, P. A. (1992). *When partners become parents: The big life change for couples.* New York: Basic Books.

Cowan, P. (1978). *Piaget, with feeling: Cognitive, social, and emotional dimensions.* New York: Holt, Rhinehart & Winston.

Cowan, P. (1991). Individual and family life transitions: A proposal for a new definition. In P. Cowan & E. M. Hetherington (Eds.), *Advances in family research (Vol. 2).* Hillsdale, NJ: Erlbaum.

Cowgill, D., & Holmes, L. (1972). *Aging and modernization.* New York: Appleton-Century-Crofts.

Cox, H., & Hammonds, A. (1988). Religiosity, aging, and life satisfaction. *Journal of Religion and Aging, 5*, 1–21.

Craik, F. I. M., & Byrd, M. (1982). Aging and cognitive deficits: The role of attentional resources. In F. I. M. Craik & S. Trehub (Eds.), *Aging and cognitive process.* New York: Plenum.

Craik, F. I. M., & McDowd, J. M. (1987). Age differences in recall and re-cognition. *Journal of Experimental Psychology: Learning, Memory, and Cognition, 13*, 474–479.

Crews, F. (1957). *The tragedy of manners: Moral drama in the later novels of Henry James.* Hornden, CT: Archon Books.

Crockett, W. H., & Hummert, M. L. (1987). Perceptions of aging and the elderly. In K. W. Schaie (Ed.), *Annual review of gerontology and geriatrics* (Vol. 7, pp. 217–241). New York: Springer Publishing.

Cumming, E., & Henry, W. (1961). *Growing old: The process of disengagement.* New York: Basic Books.

Cunningham, W., & Tomer, A. (1990). Intellectual abilities and age: Concepts, theories and analyses. In E. A. Lovelace (Ed.), *Aging and cognition: Mental processes, self-awareness and interventions* (pp. 379–406). New York: Elsevier Science Publishers.

Curror, S., Skoe, E., & Pratt, M. (1994, July). *Gender differences in care reasoning in older adults.* Paper presented at the Canadian Psychological Association Meetings, Penticton, British Columbia.

Damon, W. (1981). Exploring children's social cognition on two fronts. In J. H. Flavell & L. Ross (Eds.), *Social cognitive development: Frontiers and possible futures* (pp. 154–175). New York: Cambridge University Press.

Danigelis, N., & Cutler, S. (1991a). An inter-cohort comparison of changes in radical attitudes. *Research on Aging, 13*, 383–404.

Danigelis, N., & Cutler, S. (1991b). Cohort trends in attitudes about law and order: Who's leading the conservative wave? *Public Opinion Quarterly, 55*, 24–49.

Datan, N., Rodeheaver, D., & Hughes, F. (1987). Adult development and aging. *Annual Review of Psychology, 38*, 153–180.

David, D. (1990). Reminiscence, adaptation, and social context in old age. *International Journal of Aging and Human Development, 30*, 175–188.

Deaux, K., & Emswiller, T. (1974). Explanations of successful performance on sex-linked tasks: What is skill for the male is luck for the female. *Journal of Personality & Social Psychology, 29*, 80–85.

Demos, J. (1978). Old age in early New England. *American Journal of Sociology, 84*, 248–287.

Denney, N. W. (1982). Aging and cognitive development. In B. B. Wolman (Ed.), *Handbook of developmental psychology,* (pp. 807–827). San Diego, CA: Academic Press.

Denney, N. W. (1989). Everyday problem solving: Methodological issues, research findings, and a model. In L. W. Poon, D. C. Rubin, & B. A. Wilson (Eds.), *Everyday cognition in adulthood and late life* (pp. 437–456). Cambridge: Cambridge University Press.

Denney, N. W., & Palmer, A. M. (1981). Adult age differences in traditional and practical problem-solving measures. *Journal of Gerontology, 36*, 323–328.

Denney, N. W., & Pearce, K. A. (1989). A developmental study of practical problem-solving in adults. *Psychology and Aging, 4*, 438–442.

Denney N. W., Pearce, K. A., & Palmer, A. M. (1982). A developmental study of adults' performance. *Experimental Aging Research, 8*, 115–118.

Deutsch, F., Zalenski, C., & Clark, M. (1986). Is there a double standard of aging? *Journal of Applied Social Psychology, 16*, 771–785.

deVries, B., & Walker, L. (1986). Moral reasoning and attitudes toward capital punishment. *Developmental Psychology, 22*, 509–513.

Diamond, P. & Hausman, J. (1984). The retirement and unemployment behavior of older men. In H. Aaron & G. Burtless (Eds.), *Retirement and economic behavior* (pp. 97–134). Washington, DC: The Brookings Institute.

Dittmann-Kohli, F. (1990). The construction of meaning in old age: Possibilities and constraints. *Aging and Society, 10*, 279–291.

Dittmann-Kohli, F., Lachman, M. E., Kliege, R., & Baltes, P. (1991). Effects of cognitive training and testing on intellectual efficacy beliefs in elderly adults. *Journal of Gerontology, 46*, 162–164.

Dixon, R. (1992). Contextual approaches to adult intellectual development. In R. Sternberg and C. Berg (Eds.), *Intellectual development*. New York: Cambridge University Press.

Dixon, R., & Hultsch, D. (1984). The metamemory in adulthood (MIA) instrument. *Psychological Documents, 14*, 3.

Dodge, K. A., Pettit, G. S., McClaskey, C. L., & Brown, M. M. (1986). Social competence in children. *Monographs of the Society for Research in Child Development, 51*, 1–85.

Dolen, L. S., & Bearison, D. J. (1982). Social interaction and social cognition in aging: A contextual analysis. *Human Development, 25*, 430–442.

Duff, R. W., & Hong, L. K. (1980). *Quality and quantity of social interactions and the life satisfaction of older Americans.* Paper presented at the annual meeting of the Gerontological Society of America, San Diego.

Edinger, L. (1985). Politics of the aged: Orientations and behavior in major liberal democracies. *Zeitschrift für Gerontologie, 18*, 58–64.

Eisenberg, N. & Lennon, R. (1983). Sex differences in empathy and related capacities. *Psychological Bulletin, 49*, 100–131.

Ekerdt, D., Baden, L., Bossé, R., & Dibbs, E. (1983). The effect of retirement on physical health. *American Journal of Public Health, 73*, 779–783.

Ekerdt, D., Bossé, R., & Levkoff, S. (1985). An empirical test for phases of retirement: Findings from the Normative Aging Study. *Journal of Gerontology, 40*, 95–101.

Elkind, D. (1967). Egocentrism in adolescence. *Child Development, 38*, 1025–1034.

Elkind, D. (1974). *Children and adolescence* (2nd ed.). New York: Oxford University Press.

Emery, O. (1985). Language and aging. *Experimental Aging Research, 11*, 3–60.

Emery, O. (1986). Linguistic decrement in normal aging. *Language and Communication, 6*, 47–64.

Enright, R. D., Roberts, P., & Lapsley, D. K. (1983). Belief discrepancy reasoning in the elderly. *International Journal of Aging and Human Development, 17*, 213–221.

Erber, J. T., Szuchman, L. T., & Rothberg, S. T. (1990). Everyday memory failure: Age differences in appraisal and attribution. *Psychology and Aging, 5*, 236–241.

Ericsson, K. A., & Simon, H. A. (1984). *Protocol analysis: Verbal reports.* Cambridge, MA: MIT Press.

Erikson, E. (1950). *Childhood and society.* New York: W. W. Norton.

Erikson, E. (1982). *The life cycle completed: Review.* New York: W. W. Norton.

Erikson, E. H., Erikson, J. M., & Kivnick, H. Q. (1986). *Vital involvement in old age: The experience of old age in our time.* New York: W. W. Norton.

Feier, C., & Gerstman, L. (1980). Sentence comprehension abilities throughout the adult life span. *Journal of Gerontology, 35*, 727–728.

Ferrara, R., Brown, A., & Campione, J. (1986). Children's learning and transfer of inductive reasoning rules: Studies of proximal development. *Child Development, 57*, 1087–1099.

Festinger, L. (1954). A theory of social comparison processes. *Human Relations, 7*, 117–140.

Festinger, L. (1957). *A theory of cognitive dissonance.* New York: Harper & Row.

Field, D., & Millsap, R. E. (1991). Personality in advanced old age: Continuity or change. *Journal of Gerontology, 46*, 299–308.

Finch, C. (1989). The brain, genes, and aging. In V. L. Bengtson & K. W. Schaie (Eds.), *The course of later life* (pp. 1–14). New York: Springer.

Fine, M., & Norris, J. E. (1994). *A perceptual and interactional study of family functioning.* Manuscript submitted for publication.

Fischer, K. W., & Pipp, S. L. (1984). Processes of cognitive development: Optimal level and skill acquisition. In R. J. Sternberg (Ed.), *Mechanisms of cognitive development* (pp. 45–80). New York: W. H. Freeman.

Fisher, C. B., Reid, J. D., & Melendez, M. (1989). Conflict in families and friendships of later life. *Family Relations, 38*, 83–89.

Fiske, S. T. (1993). Social cognition and social perception. *Annual Review of Psychology, 44*, 155–194.

Fiske, S. T., & Taylor, S. E. (1984). *Social cognition.* Reading, MA: Addison-Wesley.

Fiske, S. T., & Taylor, S. E. (1991). *Social cognition (2nd ed.).* Reading, MA: Addison-Wesley.

Fitzgerald, J. M., & Martin-Louer, P. (1983–1984). Person-perception in adulthood: A categories analysis. *International Journal of Aging and Human Development, 18*, 197–205.

Fivush, R. (1991). The social construction of personal narratives. *Merrill-Palmer Quarterly, 37*, 59–81.

Flavell, J. H. (1985). *Cognitive development: 2nd Edition*. Englewood Cliffs, NJ: Prentice-Hall.

Flavell, J. H., & Wohlwill, J. F. (1969). Formal and functional aspects of cognitive development. In D. Elkind & J. H. Flavell (Eds.), *Studies in cognitive development: Essays in honor of Jean Piaget* (pp. 67–120). New York: Oxford University Press.

Foa, U., & Foa, E. (1974). *Societal structures of the mind*. Springfield, IL.: Charles C. Thomas.

Fodor, J. (1982). *Modularity of mind*. Cambridge, MA: MIT Press.

Folkman, S., Lazarus, R., Pimley, S., & Novacek, J. (1987). Age differences in stress and coping processes. *Psychology and Aging, 2*, 171–184.

Forbes, S. (1985). *Families coping with an elder's care and related decisions*. Unpublished master's thesis, University of Guelph.

Fowler, J. (1981). *Stages of faith*. New York: Harper & Row.

Franzke, A. W. (1987). The effectiveness of assertiveness training on older adults. *Gerontologist, 27*, 13.

Fredrickson, B. L., & Carstensen, L. L. (1990). Choosing social partners: How old age and anticipated endings make people more selective. *Psychology and Aging, 5*, 335–347.

Fries, J. E. (1980). Medical perspectives upon successful aging. In P. B. Baltes & M. M. Baltes (Eds.), *Successful aging: Perspectives from the behavioural sciences*. Cambridge: Cambridge University Press.

Furstenberg, A.-L. (1989). Older people's age self-concept. *Social casework: The Journal of Contemporary Social Work*.

Gallup, G. (1984). *Religion in America*. Princeton, NJ: Princeton Religious Research Center.

Gardner, H. (1973). *The arts and human development*. New York: Wiley.

Gardner, H. (1985). *The mind's new science: A history of the cognitive revolution*. New York: Basic Books.

Gelman, R. (1969). Conservation acquisition: A problem of learning to attend to relevant attributes. *Journal of Experimental Child Psychology, 7*, 167–187.

Gelman, R. (1978). Cognitive development. *Annual Review of Psychology, 29*, 297–382.

Gelman, R., & Baillargeon, R. (1983). A review of some Piagetian concepts. In J. H. Flavell & E. M. Markman (Eds.), *Handbook of child psychology: Vol. 3. Cognitive development* (pp. 167–230). New York: Wiley.

Gerbner, G., Gross, L., Signorielli, N., & Morgan, M. (1980). Aging with television: Images on television drama and conceptions of social reality. *Journal of Communication, 30*, 37–47.

Gibbs, J. C. (1979). Kohlberg's moral stage theory: A Piagetian revision. *Human Development, 22*, 89–112.

Gibson, R. (1987). Reconceptualizing retirement for Black Americans. *The Gerontologist, 27*, 691–698.

Gibson, R. (1991). The subjective retirement of Black Americans. *Journal of Gerontology, 46*, S204–209.

Gignac, M. A. M. (1991). *Recognizing the perspective-affect link: An alternative path to contentment*. Unpublished doctoral dissertation, University of Waterloo, Waterloo, Ontario.

Gilligan, C. (1982). *In a different voice: Psychological theory and woman's development*. Cambridge, MA: Harvard University Press.

Gilligan, C., & Atanucci, J. (1988). Two moral orientations: Gender differences and similarities. *Merrill-Palmer Quarterly, 34*, 223–237.

Glenn, N. (1974). Aging and conservatism. *Annals of the American Academy of Political and Social Science, 415*, 176–186.

Goethals, G., & Darley, J. (1977). Social comparison theory: An attributional approach. In J. Suls & R. Miller (Eds.), *Social comparison processes: Theoretical and empirical perspectives*. Washington, DC: Hemisphere.

Gold, D., Andres, D., Arbuckle, T., & Schwartzman, A. (1988). Measurement and correlates of verbosity in elderly people. *Journal of Gerontology: Psychological Sciences, 43*, 27–33.

Goudy, W. (1981). Changing work expectations: Findings from the Retirement History Study. *The Gerontologist, 21*, 644–649.

Gould, O. N., & Dixon, R. A. (1990). *Describing a vacation: Joint storytelling by young and old married couples*. Poster presentation at the annual convention of the Canadian Psychological Association in Ottawa.

Gould, O. N., & Dixon, R. A. (1993). How we spent our vacation: Collaborative storytelling by young and old adults. *Psychology and Aging, 8*, 10–17.

Gould, O. N., Trevithick, L., & Dixon, R. A. (1991). Adult age differences in elaborations produced during prose recall. *Psychology and Aging, 6*, 93–99.

Gould, S. J. (1982). *The mismeasure of man*. New York: W. W. Norton.

Graham, S. (1992). "Most of the subjects were white and middle class." Trends in published research on African-Americans in selected APA journals, 1970–1989. *American Psychologist, 47*, 629–639.

Gratzinger, P., Sheikh, J. I., & Friedman, L. (1990). Cognitive interventions to improve face-name recall: The role of personality trait differences. *Developmental Psychology, 26*, 889–893.

Green, S. K. (1981). Attitudes and perceptions about the elderly: Current and future perspectives. *Aging and Human Development, 13*, 95–115.

Guilford, J. P. (1965). *Fundamental statistics in psychology and education (4th ed.)*. New York: McGraw-Hills.

Gutmann, D. (1977). The cross-cultural perspective. Notes toward a comparative psychology of aging. In J. E. Birren & K. W. Schaie (Eds.), *Handbook of the psychology of aging*. New York: Van Nostrand Reinhold.

Gutmann, D. (1985). The parental imperative revisited. In J. Meacham (Ed.), *The family and individual development* (pp. 31–60). Basel, Switzerland: Karger.

Hale, S. (1990). A global development trend in cognitive processing speech. *Child Development, 61*, 653–663.

Halliday, M. A., & Hasan, R. (1976). *Cohesion in English*. London: Longman.

Hareven, T. (1982). The life course and aging in historical perspective. In T. Hareven and K. Adams (Eds.), *Aging and life course transitions: An interdisciplinary perspective*. New York: Guilford.

Hartley, A. A. (1989). The cognitive ecology of problem solving. In L. W. Poon, D. C. Rubin, & B. A. Wilson (Eds.), *Everyday cognition in adulthood and late life* (pp. 437–456). Cambridge: Cambridge University Press.

Hartley, A. A. (1992). Attention. In F. Craik and T. Salthouse (Eds.), *The handbook of aging and cognition*. Hillsdale, NJ: Erlbaum.

Hartley, J. T. (1988). Aging and individual differences in memory for written discourse. In L. L. Light & D. M. Burke (Eds.), *Language, memory, and aging* (pp. 36–57). Cambridge: Cambridge University Press.

Hasher, L., & Zacks, R. T. (1988). Working memory, comprehension, and aging: A review and a new view. In G. H. Bower (Ed.), *The psychology of learning and motivation* (Vol. 22, pp. 193–225). New York: Academic Press.

Havighurst, R., Neugarten, B., & Tobin, S. (1968). Disengagement and patterns of aging. In B. L. Neugarten (Ed.), *Middle age and aging: A reader in social psychology*. Chicago: University of Chicago Press.

Heckhausen, J., & Baltes, P. B. (1991). Perceived controllability of expected psychological change across adulthood and old age. *Journal of Gerontology, 46*, 165–173.

Heckhausen, J., Dixon, R. A., & Baltes, P. B. (1989). Gains and losses in development throughout adulthood as perceived by different adult age groups. *Developmental Psychology, 25(1)*, 109–121.

Heider, F. (1958). *The psychology of interpersonal relations*. New York: Wiley.

Heller, R., Dobbs, A. R., & Rule, B. G. (1987, June). *Expressive language ability and working memory in young and old adults*. Paper presented at the Canadian Psychological Meetings, Vancouver, British Columbia.

Helson, R., Mitchell, V., & Moane, G. (1984). Personality and patterns of adherence and non-adherence to the social clock. *Journal of Personality and Social Psychology, 46*, 1079–1096.

Helson, R., & Wink, P. (1992). Personality change in women from the early 40s to early 50s. *Psychology and Aging, 7*.

Hermans, H. J. M., Kempen, H. J. G., & van Loon, R. J. P. (1992). The dialogical self: Beyond individualism and rationalism. *American Psychologist, 47*, 23–33.

Hertzog, C., Dixon, R., & Hultsch, D. (1990). Relationships between metamemory, memory predictions, and memory task performance in adults. *Psychology & Aging, 6*, 215–227.

Hertzog, D., Dixon, R., Schulenberg, J., Hultsch, D. (1987). On the differentiation of memory beliefs from memory knowledge: The factor structure of the metamemory in adulthood scale. *Experimental Aging Research, 13*, 101–107.

Hess, T. M., & Tate, C. S. (1991). Adult age differences in explanations and memory for behavioral information. *Psychology and Aging, 6*, 86–92.

Higgins, A., Power, C., & Kohlberg, L. (1984). The relationship of moral atmosphere to judgments of responsibility. In W. Kurtines & J. Gewirtz (Eds.), *Morality, moral development, and moral behavior* (pp. 74–106). New York: Wiley.

Hochschild, A., & Machung, A. (1989). *The second shift: Working parents and the revolution at home.* New York: Viking.

Hoffman, M. (1987). The contribution of empathy to justice and moral judgment. In N. Eisenberg & J. Strayer (Eds.), *Empathy: A developmental perspective.* New York: Cambridge University Press.

Hogg, J. R., & Heller, K. (1990). A measure of relational competence for community-dwelling elderly. *Psychology and Aging, 5*, 580–588.

Holliday, S. G., & Chandler, M. J. (1986). *Wisdom: Explorations in adult competence.* Basel, Switzerland: Karger.

Holtzman, J. & Akiyama, H. (1985). What children see: The aged on television in Japan and the United States. *The Gerontologist, 25*, 62–67.

Horn, J. L. (1982a). The aging of human abilities. In B. B. Woman (Ed.), *Handbook of developmental psychology* (pp. 847–870). Englewood Cliffs, NJ: Prentice-Hall.

Horn, J. L. (1982b). The theory of fluid and crystallized intelligence in relation to concepts of cognitive psychology and aging in adulthood. In F. I. M. Craik & S. Trehub (Eds.), *Aging and cognitive processes* (pp. 237–278). New York: Plenum.

Huff, J. (1988). The disorder of naming in Alzheimer's disease. In L. L. Light & D. M. Burke (Eds.), *Language, memory, and aging* (pp. 209–220). Cambridge: Cambridge University Press.

Hultsch, D. F., & Dixon, R. A. (1984). Memory for text materials in adulthood. In P. B. Baltes & O. G. Brim, Jr. (Eds.), *Lifespan development and behavior* (Vol. 6, pp. 77–108). New York: Academic Press.

Hultsch, D. F., & Dixon, R. A. (1990). Learning and memory in aging. In J. E. Birren & K. W. Schaie (Eds.), *Handbook of the psychology of aging* (3rd ed., pp. 258–274). San Diego, CA: Academic Press.

Hummert, M. L. (1990). Multiple stereotypes of elderly and young adults: A comparison of structure and evaluations. *Psychology and Aging, 5*, 182–193.

Hunsberger, B. (1985). Religion, age, life satisfaction and perceived sources of religiousness: A study of older persons. *Journal of Gerontology, 40*, 615–620.

Hunsberger, B., McKenzie, B., Pratt, M., & Pancer, S. M. (1993). Religious doubt: A social psychological analysis. *Research in the Social Scientific Study of Religion, 5*, 27–51.

Hunt, E. (1978). Mechanics of verbal ability. *Psychological Review, 85*, 109–130.

Ingersoll-Dayton, B., & Antonucci, T. C. (1988). Reciprocal and nonreciprocal social support: Contrasting sides of intimate relationships. *Journal of Gerontology, 43*, 565–573.

Irion, J. C., & Blanchard-Fields, F. (1987). A cross-sectional comparison of adaptive coping in adulthood. *Journal of Gerontology, 42*, 502–504.

Isquick, M. F. (1981). Training older people in empathy: Effects on empathy, attitudes, and self-exploration. *International Journal of Aging and Human Development, 13*, 1–13.

Jackson, J. (1970). Aged Negroes: Their cultural departures from statistical stereotypes and rural-urban differences. *The Gerontologist, 10*, 140–145.

Jennings, W., Kilkenny, R., & Kohlberg, L. (1987). Moral development theory and practice for youthful and adult offenders. In W. S. Laufer & J. M. Day (Eds.), *Personality theory, moral development and criminal behavior*. Lexington, MA: Lexington Books.

Johnson, C. L., & Barer, B. M. (1992). Patterns of engagement and disengagement among the oldest old. *Journal of Aging Studies, 6*, 351–364.

Johnson, J., & Newport, E. (1989). Critical periods effects in second language learning: The influence of maturational state on the acquisition of English as a second language. *Cognitive Psychology, 21*, 60–99.

Johnson, M., & Raye, C. (1981). Reality monitoring. *Psychological Review, 88*, 67–85.

Jones, D. C., & Vaughn, K. (1990). Close friendships among senior adults. *Psychology and Aging, 5*, 451–457.

Jones, E. E., & Davis, K. E. (1965). From acts to dispositions: The attribution process in person perception. In L. Berkowitz (Ed.), *Advances in experimental social psychology* (Vol. 2, pp. 219–266). New York: Academic Press.

Kahana, E., Midlarsky, E., & Kahana, B. (1987). Beyond dependency, autonomy and exchange: Prosocial behavior in late life adaptation. *Social Justice Research, 1*, 439–459.

Kail, R., & Bisanz, J. (1982). Information processing and cognitive development. In H. W. Reese (Ed.), *Advances in child development and behavior* (Vol. 17, pp. 45–82). New York: Academic Press.

Kakar, S. (1978). *The inner world: A psychoanalytic study of childhood and society in India*. New York: Oxford University Press.

Kalish, R. A., & Knudtson, F. W. (1976). Attachment versus disengagement: A life-span conceptualization. *Human Development, 19*, 182–196.

Karuza, J., Zevon, M., Gleason, T., Karuza, C., & Nash, L. (1990). Models of helping and coping, responsibility attributions, and well-being in community elderly and their helpers. *Psychology and Aging, 5*, 194–208.

Kausler, D. H. (1991). *Experimental psychology and human aging* (3rd ed.). New York: Wiley.

Kausler, D. H., & Hakami, M. K. (1983). Memory for topics of conversation: Adult age differences and intentionality. *Experimental Aging Research, 9*, 153–157.

Kelley, H. H. (1972). Causal schemata and the attribution process. In E. E. Jones, D. E. Kanouse, H. H. Kelley, R. E. Nisbett, S. Valins, &

B. Weiner (Eds.), *Attribution: Perceiving the causes of behavior* (pp. 1–26). New York: General Learning Press.

Kelly, G. A. (1955). *The psychology of personal constructs*. New York: Norton.

Kemper, S. (1986). Imitation of complex syntactic constructions by elderly adults. *Applied Psycholinguistics, 7*, 277–287.

Kemper, S. (1987). Life-span changes in syntactic complexity. *Journal of Gerontology, 42*, 323–328.

Kemper, S. (1988). Geriatric psycholinguistics: Syntactic limitations of oral and written language. In L. Light & D. Burke (Eds.), *Language, memory, and aging* (pp. 58–76). Cambridge: Cambridge University Press.

Kemper, S. (1990). Adults' diaries: Changes made to written narratives across the life span. *Discourse Process, 13*, 207–223.

Kemper, S. (1992). Language and aging. In F. Craik & T. Salthouse (Eds.), *The handbook of aging and cognition*. Hillsdale, NJ: Erlbaum.

Kemper, S., Kynette, D., & Norman, S. (1992). Age differences in spoken language. In R. West and J. Sinnott (Eds.), *Everyday memory and aging*.

Kemper, S., Rash, S., Kynette, D., & Norman, S. (1990). Telling stories: The structure of adults' narratives. *European Journal of Cognitive Psychology, 2*, 205–228.

Kennaley, D., Pratt, M., & Ryan, E. (1994, May). *Patronizing speech by caregivers to assertive versus passive elderly: Evaluations by nursing home staff and residents*. Paper presented at the Second International Conference on Communication, Aging, and Health, Hamilton, Ontario.

Kenrick, D., & Trost, M. (1989). A reproductive exchange model of heterosexual relationships. In C. Hendrick (Ed.), *Review of personality and social psychology: Close relationships (Vol. 10)*. Newbury Park, CA: Sage.

Kessen, W. (1965). *The child*. New York: Wiley.

Kitchener, K. S., & King, P. M. (1981). Reflective Judgment: Concepts of justification and their relationship to age and education. *Journal of Applied Developmental Psychology, 2*, 89–116.

Kite, M. E., Deaux, K., & Miele, M. (1991). Stereotypes of young and old: Does age outweigh gender? *Psychology and Aging, 6(1)*, 19–27.

Kite, M. E., & Johnson, B. T. (1988). Attitudes toward older and younger adults: A meta-analysis. *Psychology and Aging, 3*, 233–244.

Kliegl, R., Smith, J., & Baltes, P. B. (1990). On the locus and process of magnification of age differences during mnemonic training. *Developmental Psychology, 26*, 894–904.

Kliegl, R., Smith, J., Heckhausen, J., & Baltes, P. B. (1987). Mnemonic training for the acquisition of skilled digit memory. *Cognition and Instruction, 4*, 203–223.

Koenig, H. G. (1992). Religion and mental health in later life. In J. Schumaker (Ed.), *Religion and mental health*. Oxford, England: Oxford University Press.

Koenig, H., Kvale, J., & Ferrel, C. (1988). Religion and well-being in later life. *The Gerontologist, 28*, 18–28.

Kogan, N. (1979). Beliefs, attitudes, and stereotypes about old people: A new look at some old issues. *Research on Aging, 1*, 11–36.

Kogan, N., & Mills, M. (1992). Gender influences on age cognitions and preferences: Sociocultural or sociobiological? *Psychology and Aging, 7*, 98–106.

Koh, J., & Bell, W. (1987). Korean elders in the United States: Intergenerational relations and living arrangements. *The Gerontologist, 27*, 66–71.

Kohlberg, L. (1969). Stage and sequence: The cognitive-developmental approach to socialization. In D. A. Goslin (Ed.), *Handbook of socialization: Theory and research* (pp. 347–480). San Diego, CA: Academic Press.

Kohlberg, L. (1973). Continuities in childhood and adult moral development revisited. In P. B. Baltes & K. W. Schaie (Eds.), *Life-span developmental psychology: Personality and socialization* (pp. 180–204). New York: Academic Press.

Kohlberg, L. (1976). Moral stages and moralization: The cognitive-developmental approach. In T. Lickona (Ed.), *Moral development and behavior: Theory, research, and social issues.* New York: Holt, Rinehart, & Winston.

Kohlberg, L. (1981). *The philosophy of moral development: Moral stages and the idea of justice. Vol. 1: Essays on moral development.* San Francisco: Harper & Row.

Kohlberg, L. (1984). *The psychology of moral development, Volume 2.* San Francisco: Harper & Row.

Kohlberg, L., & Candee, D. (1984). The relationship of moral judgment to moral action. In W. M. Kurtines & J. L. Gewirtz (Eds.), *Morality, moral behavior and moral development: Basic issues in theory and research* (pp. 52–72). New York: Wiley.

Kohlberg, L., & Higgins, A. (1984). Continuities and discontinuities in childhood and adult development revisited – again. In L. Kohlberg (1984), *The psychology of moral development. (Vol. 2).* (pp. 426–497). New York: Harper & Row.

Konner, M. (1982). *The tangled wing: Biological constraints on the human spirit.* New York: Harper & Row.

Konner, M. (1990). *Why the reckless survive.* New York: Penguin Books.

Kozma, A., Stones, M. J., & McNeil, J. K. (1991). *Psychological well-being in later life.* Toronto: Butterworths.

Kramer, D. A. (1990). Conceptualizing wisdom: The primacy of affect-cognition relations. In R. Sternberg (Ed.), *Wisdom: Its nature, origins, and development* (pp. 279–313). Cambridge: Cambridge University Press.

Kramer, D. A., Kalbaugh, P., & Goldston, R. (1992). A measure of paradigm beliefs about the social world. *Journal of Gerontology, 47*, P180–189.

Kramer, D. A., & Woodruff, D. S. (1986). Relativistic and dialectical thought in three adult age-groups. *Human Development, 29*, 280–290.

Krause, N. (1993). Measuring religiosity in later life. *Research on Aging, 15*, 170–197.

Krause, N., & Markides, K. (1990). Measuring social support among older adults. *International Journal of Aging and Human Development, 30*, 37–53.

Krebs, D., Vermeulen, S., Carpendale, J., & Denton, K. (1991). Structural and situational influences on moral judgment. In W. Kurtines & J. Gewirtz (Eds.), *Handbook of moral behavior and development*. Hillsdale, NJ: Erlbaum.

Kreutzer, M., Leonard, D., & Flavell, J. (1975). An interview study of children's knowledge about memory. *Monographs of the Society for Research in Child Development, 40*, (1, Serial No. 159).

Krosnick, J., & Alwin, D. (1989). Aging and susceptibility to attitude change. *Journal of Personality and Social Psychology, 57*, 417–425.

Krueger, J. & Heckhausen, J. (1993). Personality development across the adult life span: Subjective conceptions vs cross-sectional contrasts. *Journal of Gerontology, 48*, 100–108.

Kuhn, D. (1989). Children and adults as intuitive scientists. *Psychological Review, 96*, 674–689.

Kuhn, D. (1991). *The skills of argument*. Cambridge: Cambridge University Press.

Kuhn, D., Pennington, N., & Leadbeater, B. (1983). Adult thinking in developmental perspective. In P. B. Baltes & O. G. Brim, Jr. (Eds.), *Life-span development and behavior* (Vol. 5, pp. 158–195.) New York: Academic Press.

Kuhn, T. S. (1962). *The structure of scientific revolutions*. Chicago: University of Chicago Press.

Kuypers, J. A. (1971). Internal-external locus of control and ego-functioning correlates in the elderly. *Gerontologist, 12*, 168–173.

Kuypers, J. A., & Bengtson, V. L. (1973). Social breakdown and competence: A model of normal aging. *Human Development, 16*, 181–201.

Laboratory of Comparative Human Cognition, (1983). Culture and cognitive development. In W. Kessen (Ed.), History, theory, and methods: Vol. 1. P. H. Mussen (Gen. Ed.), *Handbook of child psychology* (4th ed.). New York: Wiley.

Labouvie-Vief, G. (1982). Growth and aging in a life span perspective. *Human Development, 25*, 65–88.

Labouvie-Vief, G. (1985). Intelligence and cognition. In J. E. Birren & K. W. Schaie (Eds.), *Handbook of the psychology of aging* (2nd ed., pp. 500–530). New York: Van Nostrand Reinhold.

Labouvie-Vief, G. (1990). Modes of knowledge and organization of development. In M. L. Commons, C. Armon, F. A. Richards, & J. Sinnott (Eds.), *Beyond formal operations 2. The development of adolescent and adult thinking and perception* (pp. 43–62). New York: Praeger.

Labouvie-Vief, G., DeVoe, M., & Bulka, D. (1989). Speaking about feelings: Conceptions of emotion across the life span. *Psychology and Aging, 4(4)*, 425–437.

Labouvie-Vief, G., Hakim-Larson, J., & Hobart, C. J. (1987). Age, ego level, and the life-span development of coping and defense processes. *Psychology and Aging, 2(3)*, 286–293.

Labov, W., & Waletzsky, J. (1967). Narrative analysis: Oral versions of personal experience. In J. Helm (Ed.), *Essay on the verbal and visual arts*. Seattle: University of Washington Press.

Lachman, M. E. (1986). Locus of control in aging research: A case for multidimensional and domain-specific assessment. *Psychology and Aging, 1*, 34–40.

Langer, E. J., & Rodin, J. (1976). The effects of choice and enhanced personal responsibility for the aged: A field experiment in an institutional setting. *Journal of Personality & Social Psychology, 34*, 191–198.

Lapsley, D. K., & Quintana, S. M. (1989). Mental capacity and role taking: A structural equations approach. *Merrill-Palmer Quarterly, 35*, 143–163.

Larson, R. (1978). Thirty years of research on the subjective well-being of older Americans. *Journal of Gerontology, 33*, 109–125.

Larson, R., Zuzanek, J., & Mannell, R. (1985). Being alone versus being with people: Disengagement in the daily experience of older adults. *Journal of Gerontology, 3*, 375–381.

Lawton, M. P. (1972). The dimensions of morale. In D. B. Kent, R. Kastenbaum & S. Sherwood (Eds.), *Research, planning and action for the elderly*. New York: Behavioral Publications.

Lawton, M. P. (1980). *Environment and aging*. Albany, NY: Center for the Study of Aging.

Lazarus, R. S. & Golden, G. Y. (1981). The function of denial in stress, coping, and aging. In J. L. McGaugh & S. K. Kiesler (Eds.), *Aging: Biology and behavior*. New York: Academic Press.

Learman, L., Avorn, J., Everitt, D., & Rosenthal, R. (1990). Pygmalion in the nursing home. *Journal of the American Geriatrics Society, 38*, 797–803.

Leont'ev, A. N. (1981). The problem of activity in psychology. In J. V. Wertsch (Ed.), *The concept of activity in Soviet psychology* (pp. 37–71). Armonk, NY: Sharpe.

Lerner, M. J. (1981). The justice motive in human relations: Some thoughts on what we know and need to know about justice. In M. J. Lerner & S. C. Lerner (Eds.), *The justice motive in social behavior: Adapting to times of scarcity and change* (pp. 11–35). New York: Plenum.

Lerner, M. J., & Gignac, M. A. M. (1992). Is it coping or is it growth? A cognitive-affective model of contentment in the elderly. In L. Montada, S. H. Fillip, & M. J. Lerner (Eds.), *Life crises and experiences of loss in adulthood*. Hillsdale, NJ: Erlbaum.

Lerner, M. J., Somers, D. G., Reid, D., & Tierney, M. (1988). The social psychology of individual and social dilemmas: Egocentrically biased cognitions among filial caregivers. In S. Spacapan & S. Oskamp (Eds.), *The social psychology of aging: Claremont symposium on applied and social psychology*. Newbury Park, CA: Sage.

Lerner, R. M. (1984). *On the nature of human plasticity*. New York: Cambridge University Press.

Levin, J., & Levin, W. C. (1981). Willingness to interact with an old person. *Research on Aging, 3*, 211–217.

Levine, C., Kohlberg, L., & Hewer, A. (1985). The current formulation of Kohlberg's theory and a response to critics. *Human Development, 28*, 94–100.

Levinson, D. J. (1978). *The seasons of a man's life.* New York: Ballantine Books.

Light, L. L. (1991). Memory and aging: Four hypotheses in search of data. *Annual Review of Psychology, 42*, 333–376.

Light, L. L., & Albertson, S. A. (1988). Comprehension of pragmatic implications in young and old adults. In L. L. Light & D. M. Burke (Eds.), *Language, memory, and aging* (pp. 131–153). New York: Cambridge University Press.

Light, L. L., & Burke, D. M. (1988). Patterns of language and memory in old age. In L. L. Light & D. M. Burke (Eds.), *Language, memory, and aging* (pp. 244–271). Cambridge: Cambridge University Press.

Light, L. L., & Capps, J. L. (1986). Comprehension of pronouns in young and older adults. *Developmental Psychology, 22*, 580–585.

Lindsay, C. (1987). The decline in employment among men aged 55–64. *Canadian Social Trends*, Spring, 12–15.

Linville, P. (1982). The complexity-extremity effect and age-based stereotyping. *Journal of Personality and Social Psychology, 42*, 211.

List, J. A. (1986). Age and schematic differences in the reliability of eyewitness testimony. *Developmental Psychology, 22*, 50–59.

Livesley, W. J., & Bromley, D. B. (1974). *Person perception in childhood and adolescence.* London: Wiley.

Lonky, E., Kaus, C. R., & Roodin, P. A. (1984). Life experience and mode of coping: Relation to moral judgment in adulthood. *Developmental Psychology, 20*, 1159–1167.

Lonky, E., Reihman, J., & Serlin, R. (1981). Political values and moral judgment in adolescence. *Youth and Society, 12*, 423–441.

Looft, W. R. (1972). Egocentrism and social interaction across the life span. *Psychological Bulletin, 78*, 73–92.

Looft, W. R., & Charles, D. C. (1971). Egocentrism and social interaction in young and old adults. *Aging and Human Development, 2*, 21–28.

Lovelace, E. (1990). Aging and metacognitions concerning memory function. In E. Lovelace (Ed.), *Aging and cognition: Mental processes, self awareness, and interventions* (pp. 157–188). Amsterdam: Elsevier.

Lowenthal, M. F. (1968). Social isolation and mental illness in old age. In B. L. Neugarten (Ed.), *Middle age and aging* (pp. 220–234). Chicago: University of Chicago Press.

Lowenthal, M. F., & Haven, C. (1968). Interaction and adaptation: Intimacy as a critical variable. In B. Neugarten (Ed.), *Middle age and aging.* Chicago: University of Chicago Press.

Luborsky, M., & Rubenstein, R. (1987). Ethnicity and lifetimes: Self-concepts and situational contexts of ethnic identity in late life. In D. Gelfand and C. Barresi (Eds.), *Ethnic dimensions of aging*. New York: Springer.

Luria, A. (1976). *Cognitive development: Its cultural and social foundations*. Cambridge, MA: Harvard University Press.

Luszcz, M. A. (1989). Theoretical models of everyday problem-solving. In J. Sinnott (Ed.), *Everyday problem-solving: Theory and applications* (pp. 24–39). New York: Praeger.

Lutsky, N. S. (1980). Attitudes toward old age and elderly persons. In C. Eisdorfer (Ed.), *Annual review of gerontology and geriatrics* (Vol. 1, pp. 287–336). New York: Springer Publishing.

Maddox, G. L. (1963). Activity and morale: A longitudinal of selected elderly subjects. *Social Forces, 42*, 195–204.

Maddox, G. L., & Douglas, E. (1974). Aging and individual differences. *Journal of Gerontology, 29*, 555–563.

Main, M., Kaplan, N., & Cassidy, J. (1985). Security in infancy, childhood, and adulthood: A move to the level of representation. *Monographs of the Society for Research in Child Development, 50*, 66–104.

Malatesta, C. Z., Izard, C. E., Culver, C., & Nicolich, M. (1987). Emotion communication skills in young, middle-aged, and older women. *Psychology and Aging, 2*, 193–203.

Malatesta-Magai, C., Jonas, R., Shepard, B., & Culver, L. C. (1992). Type A behavior pattern and emotion expression in younger and older adults. *Psychology and Aging, 7*, 551–561.

Mandler, J. (1984). *Stories, scripts, and scenes: Aspects of schema theory*. Hillsdale, NJ: Erlbaum.

Manheimer, R. J. (1992). In search of the gerontological self. *Journal of Aging Studies, 4*, 319–332.

Marcia, J. E. (1966). Development and validation of ego identity status. *Journal of Personality & Social Psychology, 3*, 551–558.

Markides, K., Levin, J., & Ray, L. (1987). Religion, aging, and life satisfaction: An eight-year, three-wave longitudinal study. *The Gerontologist, 27*, 660–664.

Markus, H., & Nurius, P. (1986). Possible selves. *American Psychologist, 41*, 954–969.

Marshall, V. G. (1974). *The life review as a social process*. Paper presented at the annual meeting of the Gerontological Society, Portland.

Marshall, V. W. (1978–1979). No exit: A symbolic interactionist perspective on aging. *International Journal of Aging and Human Development, 9*, 345–358.

Marshall, V. W. (1980). *Last chapters: A sociology of aging and dying*. Monterey, CA: Brooks Cole.

Marshall, V. W. (1986). Dominant and emerging paradigms in the social psychology of aging. In V. W. Marshall (Ed.), *Later life: The social psychology of aging*. Beverly Hills: Sage.

Martin Matthews, A. (1991). *Widowhood in Canada*. Toronto: Butterworths.

Matthews, S. H. (1983). Definitions of friendships and the consequences in old age. *Aging and Society, 3*, 141–155.

Matthews, S. H. (1986). Friendships in old age: Biography and circumstance. In V. W. Marshall (Ed.), *Later life: The social psychology of aging* (pp. 233–269). Beverly Hills: Sage.

McAdams, D. (1985). *Power, intimacy, and the life story*. New York: Guilford.

McAdams, D., & de St Aubin, E. (1992). A theory of generativity and its assessment through self-report, behavioral acts, and narrative themes in autobiography. *Journal of Personality and Social Psychology, 62*, 1003–1015.

McAdams, D., de St Aubin, E., & Logan, R. (1993). Generativity among young, midlife, and older adults. *Psychology and Aging, 8*, 221–230.

McDonald, P. L., & Wanner, R. A. (1990). *Retirement in Canada*. Toronto: Butterworths.

McDowd, J. M., & Birren, J. E. (1990). Aging and attentional processes. In J. E. Birren & K. W. Schaie (Eds.), *Handbook of the psychology of aging* (3rd ed., pp. 222–233). San Diego, CA: Academic Press.

McFarland, C., Ross, M., & Giltrow, M. (1992). Biased recollections in older adults: The role of implicit theories of aging. *Journal of Personality and Social Psychology, 62*.

McFarland, R. A. (1956). Functional efficiency, skills and employment. In J. E. Anderson (Ed.), *Psychological aspects of aging*. Washington, DC: American Psychological Association.

McGue, M., Hirsch, B., & Lykken, D. T. (1993). Age and the self-perception of ability: A twin study analysis. *Personality and Aging, 8*, 72–80.

Meacham, J. A., & Emont, N. C. (1989). The interpersonal basis of everyday problem-solving. In J. Sinnott (Ed.), *Everyday problem-solving: Theory and applications* (pp. 7–23). New York: Praeger.

Mergler, N. L., Faust, M., & Goldstein, M. D. (1985). Storytelling as an age-dependent skill. *International Journal of Aging and Human Development, 20*, 205–228.

Mergler, N. L., & Goldstein, M. D. (1983). Why are there old people? Senescence as biological and cultural preparedness for the transmission of information. *Human Development, 26*, 72–90.

Meyer, B. J. F. (1987). Reading comprehension and aging. In K. W. Schaie (Ed.), *Annual review of gerontology and geriatrics: Vol. 7* (pp. 93–115). New York: Springer.

Meyer, B. J., Young, C., & Bartlett, B. (1989). *Memory improved: Reading and memory enhancement across the life span through strategic text structures*. Hillsdale, NJ: Erlbaum.

Middleton, D., & Edwards, D. (1990). *Collective remembering*. London: Sage.

Midlarsky, E., & Hannah, M. E. (1989). The generous elderly: Naturalistic studies of donations across the lifespan. *Psychology and Aging, 4*, 346–351.

Miller, P., Kessel, F., & Flavell, J. (1970). Thinking about people thinking about people thinking about. . . . : A study of social cognitive development. *Child Development, 41*, 613–623.

Moberg, D. (1970). Religion in the later years. In A. M. Hoffman (Ed.), *The daily needs and interests of older persons.* Springfield, IL: Charles Thomas.

Morse, C. K. (1993). Does variability increase with age? An archival study of cognitive measures. *Psychology and Aging, 8*, 156–164.

Murphy, J. M., & Gilligan, C. (1980). Moral development in late adolescent and adulthood: A critique and reconstruction of Kohlberg's theory. *Human Development, 23*, 77–104.

Murrell, K. F. H., & Griew, S. (1965). Age, experience, and speed of response. In A. T. Welford & J. E. Birren (Eds.), *Behavior, aging, and the nervous system.* Springfield, IL: Thomas.

Neugarten, B. L., & Datan, N. (1973). Sociological perspectives on the life cycle. In P. B. Baltes & K. W. Schaie (Eds.), *Life-span developmental psychology: Personality and socialization* (pp. 53–69). New York: Academic Press.

Neugarten, B. L., & Hagestadt, G. (1976). Age and the life course. In R. H. Binstock & E. Shanas (Eds.), *Handbook of aging and the social sciences.* New York: Van Nostrand Reinhold.

Neugarten, B. L., Havighurst, R. S., & Tobin, S. S. (1961). The measurement of life satisfaction. *Journal of Gerontology, 16*, 134–143.

Newcomb, T., Koenig, K., Flacks, R., & Warwick, D. P. (1967). *Persistence and change: Bennington College and its students after 25 years.* New York: Wiley.

Nisbett, R., & Ross, L. (1980). *Human inference: Strategies and shortcomings of social judgment.* Englewood Cliffs, NJ: Prentice-Hall.

Norris, J. E. (1979). *Social disengagement in aging: Controversial, but measurable.* Unpublished doctoral thesis, University of Waterloo, Waterloo, Ontario, Canada.

Norris, J. E. (1987). Psychological processes in the development of late-life social identity. In V. W. Marshall (Ed.), *Aging in Canada: Social perspectives*, 2nd ed. Toronto: Fitzhenry & Whiteside.

Norris, J. E. (1990). *Peer relationships of the never-married.* Paper presented at the annual meeting of the Canadian Association on Gerontology, Victoria, BC.

Norris, J. E. (1993). "Why not think Carnegie Hall?" Working and retiring among older professionals. *Canadian Journal on Aging, 12*, 182–199.

Norris, J. E. (1994). Effects of marital disrupton on older adults: Widowhood. In L. Ploufe (Ed.), *Writings in gerontology – Late life marital disruptions.* Ottawa: National Advisory Council on Aging.

Norris, J. E., & Forbes, S. J. (1987). *Cohesion and adaptability in caregiving families.* Paper presented at the annual meeting of the Gerontological Society of America, Washington, DC.

Norris, J. E., & Pratt, M. W. (1980). *Adult usage of Kelley's causal schemes.* Paper presented at the annual meeting of the Canadian Association on Gerontology, Saskatoon, Saskatchewan.

Norris, J. E., & Rubin, K. (1984). Peer interaction and communication: A life-span perspective. In P. Baltes & O. G. Grim (Eds.), *Life-span development and behavior* (Vol. 6, pp. 355–391). New York: Academic Press.

Norris, J. E., & Tari, A. J. (1985, February). *A qualitative approach to the study of the grandparenting experience.* Paper presented at the annual meeting of the Ontario Psychological Association, Ottawa.

Norris, J. E., & Tindale, J. A. (1994). *Among generations: The cycle of adult relationships.* New York: Freeman.

Novak, M. (1993). *Aging & society: A Canadian perspective.* Toronto: Nelson.

Nurmi, J.-E., Pullianen, H., & Salmela-Aro, K. (1992). Age differences in adults' control beliefs related to life goals and concerns. *Psychology and Aging, 7,* 194–196.

Obler, L. (1980). Narrative discourse style in the elderly. In L. Obler & M. Albert (Eds.), *Language and communication in the elderly* (pp. 75–90). Lexington, MA: D. C. Health.

Obler, L. (1989). Language beyond childhood. In J. B. Gleason (Ed.), *The development of language (2nd ed.).* (pp. 275–302). Columbus, OH: Merrill Publishing.

Olson, J., & Zanna, M. (1993). Attitudes and attitude change. *Annual Review of Psychology, 44,* 117–154.

Orasanu, J., Boykin, A. W., & the Laboratory of Comparative Human Cognition (1977). A critique of social standardization. *Social Policy, 8,* 61–67.

Osberg, L. (1988). *Is it retirement or unemployment? The constrained labour supply of older Canadians.* Ottawa: Health and Welfare Canada.

Oskamp, S. (1991). *Attitudes and opinions. (2nd Ed.).* Englewood Cliffs, NJ: Prentice-Hall.

Overton, W., & Newman, J. (1982). Cognitive development: A competence-activation/utilization approach. In T. Field, A. Huston, H. Quay, L. Troll, & G. Finley (Eds.), *Review of human development.* (pp. 217–241). New York: Wiley.

Palmore, E. B. (1977). Facts on aging: A short quiz. *Gerontologist, 17,* 315–320.

Palmore, E. B. (1982). Predictors of the longevity difference: A 25-year follow-up. *Gerontologist, 22,* 513–518.

Palmore, E. B., Burchett, B., Fillenbaum, G., George, L., & Wallman, L. (1985). *Retirement: Causes and consequences.* New York: Springer.

Pancer, S. M., & Westhues, A. (1989). A developmental stage approach to program planning and evaluation. *Evaluation Review, 13,* 56–77.

Papalia, D. (1972). The stages of several conservation abilities across the lifespan. *Human Development, 15,* 229–243.

Park, D. (1992). Applied cognitive aging research. In F. I. M. Craik & T. Salthouse (Eds.), *The handbook of aging and cognition.* Hillsdale, NJ: Erlbaum.

Parke, R. (1979). Interactional designs. In R. B. Cairns (Ed.), *The analysis of social interactions: Methods, issues, and illustrations* (pp. 15–35). Hillsdale, NJ: Erlbaum.

Passuth, P., & Cook, F. (1985). Effects of television viewing on knowledge and attitudes about older adults: A critical reexamination. *The Gerontologist, 25*, 69–77.

Peevers, B., & Secord, P. (1973). Developmental changes in attribution of descriptive concepts to persons. *Journal of Personality and Social Psychology, 27*, 120–128.

Perlmutter, M. (1978). What is memory aging the aging of? *Developmental Psychology, 14*, 330–345.

Perry, W. G. (1970). *Forms of intellectual and ethical development in the college years.* New York: Holt, Rinehart & Winston.

Peterson, C., & McCabe, A. (1983). *Developmental psycholinguistics.* New York: Plenum.

Petrowsky, M. (1976). Marital status, sex and the social networks of the elderly. *Journal of Marriage and the Family, 38*, 749–756.

Phifer, J. (1990). Psychological distress and somatic symptoms after natural disaster: Differential vulnerability among older adults. *Psychology and Aging, 5*, 412–420.

Piaget, J. (1926). *The language and thought of the child.* London: Routledge and Kegan Paul.

Piaget, J. (1970). Piaget's theory. In P. M. Mussen (Ed.), *Carmichael's manual of child psychology.* New York: Wiley.

Piaget, J. (1972). Intellectual evolution from adolescence to adulthood. *Human Development, 15*, 1–12.

Piaget, J., & Inhelder, B. (1969). *Psychology of the child.* New York: Basic Books.

Plomin, R., & McClearn, G. E. (1990). Human behavioral genetics of aging. In J. E. Birren & K. W. Schaie (Eds.), *Handbook of the psychology of aging* (3rd ed., pp. 67–78). San Diego, CA: Academic Press.

Poon, L., Martin, P., Clayton, G., Messner, S., Noble, C., & Johnson, M. (1992). The influences of cognitive resources on adaptation and old age. *International Journal of Aging and Human Development, 34*, 31–46.

Porter, C., & Suedfeld, P. (1981). Integrative complexity in the correspondence of literary figures: Effects of personal and social stress. *Journal of Personality and Social Psychology, 40*, 321–330.

Pratt, M. W. (1975). *Learning the what and why of others: A developmental study of person perception and attribution.* Unpublished Ed.D. dissertation, Harvard University.

Pratt, M. W. (1991). *Integrative complexity and thinking about personal relationships.* In P. Suedfeld (Chair), New directions in research on integrative complexity. Symposium presented at the American Psychological Association Meetings, San Francisco, August.

Pratt, M. W. (1992). *Older but wiser? A longitudinal study of mature adult thinking about the social domain.* Paper presented at the International Congress of Psychology, Brussels, July.

Pratt, M. W., & Bates, K. (1982). Young editors: Preschoolers' evaluation and production of ambiguous messages. *Developmental Psychology, 18*, 30–42.

Pratt, M. W., Boyes, C., Robins, S., & Manchester, J. (1989). Telling tales: Aging, working memory, and the narrative cohesion of story re-tellings. *Developmental Psychology, 25*, 628–635.

Pratt, M. W., Bumstead, D., & Raynes, N. (1976). Attendant staff speech to the institutionalized retarded: Language use as a measure of the quality of care. *Journal of Child Psychology and Child Psychiatry, 17*, 133–144.

Pratt, M. W., Diessner, R., Hunsberger, B., Pancer, S. M., & Savoy, K. (1991). Four pathways in the analysis of adult development and aging: Comparing analyses of reasoning about personal life dilemmas. *Psychology and Aging, 7*, 666–675.

Pratt, M. W., Golding, G., & Hunter, W. J. (1983). Aging as ripening: Character and consistency of moral judgment in young, mature, and older adults. *Human Development, 26*, 277–288.

Pratt, M. W., Golding, G., Hunter, W., & Norris, J. (1988). From inquiry to judgment: Age and sex differences in patterns of adult moral thinking and information-seeking. *International Journal of Aging and Human Development, 27*, 115–130.

Pratt, M. W., Golding, G., Hunter, W., & Sampson, R. (1988). Sex differences in adult moral orientations. *Journal of Personality, 56*, 373–391.

Pratt, M. W., Golding, G., & Kerig, P. (1987). Lifespan differences in adult thinking about hypothetical and personal moral issues. *International Journal of Behavioral Development, 10*, 359–375.

Pratt, M. W., Hunsberger, B., Pancer, S. M., & Pratt, A. (1994). *Perspective-taking and moral reasoning in maturity: A longitudinal study*. Paper presented at the Canadian Psychological Association Meetings, Penticton, British Columbia.

Pratt, M. W., Hunsberger, B., Pancer, S. M., Roth, D., & LaPointe, N. (1990, November). *Reflections on religion: Aging and cognitive style variations in adult thinking about religious issues*. Paper presented at the Society for the Scientific Study of Religion Conference, Virginia Beach, Virginia.

Pratt, M. W., Hunsberger, B., Pancer, S. M., & Roth, D. (1992). Reflections on religion: Aging, belief orthodoxy, and interpersonal conflict in the complexity of adult thinking about religious issues. *Journal for the Scientific Study of Religion, 31*, 514–522.

Pratt, M. W., Hunsberger, B., Pancer, S. M., Roth, D., & Santolupo, S. (1993). Thinking about parenting: Reasoning about developmental issues across the lifespan. *Developmental Psychology*,

Pratt, M. W., Kerig, P., Cowan, P. A., & Cowan, C. P. (1988). Mothers and fathers teaching three-year-olds: Authoritative parenting and adults' scaffolding of young children's learning. *Developmental Psychology, 24*, 732–739.

Pratt, M. W., Pancer, S. M., Hunsberger, B., & Manchester, J. (1990). Reasoning about the self and relationships in maturity: An integrative complexity analysis of individual differences. *Journal of Personality and Social Psychology, 59(3)*, 575–581.

Pratt, M. W., & Robins, S. (1991). That's the way it was: Age differences in the structure and quality of adults' personal narratives. *Discourse Process, 14*, 73–85.

Pratt, M. W., Roth, D., Cohn, D., Cowan, P. A., & Cowan, C. P. (1991). *Connecting the generations: Adults' complexity of reasoning about family of origin, attachment security, and quality of parenting.* Paper presented at the Society for Research in Child Development Meetings, Seattle, April.

Quadagno, J. (1982). *Aging in early industrial society.* New York: Academic Press.

Ramig, L. A. (1986). Aging speech: Physiological and sociological aspects. *Language and Communication, 6*, 25–34.

Reich, P. (1986). *Language development.* Englewood Cliffs, NJ: Prentice-Hall.

Reisman, J. M. (1981). Adult friendships. In S. W. Duck & R. Gilmour (Eds.), *Personal relationships, Vol. 2: Developing relationships* (pp. 205–230). London: Academic Press.

Reker, G. (1990). *Aging, optimism and wellness promotion.* Unpublished manuscript, Department of Psychology, Trent University, Peterborough, Ontario.

Reker, G., & Wong, P. (1985). Personal optimism, physical and mental health: The triumph of successful aging. In J. Birren & J. Livingston (Eds.), *Cognition, stress, and aging* (pp. 134–173). Englewood Cliffs, NJ: Prentice-Hall.

Renaud, V. & Badets, J. (1993). Ethnic diversity in the 1990s. *Canadian Social Trends*, Statistics Canada Cat. 11–008E, 18–23.

Rest, J. (1979). *Development in judging moral issues.* Minneapolis: University of Minnesota Press.

Rest, J. (1983). Morality. In P. Mussen (Gen. Ed.), *Manual of child psychology* (4th ed., Vol. 3, pp. 556–629). New York: Wiley.

Riegel, K. (1975). Adult life crises: A dialectical interpretation of development. In N. Datan & L. H. Ginsberg (Eds.), *Life-span developmental psychology: Normative life crises.* New York: Academic Press.

Riegel, K. F., & Riegel, R. M. (1972). Development, drop, and death. *Developmental Psychology, 6*, 309–316.

Riley, M., & Foner, A. (1968). *Aging and society: An inventory of research findings.* New York: Sage.

Roberto, K. A., & Scott, J. P. (1986). Equity considerations in the friendships of older adults. *Journal of Gerontology, 41*, 241–247.

Roberts, R. E. L., & Bengtson, V. L. (1990). Is intergenerational solidarity a unidimensional construct? A second test of a formal model. *Journal of Gerontology, 1*, S12–S20.

Roberts, R., & Patterson, C. (1984). Perspective taking and referential communication: The question of correspondence reconsidered. *Child Development, 54*, 1005–1014.

Robinson, D. (1990). Wisdom through the ages. In R. Sternberg (Ed.), *Wisdom: Its nature, origins, and development* (pp. 13–24). Cambridge: Cambridge University Press.

Rodin, J., & Langer, E. J. (1977). Long-term effects of a control-relevant intervention with the institutionalized aged. *Journal of Personality & Social Psychology, 35*, 897–902.

Rogers, C. R. (1980). Growing old – or older and growing. *Journal of Humanistic Psychology, 20*, 5–16.

Rogoff, B. (1990). *Apprenticeship in thinking*. London: Cambridge Press.

Roodin, P. A., Rybash, J. M., & Hoyer, W. J. (1986). Qualitative dimensions of social cognition in adulthood. *Educational Gerontology, 12*, 301–311.

Rook, K. S. (1987). Reciprocity of social exchange and social satisfaction among older women. *Journal of Personality and Social Psychology, 52*, 145–154.

Rosenmayr, L., & Kockeis, E. (1963). Propositions for a sociological theory of aging and the family. *International Social Science Journal, 15*, 410–426.

Rosenthal, C. J. (1987). Aging and intergenerational relations in Canada. In V. W. Marshall (Ed.), *Aging in Canada: Social perspectives*, 2nd ed. Toronto: Fitzhenry & Whiteside.

Rosenthal, R., & Jacobsen, L. (1968). *Pygmalion in the classroom*. New York: Holt, Rinehart, & Winston.

Ross, H. S. & Lollis, S. P. (1989). A social relations analysis of toddler peer relationships. *Child Development, 60*, 1082–1091.

Ross, L. (1981). The "intuitive scientist" formulation and its developmental implications. In L. Ross & J. Flavell (Eds.), *Social cognitive development* (pp. 1–42). New York: Cambridge University Press.

Ross, M. (1989). Relation of implicit theories to the construction of personal histories. *Psychological Review, 96*, 341–357.

Ross, N. (1980). *Buddhism: A way of life and thought*. New York: Vintage Books.

Roth, D., Pratt, M., Hunsberger, B., & Pancer, M. (1990, June). *Wisdom: Everyday judgments and formal ratings of reasoning*. Paper presented at the Canadian Psychological Meetings, Ottawa, Canada.

Rubin, A. (1988). Mass media and aging. In C. Carmichael, C. Botan, & R. Hawkins (Eds.), *Human communication and the aging process*. Prospect Heights, IL: Waveland Press.

Rubin, K. (1973). *Decentration skills in institutionalized and non-institutionalized elderly*. In Proceedings of the 81st Annual Convention of the American Psychological Association, Montreal, Canada.

Rubin, K. (1974). The relationship between spatial and communicative egocentrism in children and young and old adults. *Journal of Genetic Psychology, 125*, 295–301.

Rubin, K., Attewell, P., Tierney, M., & Tumolo, P. (1973). The development of spatial egocentrism and conservation across the life-span. *Developmental Psychology, 9*, 432–436.

Rubin, K. H., & Brown, I. D. R. (1975). A life-span look at person perception and its relationship to communicative interaction. *Journal of Gerontology, 30*, 461–468.

Rubin, K., & Krasnor, L. R. (1986). Social cognitive and social behavioral perspectives on problem-solving. In M. Perlmutter (Ed.), *Minnesota symposium on child psychology* (Vol. 18, pp. 1–68). Hillsdale, NJ: Erlbaum.

Rubin, L. (1985). *Just friends*. New York: Harper & Row.

Ruble, D. (1993). A phase model of transitions: Cognitive and motivational consequences. In M. Zanna (Ed.), *Advances in Experimental Social Psychology*.

Russell, B. (1945). *A history of western philosophy*. New York: Simon & Schuster.

Ryan, E. B. (1991). Language issues in normal aging. In R. Lubinski (Ed.), *Dementia and communication: Clinical and research implications* (pp. 84–97). Toronto: B. C. Decker Publishing.

Ryan, E. B. (1992). Beliefs about memory changes across the adult lifespan. *Journal of Gerontology: Psychological Sciences, 47*, 41–46.

Ryan, E. B., & Capadano, H. L. (1978). Age perceptions and evaluative reactions toward adult speakers. *Journal of Gerontology, 33*, 98–102.

Ryan, E. B., & Cole, R. L. (1990). Evaluative perceptions of interpersonal communication with elders. In H. Giles, N. Coupland, & J. Weimann (Eds.), *Health, communication and the elderly* (pp. 172–190). Fulbright Colloquium Series. Manchester University Press.

Ryan, E. B., Giles, H., Bartolucci, G., & Henwood, K. (1986). Psycholinguistic and social psychological components of communication by and with the elderly. *Language and Communication, 6*, 1–24.

Ryan, E. B., Kwong-See, S., Meneer, W. B., & Trovato, D. (1992). Age-based perceptions of language performance among younger and older adults. *Communication Research*.

Ryan, E. B., & Laurie, S. (1990). Evaluations of older and younger adult speakers: Influence of communication effectiveness and noise. *Psychology and Aging, 5*, 514–519.

Ryan, E. B. & Kwong-See, S. (1993). Age-based beliefs about memory changes for self and others across adulthood. *Journal of Gerontology, 48*, 199–201.

Rybash, J. M., & Hoyer, W. J., & Roodin, P. A. (1986). *Adult cognition and aging*. New York: Pergamon.

Ryff, C. D. (1984). Personality development from the inside: The subjective experience of change in adulthood and aging. In P. B. Baltes & O. G. Brim, Jr. (Eds.), *Life-span development and behavior* (Vol. 6, pp. 244–281). Orlando: Academic Press.

Ryff, C. D. (1991). Possible selves in adulthood and old age: A tale of shifting horizons. *Psychology and Aging, 6*, 286–295.

Ryff, C. D. (1993, March). The self in later life. *Gerontology News, 2*, 11.

Ryff, C. D. & Heincke, S. G. (1983). Subjective organization of personality in adulthood and aging. *Journal of Personality and Social Psychology, 44*, 807–816.

Sabat, S. R. & Harre, R. (1993). The construction and deconstruction of self in Alzheimer's disease.

Sable, P. (1989). Attachment, anxiety, and the loss of a husband. *American Journal of Orthopsychiatry, 59*, 550–556.

Salthouse, T. A. (1984). Effects of age and skill in typing. *Journal of Experimental Psychology: General, 113*, 345–371.

Salthouse, T. A. (1985). Speed of behavior and the implications for cognition. In J. E. Birren & K. W. Schaie (Eds.), *Handbook of the psychology of aging* (2nd ed., pp. 400–426). New York: Van Nostrand Reinhold.

Salthouse, T. A. (1987). The role of representativeness in age differences in analogical reasoning. *Psychology and Aging, 2*, 357–362.

Salthouse, T. A. (1988). Initiating and formalizing the theories of cognitive aging. *Psychology and Aging, 3*, 3–16.

Salthouse, T. A. (1990). Cognitive competence and expertise in aging. In J. E. Birren & K. W. Schaie (Eds.), *Handbook of the psychology of aging*, 3rd ed. San Diego: Academic Press.

Salthouse, T. A. (1990). Influence of experience on age differences in cognitive functioning. *Human Factors, 32*, 551–569.

Salthouse, T. A. (1991). Age and experience effects on the interpretation of orthographic drawings of three-dimensional objects. *Psychology and Aging, 6*, 426–433.

Sameroff, A., & Feil, L. (1985). Parental conceptions of development. In I. Sigel (Ed.), *Parental belief systems* (pp. 83–105). Hillsdale, NJ: Erlbaum.

Sansone, C. & Berg, C. A. (1993). Adapting the environment across the life span: Different process or different inputs. *International Journal of Behavioral Development, 16*, 215–241.

Santolupo, S., & Pratt, M. (in press). Age, gender, and parenting style variations in mother-adolescent dialogues and adolescent reasoning about political issues. *Journal of Research on Adolescence*.

Scarr, S., & McCartney, K. (1983). How people make their own environments: A theory of genotype environment effects. *Child Development, 54*, 424–435.

Schaie, K. W. (1965). A general model for the study of developmental problems. *Psychological Bulletin, 64*, 92–107.

Schaie, K. W. (Ed.). (1983). *Longitudinal studies of adult psychological development*. New York: Guilford Press.

Schaie, K. W. (1990). Intellectual development in adulthood. In J. E. Birren & K. W. Schaie (Eds.), *Handbook of the psychology of aging* (3rd ed., pp. 291–309). San Diego, CA: Academic Press.

Schaie, K. W., & Hertzog, C. (1983). Fourteen-year cohort-sequential studies of adult intelligence. *Developmental Psychology, 19*, 531–543.

Schaie, K. W., & Willis, S. L. (1991). Adult personality and psychomotor performance: Cross-sectional and longitudinal analyses. *Journal of Gerontology, 46,* 275–284.

Schlesinger, Jr., A. (1992). *The disuniting of America.* New York: W. W. Norton.

Schludermann, E. H., Schludermann, S. M., Merryman, P. W., & Brown, B. W. (1983). Halstead's studies in the neuropsychology of aging. *Archives of Gerontology and Geriatrics, 2,* 49–172.

Schmidt, D. F., & Botwinick, J. (1989). A factorial analysis of the age de-differentiation hypothesis. In V. L. Bengtson & K. W. Schaie (Eds.), *The course of later life: Research and reflection* (pp. 87–92). New York: Springer.

Schneider, D., Hastorf, A., & Ellsworth, P. (1979). *Person perception* (2nd ed.). Reading, Mass.: Addison-Wesley.

Schonfield, D. (1982). Attention switching in higher mental process. In F. I. M. Craik & S. E. Trehub (Eds.), *Aging and cognitive processes* (pp. 309–316). New York: Plenum.

Schrootes, J. J. F., & Birren, J. E. (1990). Concepts of time and aging in science. In J. E. Birren & K. W. Schaie (Eds.), *Handbook of the psychology of aging* (3rd ed., pp. 45–64). San Diego, CA: Academic Press.

Schultz, N. R., & Hoyer, W. J. (1976). Feedback effects on spatial egocentrism in old age. *Journal of Gerontology, 31,* 72–75.

Schulz, R., & Ewen, R. (1988). *Adult development and aging.* New York: Macmillan.

Schwartz, S. H. (1977). Normative influences on altruism. In L. Berkowitz (Ed.), *Advances in experimental social psychology* (Vol. 10). New York: Academic Press.

Sears, D. (1981). Life-stage effects on attitude change, especially among the elderly. In S. Kiesler, J. Morgan, & V. Oppenheimer (Eds.), *Aging: Social change.* New York: Academic Press.

Seccombe, K., & Lee, G. (1986). Gender differences in retirement satisfaction and its antecedents. *Research on Aging, 8,* 426–440.

Selman, R. (1980). *The growth of interpersonal understanding.* New York: Academic Press.

Shaffer, D. R. (1989). *Developmental psychology (2nd Ed.)* Pacific Grove, CA: Brooks/Cole.

Shulik, R. (1979). *Faith development, moral development and old age: An assessment of Fowler's faith development paradigm.* Unpublished doctoral dissertation, University of Chicago, Chicago, Illinois.

Shultz, T. R., Butkowsky, I., Pearce, J., & Shanfield, H. (1974). Development of schemes for the attribution of multiple psychological causes. *Developmental Psychology, 11,* 502–510.

Siegler, J. S., George, L. K., & Okun, M. A. (1979). A cross-sequential analysis of adult personality. *Developmental Psychology, 15,* 350–351.

Siegler, R. (1991). *Children's thinking (2nd Ed.)* Englewood Cliffs, NJ: Prentice-Hall.

Simon, S., Walsh, D., Regnier, V., & Krauss, I. (1992). Spatial cognition and neighborhood use: The relationship in older adults. *Psychology and Aging,* 7, 389–394.

Singleton, S. (1983). Age, skill, and management. *International Journal of Aging and Human Development,* 17, 15–23.

Sinnott, J. D. (1982). Correlates of sex roles of older adults. *Journal of Gerontology,* 37, 587–594.

Sinnott, J. D. (1984). Post-formal reasoning: The relativistic stage. In M. L. Commons, F. A. Richards, & C. Armon (Eds.), *Beyond formal operations: Late adolescent and adult cognitive development.* New York: Praeger.

Sinnott, J. D. (1989). General systems theory: A rationale for the study of everyday memory. In L. W. Poon, D. C. Rubin, & B. A. Wilson (Eds.), *Everyday cognition in adulthood and late life* (pp. 59–70). Cambridge: Cambridge University Press.

Skaff, M. M. & Pearlin, L. I. (1992). Caregiving: Role engulfment and the loss of self. *Gerontologist,* 32, 656–664.

Skoe, E. (1993). *The ethic of care interview manual.* Unpublished manuscript, University of Tromso, Norway.

Skoe, E., & Diessner, R. (in press). Ethic of care, justice, identity and gender – an extension and replication. *Merrill-Palmer Quarterly.*

Skoe, E., & Marcia, J. (1991). A care-based measure of morality and its relation to ego identity. *Merrill-Palmer Quarterly,* 37, 289–304.

Skoe, E., Pratt, M., & Curror, S. (in preparation). Ethic of care and real-life moral dilemma content in elderly men and women.

Slawinski, E., Hartel, D., & Kline, D. (1993). Self-reported hearing problems in daily life throughout adulthood. *Psychology and Aging,* 8, 552–561.

Smith, J., & Baltes, P. B. (1990). Wisdom-related knowledge: Age/cohort differences in response to life-planning problems. *Developmental Psychology,* 26, 494–505.

Smith, M. C. (1975). Children's use of the multiple sufficient cause schema in social perception. *Journal of Personality and Social Psychology,* 32, 737–742.

Smith, S. W., Rebok, G. W., Smith, W. R., Hall, S. E., & Alvin, M. (1983). Adult age differences in the use of story structure in delayed free recall. *Experimental Aging Research,* 9, 191–195.

Snow, R. E. (1980). Aptitude processes. In R. E. Snow, P. A. Frederico, & W. E. Montague (Eds.), *Aptitude, learning, and instruction: Cognitive process analyses of aptitude* (Vol. 1, pp. 27–63). Hillsdale, NJ: Erlbaum.

Sontag, S. (1979). The double standard of aging. In J. Williams (Ed.), *Psychology of women.* San Diego, CA: Academic Press.

Spearman, C. (1904). "General intelligence": Objectively determined and measured. *American Journal of Psychology,* 15, 201–292.

Spilich, G. J. (1983). Life-span components of text-processing: Structural and procedural differences. *Journal of Verbal Learning and Verbal Behavior,* 22, 231–244.

Spivack, G., Platt, J. J., & Shure, M. B. (1976). *The problem-solving approach to adjustment*. San Francisco: Jossey-Bass.

Stagner, R. (1985). Aging in industry. In J. E. Birren & K. W. Schaie (Eds.), *Handbook of the psychology of aging* (2nd ed., pp. 789–817). New York: Van Nostrand Reinhold.

Sternberg, R. (1985). *Beyond IQ: A triarchic theory of human intelligence*. Cambridge: Cambridge University Press.

Sternberg, R. (1986). A triangular theory of love. *Psychological Review, 93*, 119–135.

Sternberg, R. (1990). *Wisdom: Its nature, origins, and development*. Cambridge: Cambridge University Press.

Sternberg, R., & Wagner, B. (Eds.) (1986). *Practical intelligence: Nature and origins of competence in the everyday world*. Cambridge: Cambridge University Press.

Stine, E. L., Wingfield, A., & Poon, L. W. (1989). Speech comprehension and memory through adulthood: The roles of time and strategy. In L. W. Poon, D. C. Rubin, & B. A. Wilson (Eds.), *Everyday cognition in adulthood and late life* (pp. 195–229). New York: Cambridge University Press.

Stoller, E. P. (1985). Exchange patterns in the informal support networks of the elderly: The impact of reciprocity on morale. *Journal of Marriage and the Family, 47*, 335–342.

Stone, L. O. & Frenken, H. (1988). *Canada's seniors*. Cat. No. 98–121. Ottawa: Minister of Supply and Services.

Storr, A. (1988). *Solitude: A return to the self*. New York: Free Press.

Suedfeld, P., & Piedrahita, L. (1984). Intimations of mortality: Integrative simplification as a precursor of death. *Journal of Personality and Social Psychology, 47*, 848–852.

Suls, J., & Mullen, B. (1982). From the cradle to the grave: Comparison and self-evaluation across the lifespan. In J. Suls (Ed.), *Psychological perspectives on the self* (Vol. 1), (pp. 97–125). Hillsdale, NJ: Erlbaum.

Szinovacz, M. (1989). Women and retirement. In B. Hess & E. Markson (Eds.), *Growing old in America*. New Brunswick, NJ: Transaction Publishers.

Tapp, J., & Kohlberg, L. (1971). Developing senses of law and legal justice. *Journal of Social Issues, 27*, 65–91.

Taranto, M. A. (1989). Facets of wisdom: A theoretical synthesis. *International Journal of Aging and Human Development, 29*, 1–21.

Taylor, J. E. & Norris, J. E. (1993). *The response of mid-life women to maternal death: Grief reaction and attachment status*. Manuscript submitted for publication.

Taylor, R. N. (1975). Age and experience as determinants of managerial information processing and decision making performance. *Academy of Management Journal, 18*, 74–81.

Taylor, R., & Chatters, L. (1986). Church-based informal support networks among elderly Blacks. *The Gerontologist, 26*, 637–642.

Tesch, S. A. (1989). Early-life development and adult friendship. In R. G. Adams & R. Blieszner (Eds.), *Older adult friendship* (pp. 89–107). Newbury Park, CA: Sage.

Tetlock, P. E. (1986). A value pluralism model of ideological reasoning. *Journal of Personality and Social Psychology, 50*, 865–875.

Tetlock, P. E. (in press). An alternative model of judgment and choice: People as politicians. *Theory and Psychology*.

Thomae, H. (1980). Personality and adjustment to aging. In J. E. Birren & R. B. Sloane (Eds.), *Handbook of mental health and aging*. Englewood Cliffs, NJ: Prentice-Hall.

Thompson, M., Norris, F., & Hanacek, B. (1993). Age differences in the psychological consequences of Hurricane Hugo. *Psychology and Aging, 8*, 606–616.

Tindale, J. A. (1991). *Writings in Gerontology. No.9: Older workers in an aging work force*. Ottawa: National Advisory Council on Aging.

Tindale, J. A. (1993). Participant observation as a method for evaluating a mental health promotion program with older persons. *Canadian Journal on Aging, 12*, 200–215.

Tran, T. V. (1990). Language acculturation among old Vietnamese adults. *The Gerontologist, 30*, 94–99.

Triandis, H. C. (1989). The self and social behavior in differing cultural contexts. *Psychological Review, 96*, 506–520.

Tulving, E. (1985). Memory and consciousness. *Canadian Psychology, 26*, 1–11.

Turiel, E. (1983). *The development of social knowledge: Morality and convention*. Cambridge: Cambridge University Press.

Tversky, A., & Kahneman, D. (1973). Availability: A heuristic for judging frequency and probability. *Cognitive Psychology, 5*, 207–232.

Tyler, T., & Schuller, R. (1991). Aging and attitude change. *Journal of Personality and Social Psychology, 61*, 689–697.

Unger, R. K. (1979). *Male and female: Psychological perspectives*. New York: Harper & Row.

United Nations. (1984). *Periodical on Aging. 1(1)*. New York. Department of International Economics and Social Affairs.

Vygotsky, L. S. (1978). *Mind in society*. Cambridge, MA: MIT Press.

Waldman, D. A., & Avolio, B. J. (1986). A meta-analysis of age differences in job performance. *Journal of Applied Psychology, 71*, 33–38.

Walker, L. (1984). Sex differences in the development of moral reasoning. *Child Development, 55*, 677–691.

Walker, L. (1988). The development of moral reasoning. *Annals of Child Development, 5*, 33–78.

Walker, L. (1989). A longitudinal study of moral reasoning. *Child Development, 60*, 157–166.

Walker, L., DeVries, B., & Trevethan, S. (1987). Moral stages and moral orientations in real-life and hypothetical dilemmas. *Child Development, 58*, 842–858.

Walker, L., & Taylor, J. (1991). Family interactions and the development of moral reasoning. *Child Development, 62*, 264–283.

Wallace, J. B. (1992). Reconsidering the life review. The social construction of talk about the past. *Gerontologist, 32*, 120–125.

Walsh, R. P., & Connor, C. L. (1979). Old men and young women: How objectively are their skills assessed? *Journal of Gerontology, 34*, 561–568.

Walster, E., & Berscheid, E. (1978). *Equity: Theory and research.* Boston: Allyn & Bacon.

Warr, P. (1992). Age and occupational well-being. *Psychology and Aging, 7*, 37–45.

Warren, R. M., & Warren, R. P. (1970). Auditory illusions and confusions. *Scientific America, 223*, 30–36.

Warren-Leubecker, A., & Bohannon, J. (1989). Pragmatics: Language in social contexts. In J. B. Gleason (Ed.), *The development of language.* Columbus, OH: Merrill Publishing.

Watson, P., Howard, R., Hood, R., & Morris, R. (1988). *Age and religious orientation. Review of Religious Research, 29*, 271–280.

Weiland, S. (1992). Criticism between literature and gerontology. *Critical Gerontology.* New York: Springer.

Wentowski, G. J. (1981). Reciprocity and the coping strategies of older people: Cultural dimensions of network building. *Gerontologist, 21*, 600–609.

Wertsch, J. V. (1991). *Voices of the mind.* Cambridge, MA: Harvard University Press.

Wheeler, E. G. (1980). Assertive training groups for the aging. In S. S. Sargent (ed.), *Nontraditional therapy and counselling with the aging.* New York: Springer.

Whitbourne, S. K. (1987). Personality development in adulthood and old age: Relationships among identity style, health and well-being. In K. W. Schaie (Ed.), *Annual review of gerontology and geriatrics: Vol. 7.* New York: Springer.

White, C. B. (1988). Age, education, and sex effects on adult moral reasoning. *International Journal of Aging and Human Development, 27*, 271–281.

White, N., & Cunningham, W. R. (1988). Is terminal drop pervasive or specific? *Journal of Gerontology: Psychological Sciences, 43*, 141–144.

Williams, S. A., Denney, N. W., & Schadler, M. (1983). Elderly adults' perception of their own cognitive development during the adult years. *International Journal of Aging and Human Development, 16*, 147–158.

Willis, S. (1990). Introduction to the special selection on cognitive training in later adulthood. *Developmental Psychology, 26*, 875–878.

Willis, S. L., & Schaie, K. W. (1986). Practical intelligence in later adulthood. In R. J. Sternberg and R. K. Wagner (Eds.), *Practical intelligence: Origins of competence in the everyday world* (pp. 236–268). Cambridge: Cambridge University Press.

Wong, P. T. P., & Watt, L. M. (1991). What types of reminiscence are associated with successful aging? *Psychology and Aging, 6*, 272–279.

Wood, L. A. (1986). Loneliness. In R. Harre (Ed.), *The social construction on emotions* (pp. 184–208). Oxford: Blackwell.

Wood, L., & Ryan, E. (1991). Talk to elders: Social structure, attitudes and forms of address. *Aging and Society, 11*, 167–187.

Wright, P. H. (1989). Gender differences in adults' same- and cross-gender friendships. In R. G. Adams & R. Bleiszner (Eds.), *Older adult friendships* (pp. 197–221). Newbury Park, CA: Sage.

Wrightsman, L. (1988). *Personality development in adulthood*. Newbury Park, CA: Sage.

Yarmey, A. D. (1984). Accuracy and credibility of the elderly witness. *Canadian Journal of Aging, 3*, 79–90.

Yesavage, J. A., Sheikh, J. I., Friedman, L., & Tanke, E. (1990). Learning mnemonics: Roles of aging and subtle cognitive impairment. *Psychology and Aging, 5*, 133–137.

Zabrucky, K., Moore, D., & Schultz, N. R., Jr. (1987). Evaluation of comprehension in young and old adults. *Developmental Psychology, 23*, 39–43.

Subject Index

abilities, 143–144
  and practice, 143–144
  crystallized, 27, 179–180
  fluid, 27, 179–180
altruism, 170–171
attachment, 98, 103–104,
    105–106, 107, 110
attitudes, 118
attribution theory, 45

behavior genetics, 15

caregiving, 105–106
cognition, 5–6
cognitive competence, 8–9,
    25–26, 32
cognitive performance, 25–26,
    32
  compensation and, 30
  processing rate and, 29
  reserve capacity and, 25
  resource theory and, 29
  training and, 25–26
cognitive stages, 17–19
  generality of, 17–18
  hierarchy of, 17–18
  post-formalist model and, 32,
    48–49, 158–159
  regression in later life, 31–32,
    181
  universality of, 17–19

communication in aging,
    176–202
  and conversation, 196–197
  competence vs. performance,
    189
  hearing loss and, 182
  pronoun use and, 184–187
  syntax and, 187–190
  working memory and, 186–189
community
  sense of, 126–129
competence
  cognitive, see cognitive
    competence
  social, 96, 104
control
  perceived, 49–52, 60
coping
  and control, 51–52
  with old age, 46–50
  with stress, 154

decision-making, 143–156, 162
  development of, 143–144
development, 13–18
  continuity in, 17
  environmental influences,
    14–16
  genetic influences, 14–16
  genetic-environmental
    interactions, 14–15

Author Index